OUR SECRET CODE
GIVE TERRY A BONE

Babes van Dillen Clinton —

THE NETHERLANDS
(Holland)

0 10 20 30 40
MILES

NORTH SEA

EAST FRISIAN ISLANDS

WEST FRISIAN ISLANDS

Waddenzee

GRONINGEN

Groningen *Dollart Bay*

FRIESLAND

Tjeukemeer

DRENTHE

Den Helder

NORTH HOLLAND

Alkmaar

IJsselmeer (Zuiderzee)

Zwolle

OVERIJSSEL

IJmuiden
Zaandam

Almelo

★ Amsterdam

Voorthuizen

Deventer Hengelo

Enschede

Haarlem

IJssel River

Hilversum

Apeldoorn

Amersfoort

GELDERLAND

Scheveningen
The Hague ★

Utrecht

Gouda UTRECHT

Arnhem

SOUTH HOLLAND

Rotterdam

Lek River *Lower Rhine*

Nijmegen

Vlaardingen

Waal River

Dordrecht

Maas River

BIESBOSCH

GERMANY

Drimmelen NORTH BRABANT

ZEELAND

Breda

Tilburg

Helmond

Roosendaal

Eindhoven

Venlo

Schedlt R.

LIMBURG

Antwerp

Rhine River

BELGIUM

Heerlen

Brussels

Maasctricht

BABES VAN DILLEN CLINTON
OUR SECRET CODE
GIVE TERRY A BONE
A TRUE STORY OF NAZI OCCUPIED HOLLAND

Blue Tulip Press

"Give Terry a Bone"
Our secret code

Published by:
Blue Tulip Press
110 South El Camino Real #113
San Mateo, California 94402

Library of Congress Cataloging-in-Publication Data

Dillen Clinton, Babes van
    Give Terry a Bone.

    1. Dillen Clinton, Babes van
2. World War, 1939-1945 — Underground movements —
Netherlands. 3. World War, 1939-1945 — Personal
narratives, Dutch. 4. Guerrillas — Netherlands
— Biography. I. Title.
D802.N4D53 1986   940.53'492   86-6857
ISBN 0-9616163-0-X

Cover by Kyle Bogertman

Color photograph on back inside cover by Erik van Dillen

Printed in the United States of America

To Paul and Erik

"Love You With All My Heart"

FOREWORD

by Keith Fuller, Past President,
The Associated Press

For a protracted period of time after World War II most countries that had been occupied by the Nazi forces went through a period of introspection questioning whether they, as a people, had shown a reasonable and proper amount of harassment and defiance of the enemy.

In my capacity as president of The Associated Press I became aware of this, when I visited the various European countries that had been occupied and heard the question raised in conversation.

From Associated Press news people, mostly natives of their own country, I became aware that there was an undercurrent of dissatisfaction in a few of these countries as to the image they had portrayed as being less than hostile to the occupying force.

I am not aware that we Americans gave much, if any, thought to this line of questioning. We knew there were collaborators in all countries, just as we knew how bravely other segments of these populations had performed.

France, for example, had the Laval government as a national shame while the other extreme found some of the most effective underground fighters in the war operating in Normandy, Britanny and the Pas de Calais area.

On my first visit to Copenhagen I was told by people I met — mainly in journalistic circles — that the Danes were sensitive to a perceived notion that the free World had the idea they could have been a bit more aggressive against the enemy. I pass no judgment on the matter; I would suspect that for every Danish passivist there was a Danish hero.

But over a matter of years I had the feeling that among Europeans — including the British — there was a notion that the Norwegians got top marks for their hostility and sabotage against the Germans.

The Dutch, too, ranked high as did the Normans and Bretons. The Dutch won the acclaim of many Jewish people as being particularly sympathetic to the plight of the Jews in Holland.

Many wars, declared and undeclared, have been fought since the jubilant Victory-in-Europe day May 6, 1945. The issue of who did what in Europe against Hitler is not an issue today. Certainly enough people had the courage and determination to eradicate the Nazi scourge.

I was reminded of these matters as I read the fascinating pages of this true account of the life of a brave, young Dutch woman during the German occupation of Holland. As her story unfolded it occurred to me that her book would put to rest the absurd idea of trying to label an entire population as "brave" or "effective" or "collaborative" in terms of wartime behavior.

She dealt with the latent question with such objectivity and such patent honesty that I mentally shouted "great" and I straight away sat down and wrote to some of my former colleagues in Europe about it.

What Babes van Dillen Clinton has done is to tell her story chronicling the wonderfully brave acts of some of her Dutch acquaintances and the treachery of others. She loathes those who turned against their own people for Nazi favors as much as she took pride in the reckless bravery of other Dutch people.

While the author was living the drama of her experiences, I was, for a good deal of that time, flying from England against Germany as a B-17 crew member in the Eighth Airforce (Corps). In 1944, a bleak year for her in Holland, I was in a German prison camp not too many miles from her milieu. Though we would not meet for some three decades later, we had a kinship even then. The kinship is still felt by the millions whose lives were touched by the horror and majesty of World War II. Majesty? Yes. So many good people sacrificed so much for a simple choice of right over wrong it was indeed a majestic experience.

For me, the story and the telling of it both were a delightful trip back in time to a period when there was no normalcy in the world except untold millions being challenged each day to live with sacrifice.

Keith Fuller
South Carolina
Nov. 15, 1985

INTRODUCTION

Why did I write this book? First I wanted to answer the many people who asked me what did I do when the Germans suddenly invaded our neutral Holland. Invariably their second question was, "Why did you hate the Nazis so much; what did they do to you?"

When I would tell some of the reasons, they would be fascinated. But, because they did not know the whole story, especially the early events, they did not understand. This prompted me to write from the very beginning — from May 10, 1940 on, and tell what I saw happen during those five Nazi occupation years. I wrote my thoughts and experiences of that time.

Then, of course, I wrote the story for my children, their children, and their children's children, for them to know that their ancestors made a contribution to the fight for freedom.

I have described the daily life in Holland, not only from memory, but also from six diaries, filled with newspaper clippings and photographs, in which I wrote every day. I often wish, that I had been able to write the book earlier, but I could not do it. Finally, encouraged by family and friends, I put aside my emotions and started.

There were many heinous scenes, which I could not possibly describe, as they were so horrifying that they are still deeply hidden in my heart. I admire anyone who can write about those crimes, because it should be told in all its detail. But what I have written is enough. One has to read the extreme fear, pain, and frustration in between the lines. I wanted the reader to smile once in a while and know that in all the misery there was hope and courage and great love. To every traitor there were thousands of everyday men and women who were heroes. I hope that I convey this feeling.

In the third chapter, I took some ideas of my late husband, Paul, who wrote his thoughts down right after the end of the war. I feel that he would be pleased that I did this.

Why did we do it? Why did we jeopardize our lives? It did not win the war, but we were happy just to do one small thing, and perhaps the war would end one day sooner. At the same time our dislike of the Nazis grew stronger every day and anything we could do to obstruct their advance made us feel better.

It is hard to realize what one would do if a war rages in one's own country. It made me grow up in a hurry. From a very sheltered life I was now responsible for my own actions. If I failed, the price of failure was high. It made me understand what freedom and democracy really meant, and now I feel fortunate to know that.

After the war Her Majesty Queen Wilhelmina of the Netherlands bestowed the honor on us by giving my husband and myself each a handpainted plate — our names are inscribed on the back — in recognition of fulfilling our mission for the people of Holland.

The day the war ended, the Liberator, an Allied army newspaper, expressed my feelings by writing:

"The great and glorious little people of Holland, who gave all honour to the Allied liberators, not realizing how by their own courage and sacrifice, they did much to liberate themselves."

It is this story, my book tells.

BvDC
San Mateo, California

ACKNOWLEDGEMENTS

Without the help of my family and friends, I could never have written this book.

My greatest supporter is my husband, Hart, who saw me at the typewriter every morning at six o'clock. His love, patience, and complete confidence, gave me great reasurrances. As a prominent lawyer, editor and publisher of the San Mateo Times, he scrupulously read every sentence of the manuscript, edited some, and then made me extremely happy by saying, "I like it."

Nobody gave me more moral support than my two sons and their wives. They also encouraged me to write the story, as they felt that their generation should know about it.

Paul was the first one to read the manuscript and was invaluable in analyzing its contents. He made suggestions, and made sure it stayed true to my personality.

Erik, always creative, was a big help in providing fresh ideas and usually found new avenues to explore, giving me many hours of his time.

Donna often lent a willing ear. I felt relaxed in her home as she advised me on which stories were important and should be included in the book.

Lailee, an accomplished writer, gave me the confidence that it could be done, and in her articulate way, redirected my thoughts whenever my mind was blocked.

I am very grateful to Juanita Pacifico Clark, who gave many long hours to help me edit the book the first time. Her friendship, enthusiasm, and sense of humor, were much appreciated. She became so involved with the story that she traveled to Holland to see for herself. There were other friends: Keith Fuller, recently retired President of the Associated Press, who wrote the foreword, for which I am most grateful. John Schofield, who was "there" with the 104th Infantry. Reminiscing together, we relived the liberation. It kept my memory alive.

Bill Barnard, Louana Hammett, Jennifer Hill Bassing, and my two author friends Willa Okker Iverson and Dale Fife, all gave good suggestions which improved the book. Many thanks go to Lillian Heselton, who graciously gave much of her time to type and advise. Also Virgil Wilson, managing editor, and Jack Russell, assistant to the managing editor of the San Mateo Times. Ray Zirkel, Mike Spinelli and Mike Russell for their photography; Ernie Nilsen for his artwork; Art Bouthillier, production manager; Jim Davis, head of the composing room, and Indra Dutt with other members of the staff who did the typesetting. I thank you all for your enthusiastic help.

I am very appreciative to Ronald Fouts for his invaluable assistance with the logistics of publishing a book. He freely gave of his time and knowledge. Without his help it would still be a manuscript.

In Amsterdam I received much cooperation from Edouard G. Groeneveld, librarian of the State Institute for War Documentation.

Last but not least, my faithful friend Louise who often came to visit. Noticing me constantly at the typewriter, her encouraging remarks were, "You know, I am sick and tired of the whole darn book!"

That made me hurry up and finish.

OUR SECRET CODE
GIVE TERRY A BONE

Give Terry a Bone is a true story. All names mentioned were actual people; however, I did change some names to protect the identity of the persons referred to. The fictitious names are: Gretchen, Evert and Joop, Kurt and Heinrich, Mrs. van Dam, Rolf, Robby, Piejan, Remmert, Janie, Herr Woltheim, Herman, Terwilligen, Skipper Jan, Pieter, Monique, Govert, Madelein and Guus. All resemblance or similiarity to any person, living or dead, is unintended and purely coincidental.

BvDC

1

Holland, May 1984

We drove to the south of Holland, following the same route as forty years ago. My husband and the driver sat in front of the car. I was sitting alone in the back. I wanted to be alone with my own thoughts. This time we were not stopped by Nazi guards behind wooden barricades. Instead we sped along a sleek highway, trying to find the off-ramp to the narrow winding road next to the river, on our way to Hardinxveld.

I wanted to find the brave family who during the Nazi occupation helped Paul and me escape over the rivers, to fulfill our dangerous mission. I had not been back since those days and nights when I stayed with these people who were deeply involved in the underground activities. Would they still be there?

Gazing across the endless meadows, it struck me again how green the grass is in Holland. Far away I spotted a row of windmills, their sails looking like tiny crosses black-penciled on the horizon. In those days, we had used the windmills to send secret messages by the way the sails were set, vertical or horizontal, or turned a certain way. Across the flat open countryside this secret signal could be seen for miles. It took the Nazis a long time before they caught on.

My eyes followed the entire panorama, turning toward the sky. It was unusually clear with only one white woolly cloud, a loner, floating in the blue. I expected at any moment to see two British Royal Air Force planes fly over and German flak chasing them into the safety of the cloud.

A sudden sharp curve in the road shook me. We had reached the river bank. Slowly, looking on both sides of the road, we drove over the narrow dike. The green meadows with cows and goats were on the one side, on the other side was the fast flowing Waal River, the large tributary of the Rhine. Masses of high reeds hugged the banks with here and there a clump of willow trees. A train of barges came chugging along against the strong current, on its way to Germany.

Most homes were built in the polder, the low laying meadows next to the dike, their roofs sticking out above the road. I didn't recognize any of the buildings and I was disappointed. Only in a few villages I was happy to see that the charming old brick houses and the little steepled churches were still there.

At a bend in the river we stopped and I took some pictures as this seemed to be the only place which looked even vaguely familiar to me. Just when I was resigned to the fact that I wouldn't see anything else from the past, I suddenly spotted a sign: *van Mill, Shipbuilding Yard, 1932-1982.* While staring at it, a tall young man came out of the door and crossed the yard. Instinctively I moved towards him. Somehow he looked familiar. As he slowed down and glanced at me, I asked him if any van Mills were still living here.

"Why yes," he answered with a pleasant smile, "I am Bas van Mill."

Now I knew. He reminded me of his mother!

"I am Mrs. van Dillen," I said properly, as one does in Holland, "I live in California and came to find your parents."

Silently he stared at me and I saw an expression of shock come over his face. His lips started to tremble. Haltingly, as if every word was difficult, he said, "You came, you *finally* came!"

"What do you mean?" I questioned, "Do you know me?"

"Yes. My father told me about you six years ago, when he was dying."

I looked at him and shuddered.

We were still standing in the courtyard when he continued, "Father never told us children about the war and the underground. I was only three years old when it all happened. Two weeks before he died from cancer, he called us to the side of his bed and he related the story of the trip across the rivers. He couldn't tell us fast enough."

Bas stopped to take a breath, then went on, "He told us that there was a young lady, the only woman he had helped escape across the lines, and that she now lived in America. Her name was Babes. Father said, 'I'll never forget her, and one day . . . some day . . . she'll come back.' "

I was numb . . . then goosepimples spread over my arms to my neck. I took a step closer to this Bas van Mill, who suddenly had become part of my life, and we hugged and cried, and hugged again.

"If the time my father chose to tell the story wasn't so dramatic, we would have never remembered your name," Bas went on talking softly.

I didn't know what to say. Silently we moved together towards one of the new buildings.

Finally I spoke, "It's all so new, I don't recognize anything." I was whispering as if I were still in the underground.

"We were badly bombed towards the end of the war, but here is still the old barn, and there are the steps coming down from the road. You remember those, don't you?" Bas eagerly watched the reaction on my face. Then he continued, "Two years ago we celebrated the 50th anniversary of the company. We had a special tile-painting made for this occasion. It is real Delft blue. The old house, the barn, and even the little outhouse, are painted on the tiles, just as you knew it. I still have one of them left. Would you like to have it?"

I nodded enthusiastically. He left for a minute and returned with the tile-painting. I couldn't hold back the tears as I accepted this precious gift.

We were joined by Bas' brother and together they told me about the death of their mother, just two years ago. "Her eyes were not that good any more and she started to turn into herself and dwell upon the past a lot. She really wanted to see you," they said, and continued, "We tried. We had your name broadcasted over the radio several times, hoping someone would know where you were. We even tried to get Mother on TV to talk about you, but unfortunately she died before that happened. Why didn't you come sooner?"

The question made me feel dreadful. My heart started to beat faster, my head started spinning.

"I often thought about it," I sighed. "But I was afraid your parents wouldn't remember me. Besides, my life had changed so much. Paul passed away in California and I remarried. Perhaps I also was scared to come and be disappointed." I was trying to put into words what I had thought all those years.

"Also, I felt I played such a small part in the underground."

"Not for *our* family!" Bas said, "My mother waited for you. You came two years too late!"

Too late! Too late! The words echoed in my ears and I desperately tried to hold back another flow of tears, while I started to tell them how brave and wonderful their parents had been. I told them about the trip again, while they listened attentively and I could see that they were proud of their mother and father.

When I asked, Bas told me what happened to other men of the river area. His face looked drawn when he relayed that many Resistance workers were brutally murdered by the Nazis. In their memory a small statue stands in the town of Werkendam. One of them, Kees Visser, survived the war and is still living in the same house. Wim van Veen moved his family up north, to the island of Texel, where he died a year ago.

After a cup of coffee we walked around and they showed me the plant. What was once a small wharf is now an internationally known company. Their tug-boats, patrol boats, and seagoing yachts are sailing all over the world.

When it was time to leave, I promised to come back again next year and stay longer. Exhausted from emotion, I kissed them good-bye and left reluctantly, but with an inner glow. I knew I had seen the continuation of a beautiful memory.

Back at the Hotel des Indes in The Hague, I dropped into the overstuffed chair and closed my eyes. Thoughts kept shooting through my head. How did it all happen? How did we get into this war? Could we have avoided it? Why weren't we tough when we knew that the Nazis were rearming? And that Chamberlain, who thought he could make peace forever. God, was he naive!

I felt as if a large cotton cloud was enveloping me. Slowly I sank deeper into the chair and my mind went back to the beginning . . . planes . . . bombs . . . war . . . Nazis . . . fear . . . underground . . . men . . . women . . . friends . . . screams . . . shots . . . fear . . . A procession of events passed by like a slow, silent movie, but I wasn't watching a movie . . . this was real!

I was twenty years old, blonde, slim, and full of life, sitting in my cozy bedroom of our family home in The Hague. It was a pleasantly warm evening in May. I slowly undressed and slipped into my new cotton nightgown with the lace trim. Because I felt uneasy, I could not appreciate the balmy weather and the unusually clear sky with its sprinkling of shiny stars. We had just heard that all military furloughs were cancelled and an emergency staff meeting was called for that evening. Now my friends in the army would not be coming home for the weekend. Was the situation that serious? Would we be the next to be drawn into the war? . . . Hitler had invaded country after country: Austria, Czechoslovakia, Poland, Norway, Denmark, forcing England and France to declare war six months ago. Would Hitler now violate Holland's officially declared neutrality?

I shuddered. Crawling into bed, snuggling under my thick Dutch blankets, I finally fell into a deep sleep, unaware of the evil forces preparing to attack our small country on that early Friday morning, May 10th, 1940.

Suddenly I heard a distant roaring followed by a few dull booms. I thought I was still dreaming and instinctively pulled the covers over my head to shut out the noise. But the rhythmic droning got louder and louder and the house started to shake. Leaping out of bed, I ran to the window. Oh, my God! Airplanes! Bombs!

Horrified, I saw fifty or more heavy bombers circling like giant bats against the dim morning light. Shaking and shivering, I kept on staring at the sky.

Big guns pointing skyward started to blast at the grey monsters. Just before the thunder a few little white and grey puffs of our anti-aircraft floated in the air over our city. Suddenly . . . *KABOOM!* Our house shook violently. A large bomb had exploded nearby. As my mother and sister came running upstairs to get me, I saw six planes dive over our roof with a deafening roar. They came so low that I could almost touch them. Recognizing the black hooked Nazi crosses on the wings, I gasped and clutched my chest. Now I knew what was happening!

I ran downstairs and saw my father, like a pillar of strength, standing in the dark hall and I felt safe for a moment.

Normally a nervous man, Father now seemed extremely calm. While we all hurried into the living room, he quietly turned on the radio. War! War! War! The Germans had invaded Holland! This was Hitler's Blitzkrieg! "Take the enemy by surprise," Hitler had said. "No warning, no conferences, no ultimatums!" But where were the Dutch alarms of attack? Someone must have been sleeping on the job!

"Close your windows and stay inside," the radio cautioned. But no one listened. People dashed into the street still dressed in their night clothes. Children screamed, dogs barked, soldiers from the old barracks behind our house came running past our door, army trucks screeched through the street, horns honking. It was complete bedlam!

Before I also ran outside, I rushed upstairs to get my most valuable possessions: a silver key chain with my boyfriend's regiment's emblem on it, a picture taken on the beach, a lucky charm — I needed that one right now! — a gold locket, and of course my diary. I would die if I lost any of these things!

"Watch out for paratroopers!" An excited voice on the radio wailed that large formations of German planes were swarming overhead dropping parachutists all around The Hague. Only in the newsreels at the movies had we seen the little white mushrooms floating to the ground. It all looked so harmless on the screen. It was hard to imagine that now those Krauts were literally falling out of the sky by the thousands!

My heart started pounding. I had the feeling I was going to burst. While we watched the sky a squadron of Messerschmitts suddenly came out of the clouds diving down upon us with a terrifying scream. I ducked, holding my hands over my ears to block out the earsplitting noise. The planes streaked low over the tree tops, avoiding the anti-aircraft and veering to the west. Bombs dropped, explosions followed, flames shot up in the air. Father put his arm protectively around my shoulder; my mother held our frightened cat.

"They must have hit the new barracks on the Waalsdorper Road," Father said quietly. Mother and I just nodded. By the time our guns found the range, the planes were already dots in the distance. The barracks in the dunes east of Scheveningen, a North Sea resort adjacent to The Hague, were hit. A third of the buildings were destroyed. Twenty soldiers died in their beds.

The sirens finally wailed their undulating song of warning. We all left the street, our family rushing into the shelter. At the all-clear sound, telling us it was now safe outside, we returned to the house. The phone began to ring and I heard Father answer. He put the phone down and looked at me. "They need doctors at the barracks. The stables are also hit." Knowing that the situation at the bomb site might be dreadful, he hesitated a moment before asking, "Would you like to come along?"

Of course, I knew I couldn't just stay home while the world was falling to pieces! I had to help — to help with the horses.

We drove the two miles to the military complex in the coastal dunes as quickly as we could, trying to avoid bricks and glass in the road. Dutch army trucks with wounded and dead drove slowly out of the compound. By the time we arrived at the buildings, only the horses were there. They whinnied and thrashed behind the broken-down walls, some wounded, some dying. Tears flowed down my face while I stroked a panicked stallion, his eyes rolling wildly as Father injected a pain killer. Other disoriented animals stampeded, and we had to avoid their flailing hoofs. It seemed like an eternity, but soon trained veterinarians arrived and took over. When there was nothing left for us to do, we drove home. A few straggling planes were still dropping bombs which fell behind the buildings. Fortunately no bombs reached the handful of soldiers who had flattened themselves against the dunes of this coastal area.

We didn't talk on the way home. When I saw the trucks loaded with lifeless bodies and I watched the dying horses, something died inside of me. I knew then my life was changing. Nothing would ever be the same again . . . my safe world was gone.

We used to say in Holland that, standing in the middle of the country, you could spit into Germany and Belgium, and with the right wind, even into France because our country was only 14,000 square miles, about twice as large as New Jersey. One fifth of the land is below sea level, making us chronic complainers about rain, wind, and cold. Still, we were all willing to fight for it. Once attacked, we became very patriotic. "The Last Patriotic War," someone called it.

This tiny triangular plot of land had been a well organized, clean, and healthy country. We had our troubles, but who didn't? We were not completely over the Depression but, as we later came to know . . . we had it so good!

Small though we were, the world recognized us. We had Rembrandts and other famous paintings, fine universities, four of the world's largest companies, and Rotterdam the largest harbor in the world. In spring people came from throughout the world to see acres of blooming tulips and daffodils, stare at our quaint windmills, drink our beer, eat our cheeses, and purchase sparkling diamonds in our capital, Amsterdam.

In 1940 about nine million people lived in our country, which was unfortunately situated between fighting neighbors. Declaring neutrality seemed our best defense, but this was difficult because of the mutual trade on the three large waterways, the Rhine, the Maas, and the Scheldt, which flow through Holland into the North Sea. In the Great War of 1914-'18 we had been able to stay neutral, and now in 1940, we hoped to do so again.

But Adolf Hitler had other plans. Upon becoming Reichschancellor of Germany in 1933, he blamed his nation's problems on the Versailles Treaty which he said punished Germans by withholding "Lebensraum," space to live. Few people in Holland gave this another thought. But that day bombs dropped around us and Hitler's devastating armies thundered into Belgium, Luxemburg, and Holland. We were at war; we had to fight for our lives, and we had just gone through the first horrors of it.

I followed my father into the kitchen, where he calmly started to wash his hands in the sink. I looked at him, Alexander Frederik Schoorel, physician, undisputed head of our family. He was an aristocrat, both sensitive and humble. He looked good for his 63 years, vibrant and attractive to people, especially women. The seventh of ten children of devout Protestant parents, living in the Dutch East Indies, he had chosen to be a doctor, instead of a minister like his father. He was born on the island of Ambon. We used to tease him about being born on a volcanic island, part of which later blew up and disappeared into the ocean.

After studying basic medicine in Leyden and surgery under the famous professor Korteweg in Utrecht, he began practice in Java. He became a true doctor with a deep feeling for his patients, as well as an excellent surgeon with an uncanny diagnostic talent. He never talked much, but once in a while he would tell wonderful tales to my sister and me about his medical practice in these remote islands. Smiling, he would boast that his biggest claim to fame was meeting an attractive Batavian schoolteacher, who later was shot as the cunning spy of the first World War, Mata Hari.

My mother, with her large brown eyes set above a perfect profile, had a different personality from my father. She was happy, gracious, and very wise in the ways of the world. Her ancestors were French from the time of Napoleon's reign in Holland. I remember her best as a sophisticated lady one minute and a giggling schoolgirl the next. Because my sister was five years older than I, and away at Rotterdam University, my mother and I spent a lot of time together. She taught me about art and antiques, and the beauty of nature. Besides visiting museums, I also loved to go shopping with her.

She would buy me nice clothes while chatting with everyone in the store. Then, instead of going straight home with our purchases, we would have tea and cake in some pleasant little café downtown, totally forgetting that my irritated father needed the car to visit his patients. When we came home with all our packages, my father would explode, caught between the problem of his absent automobile, and my mother's extravagance. His outbursts did not bother her too much; she just tossed her gorgeous chestnut hair, and charmed my father out of his bad mood.

As the years passed, our family grew very close. I knew my parents loved me, and that secure feeling helped me through the terrifying times which were still to come.

During the Great War, while Europe was in a turmoil, my parents lived a good life in southeast Asia. I was born on the north coast of Java in Semarang, a busy little seaport. With its restless fleet of praoes and sampangs, it was the center of inter-island trade. Our home had once been a downtown hotel. It was a sprawling, white-columned, marble-floored house surrounded by lawns with tennis courts and ten cottages for the native staff, half a mile from the Java Sea. On one side, Father built an apartment for my grandmother who always looked cool and graceful in her sarong and kabaja, having discarded European dress. On the other side of the house Father built his medical offices, complete with full operating room.

My sister Julie and I had a wonderful childhood despite the heat and mosquitos which caused such suffering to adults in the tropics. Life for us was free and easy and we played barefoot most of the time.

The intriguing world behind our house was a limitless source of wonder to me. I loved visiting the forbidden river, with its large turtles, and watching the thousands of soft bodied lizards, called tjitjaks, glued to the walls and ceiling with the tiny adhesive pads of their toes. While my mother was annoyed to find one rolled in the sugarpot, I was delighted with the little creature and held him carefully in my hands. All things that moved and breathed interested me, but nothing was more fascinating than the "charm of the snakes." The gardener, our kebon, convinced me that our family's good fortune was assured by a pair of pythons guarding us from under our house. Though I was terribly scared, I still tried to catch a glimpse of them. Even when I was six years old and we returned to Holland, I was convinced the snakes were our protectors.

My parents settled in The Hague. Father's practice soon grew, as many friends from the Far East, who had also returned to Holland, were delighted to find their doctor again.

After the Depresssion years, a new threat of war loomed over us again. It hit my parents in 1938 when they were in Baden-Baden where Father was taking a cure for arthritis. He watched the Germans feverishly prepare for war, and came home saying he would never trust them again. He was sure the Nazis would invade Holland, and being small and unprepared, we wouldn't be able to defend ourselves. With his typical Dutch trait of planning ahead and not leaving anything to chance, he realized the necessity of protecting the family. He told my mother to hoard rice, sugar, tea, and soap, and he hid extra bicycle tires in the cellar.

A picture of a bomb shelter in an American magazine made Father decide we needed one. Together with two of our neighbors, he ordered three prefabricated shelters from the United States. I never knew the cost of these things, but I remember the huge rounded corrugated steel plates arriving and our carpenter coming to set the shelter up in the backyard. It was round, like an igloo, and dug into the ground. It tore up more than three-quarters of our garden, and had about six feet of soil on top in which we grew grass. In front were three small steps leading down to a narrow door. In back was an emergency door, covered with soil. You could dig yourself out if need be. Inside was a floor of wooden planks, two benches, food provisions, a water jug and medical supplies. Father took a bottle of gin along, "for medicinal purposes," he said with a grin. The shelter might not stand a direct hit, but it could hold if the house collapsed on it. We never really thought we would have to use it, but now the war was upon us.

When we came back into the house, Mother told us that Queen Wilhelmina was on the air. We quickly trooped around the radio. In strong, well-chosen words our valiant Queen registered a "flaming protest to the world," proclaiming that "our country was at war with the German Reich after their *flagrant violation of our neutrality!*"

Holland had scrupulously guarded its neutrality. Nevertheless, even after repeatedly promising to respect our neutral stand, Nazi Germany had disregarded all rules of the Geneva conference and invaded our small country. Enraged by this unprovoked attack we now joined the western Allies.

Father sighed and said, "Well, I can't say I'm surprised. I never trusted those Krauts and Grandpa didn't either." He turned to me, "I hope to God that our Water Line will hold Hitler's troops."

He was referring to our main line defense. This surrounded the "Fortress Holland" which encompassed the three western provinces with the cities of Amsterdam, Rotterdam, The Hague, Utrecht, and Leyden. It consisted of opening dikes and flooding the lowlands. This defense had been used hundreds of years ago to deter Spanish foot soldiers but, now, against a sky full of Messerschmitts and Henkels, it no longer seemed like an effective deterrent to us.

Mother and I stood at the window, gazing into a beautiful spring morning. The chestnut trees were budding. A light green haze covered the bare branches. Nature was at her best. It seemed unreal that on such a lovely, seemingly peaceful day, evil forces were crossing our borders and falling out of the sky, hellbent to destroy us. What should we do? What can one do at home? How can we help? How can we defend ourselves? These were all unanswered questions, which we had never thought of before.

Father joined us at the window, while we watched our few fighter planes roar in defense. It seemed pretty futile, but at least we were fighting back and the enemy planes disappeared for a while. We sighed with relief. I looked at my father. He turned to my mother and calmly said, "I haven't had breakfast yet. Do you think that, for once, Gretchen could fix me an egg the way I want it, soft but not runny?"

Mother didn't answer. She was annoyed that her husband was thinking of food at this moment. Gretchen, our maid, was one of the many Germans who had come to Holland to find work after the Great War. To my father's chagrin she could never manage to boil his egg right.

My father acted abnormally unconcerned about the invasion, and I thought he probably didn't want to make us nervous. But I worried about my friends who were fighting all over Holland. Were they still alive? No breakfast for me. I wanted to find out what was really happening.

Enemy planes were still coming over and kept the sirens howling. In between raids it was quiet, and I waited for the all-clear to go outside. There I saw a Dutch army officer escorting a motley group of civilians to the police station.

"Hey Rob, what on earth are you doing?" I shouted at him unceremoniously, suddenly recognizing the officer as an old friend.

Rob turned around. "Goddamn quislings," he said, "These traitors are shooting our soldiers from the windows. The bastards! You know, those paratroopers have surrounded us. They're all over the place. They're even in Wassenaar!"

"Oh no, that close!" I suddenly lost my bravado.

Rob nodded. "Go home, Babes. You have no idea how tricky these Krauts are. They're disguised as farmers; even as Dutch soldiers. God knows where they stole those uniforms."

At that moment we heard the plaintive whine of the sirens again. I rushed home through the garden, and down into the shelter, to join my parents, when suddenly more bombs! Bang, crash,

BOOM! A burst of shells followed. The noise was deafening.

We looked at each other and turned white, shaking and shivering, waiting for the attack to end, or maybe just waiting. After another explosion we thought our home had been hit. When all was quiet again, Father asked my sister to open the door a crack to see if the house was still standing. With our eyes still large from fright we stared at the slit of daylight, holding our breath. It was deathly silent outside. Even the birds had stopped chirping. It was as if the world had stopped turning.

"It's still there," my sister announced, closing the door again. We sighed in relief.

My mother looked lovingly at each of us, as if to count her blessings. "Thank God," she said softly.

We got up still dazed, and while climbing out of our shelter I glanced at the newspaper my father had brought with him. The headlines stated boldly: GERMANS DENY THEIR SOLDIERS ARE IN DUTCH UNIFORMS OR DRESSED AS FARMERS.

"They're lying, Dad," I said to my father, pointing to the headline, "My friend *saw* them dressed as farmers!"

The bombs had fallen behind us in the open field, too close for comfort. To be nearer our shelter we decided to bring our mattresses down to the living room. While making my bed on the floor, I heard a familiar call outside. It was the explosive cry of the peacock, known only to my old school chums.

"That's Oda," said my mother, who was pasting strips of paper on the window glass to prevent shattering.

I rushed downstairs. Oda, one of my best friends, now seemed even dearer to me. Tall and slender, she stood quietly smiling in the hallway, her dark short hair in natural waves around her calm face. We embraced and after hurriedly sharing our experiences, decided we should volunteer for something like the Red Cross or so, tomorrow.

As she left Oda turned and said quizzically, "What would you do if a Kraut suddenly stepped into your house?"

I laughed. I hadn't thought of that before.

"I'll hit him with this." I picked up my tennis racket, feeling this was my best weapon.

Oda thought for a minute. "Well, I guess that's as good as you can do for now."

I smiled at her. We really weren't that worried yet, and still felt convinced we would throw the enemy out any day now. How innocent we were.

That night, ready for anything, we went to bed fully clothed. At midnight the doorbell rang. It was Mrs. van Dam, a widowed friend, complete with two suitcases full of her belongings. Bombs had blown the windows out of her apartment and she was cold, lonely and scared. We brought down a mattress for her and she stayed with us.

All through the night German planes kept flying over, followed by our gunfire. The sirens wailed constantly and forced us to our shelter, where we politely tried to let our friend enter first. Being quite heavy, she got stuck in the narrow door. Her efforts to force herself through made us giggle.

Father, usually the perfect gentleman, became a raving maniac. He saw all his efforts to have a safe place for his family ruined by this unwieldy body. Nervously he pushed and pulled, finally dragging our friend through the door. All of us piled in afterward, none the worse for wear. But Father foresaw further complications and instituted a pecking order for entering the shelter in the future: Mother first, he second, followed by my sister and I, and finally our friend last, sideways!

Our shelter was indeed a safe gathering place for the whole family. Even the dog and cat got used to it. As soon as the sirens howled, they were the first ones in, despite Father's carefully laid rules. When bombs exploded around us, our steel igloo shook violently, but had enough give to withstand the shock waves. We were never bombed directly, although other houses close by were hit and leveled to the ground.

As we kept the radio on to know what was happening in this hour of panic, we heard the appeal to turn in our weapons. Amnesty was offered for those weapons which had never been recorded under our long-time registration law.

My father did not really want to go to the police and admit that he had never registered his two revolvers, but loyalty to his country made him go, and I accompanied him. A long line of people were inside the police office, all looking somewhat sheepish. The officers stared at us all in disbelief and shook their heads. Finally, in came a young man in style. He had called a police car to carry his collection of twenty unregistered shotguns. Everybody burst out laughing. All his twenty, plus every other gun, were donated that day to the Dutch army.

The next day was Whitsunday. The weather was lovely again, just as everybody always said it was in 1914 when the Great War started. We were too tired to appreciate it. Exhausted, we didn't get up at the sound of the sirens anymore, but waited until we could hear the planes coming our way before quickly scrambling into our shelter. During the day the Germans flew over constantly, and to our surprise we saw the Royal Air Force with their red, white and blue markings on their wings, chasing the German Stukas. We learned to recognize the different planes. I even found out that Stuka stood for Sturzkampf Flugzeug, meaning "diving fighter plane" in German.

Each day became more confusing. We heard many rumors and did not know what to believe. One rumor, about the tulip festival, was probably very true. Our famous festival was held a few weeks before the attack, and it was said that many Germans who came to visit the flowers had stayed to become a Fifth Column.

We indeed wondered — where did the German flower-show visitors stay during the days between the show and the attack, and where did they get the Dutch army uniforms, which they wore while shooting our soldiers? How did they know which Dutch Nazis to release from jail the moment they invaded? We were sure they must have had some aid and support from within. This gave us a terribly unsure feeling and it was depressing to think we had traitors among ourselves. No matter what was suspected, we did see a lot of "Moffen," as we called the Germans, around suddenly, and shooting erupted in the streets. Dutch soldiers and civilians hit the dirt in the shallow trenches which had been dug in front of our house.

With paratroopers in disguise, and Dutch Nazi sympathizers running around, no one knew friend from foe. Guards were now placed at street corners. Anyone passing had to say "Scheveningen." Since Germans can't pronounce it, this was an easy way to spot the enemy. The news was still very optimistic, though, and few people realized how serious the situation was.

Hitler, who had expected to overrun Holland in twenty-four hours, found he had a tiger by the tail. Once aroused, the Dutch soldier was a fierce fighter, and for four more days we kept the Wehrmacht at bay. The main thrust of the airborne troops was in the vicinity of The Hague, with heavy shelling on the three military airfields nearby.

One of them, Valkenburg, was still under construction. This was lucky for us, because the heavy Junker transport planes got stuck in the mud, preventing more from landing.

Daily we saw more enemy planes, sometimes chased by our small but courageous air force. I cringed the first time I saw a huge Stuka divebomber being hit. Mortally wounded, it spun around with a tail of smoke growing wider with each turn. For a moment it hestiated, then dove straight down, exploding into a fiery ball of fire. People in the street cheered. Even our dignified neighbor raised his fist and shouted something about finally getting one of the sonsabitches!

I had mixed emotions about watching a German plane crash. I didn't want to see anybody killed, not even my worst enemy. But that feeling changed fast when a bomb dropped into the Bethlehem Maternity Hospital, only a few blocks away from us, killing several mothers and babies. I watched the flames and heard the screams. Soldiers kept us at a distance; the building was an inferno. I felt a rage coming over me. Slowly my fear disappeared, and I was ready to fight back.

While paratroopers surrounded us in the west, Hitler's Stosztruppen quickly advanced into the eastern part of Holland, crossing the Yssel river. Dutch troops desperately tried to halt the ferocious attack of tanks and armored cars. Completely outnumbered and having only antiquated weapons, they had no chance.

In The Hague, despite all the shooting in the streets, civilians kept running around, causing more confusion. The mailman even came with a letter from my boyfriend in the reserves. It was written before the invasion, and full of optimistic news. It made me cry bitter tears. I hoped and prayed he was still alive and was thinking of me, too.

In the meantime we had no idea what was happening in the rest of the country; thus we were still optimistic. After all, our soldiers were not doing too badly around The Hague, and it seemed like just a ghastly nightmare from which we would soon awaken. But the following day our confidence was shattered when we heard that Queen Wilhelmina had safely landed in England. We couldn't believe it. Our Queen, who had ruled our constitutional monarchy for nearly forty years, had left us! She had always said that a member of the Royal House of Orange would never forsake her people!

I was shocked and felt betrayed, at first thinking that it was just German propaganda. I could understand that Princess Juliana and her two small daughters would leave for a safer place to secure a royal succession, but the Queen leaving — it just couldn't be true!

Very few people knew Her Majesty, Queen Wilhelmina of the Netherlands. She was not just a figurehead but had a strong personality and ruled our country in her own way. Most Dutchmen saw her only once a year, on the third Tuesday of September, on her way to open Parliament. She rode through The Hague in her golden carriage pulled by eight black horses. The streets were lined with people waving little Dutch flags, small children sitting on their fathers' shoulders to see. Bigger ones hung from the lampposts to get a better view. Balconies along her route were draped with the flag, our proud red, white, and blue, along with an orange pennant for the royal House of Orange. As the coach approached, the crowd cheered, "Oranje boven! Long live the Queen!"

She would wave to us, turning back and forth like a mechanical doll, nodding her head to each side. At the Binnenhof, a large square surrounded by medieval government buildings, she would pause on the steps of the 13th-century Ridderzaal, the Hall of Knights. With its two towers, it looked like a church. There she would wave again at the throngs of loyal Dutchmen who waited in the autumn sun, "the little Orange sun that always shines on Orange Day."

During the winter I also saw her at The Hague Ice Club, an outdoor skating rink. My family was a longtime member as was the Royal Family. With only a small clubhouse, it was not a fancy rink, but just an iced meadow on the outskirts of The Hague. When we saw a special area roped off, we knew the Royal Family would soon be skating next to us. Her majesty would arrive with her ladies-in-waiting, followed by military police. The officers helped her on with her skates. They were long, wooden Frisian skates, tied to her high, black-laced boots. In her heavy winter outfit with fur collar and fur hat, she looked even more roly-poly than ever.

My friends and I watched her with outward respect, but, grinning maliciously, we made bets on how long it would be before she fell. She always fell a couple of times and was helped up quickly. Undaunted, she would start again, still managing to look very regal.

Princess Juliana learned to skate, like every other child, by holding on to a chair and pushing it over the ice. Her general education was equally democratic. The Queen realized that her daughter would eventually rule in a different world, and so Juliana was allowed to study at Leyden University where she became a member of the Women's Student Corps and took part in most student activities.

But that day General H.G. Winkelman, Commander-in-Chief of the Dutch Forces, announced that the Queen, along with some members of her cabinet, had decided to establish a government-in-exile. We discovered later that the first German paratroopers had orders to go to the Palace and capture Wilhelmina. She had left just in time.

Prince Bernard, who had accompanied his family to London the previous day, returned later and joined the Dutch and Allied Forces still valiantly defending our last stronghold in the province of Zeeland. I was impressed that he joined the actual fighting, considering that he was German himself. Later our Royal Prince managed to escape to England with the Navy and remnants of Dutch troops. He remained in England and became adviser to the Queen's exile government. Eventually he was in contact with our Resistance in Holland and became Commander of the Dutch Forces of the Interior. Princess Juliana and her two girls, Beatrix and Irene, stayed in Canada, where her third daughter Margriet was born.

It took us a long time to recover from the shock of the Royal Family's departure. It was still discussed everywhere, people disagreeing with each other. When Belgium capitulated, King Leopold III decided to stay with his people. The Germans detained him for the duration of the war. After hearing that King Leopold was confined to his home, we started to understand why Queen Wilhelmina had decided to go to London. There she was free and still able to rule the Netherlands Empire, including the still-free Dutch East Indies.

The next news was very discouraging: our outnumbered forces at the Grebbeberg were forced to retreat behind the Water Line. Germans dropped on the Maas river into rubber boats to recapture the Moerdyk bridge. Our Dutch Marines fought a savage bayonet battle in defense. We just heard bits and pieces of what was going on. Once in a while our soldiers outsmarted the Germans, but we were like the flea biting the elephant and the bitter end was near.

While negotiations for an unconditional surrender were under way, Hitler ruthlessly ordered the bombing of Rotterdam to terrify the nation. Low-flying planes unmercifully blanketed the center of this open city, in utter contempt of the Geneva Conference accords. Hundreds of innocent civilians were killed, thousands injured, and Rotterdam went up in flames.

In The Hague we could hear the dull rumble, and from my room we could see a fiery glow in the sky. It seemed the whole world was on fire. Anxiously we watched the smoke rise, grey clouds telling of the horror. With every blast we shuddered, bitter and angry at the awful realization that Rotterdam was dying. Hitler's ravaging of this city was followed by the threat to pulverize other towns if we didn't cease fire. General Winkelman announced a few hours later that "due to the Wehrmacht's superior forces, he had decided to surrender." He urged us to stay calm and have faith in the future. Long live the Queen, long live Holland!

When the surrender came, we felt lost. Our fight was over! Done! Finished! We had capitulated! We gathered in the street, weeping. Strangers embraced each other. All felt the same overwhelming sense of loss. We had fought only five days. Could we have done better?

Soon after our defeat, Hitler's mighty troops blitzed their way through Belgium, and bypassed France's "impenetrable" Maginot Line. Eighteen days for Belgium; thirty-six days for France. The allied forces miraculously escaped via Dunkirk.

We were on our own . . .

2

Only a few hours later a long convoy of mud-splattered tanks crawled into the city of The Hague. Rumbling over the old Dutch cobblestones, they sounded like a huge thunderstorm rolling in. Nazi soldiers were perched on top of the tanks. Thick brown mud was everywhere — caked on the caterpillar tracks, on the turrets, and pasted on the soldier's faces; camouflage netting and tree branches over tank and man. The mighty conquerers!

It was a shock to see the Nazis arrive as victors. It was even terrifying to see the huge whirring tanks, with large black swastikas painted on the sides, clanking down our streets. The men on top hardly looked like human beings. In their black overalls with the ominous skull-and-crossbone insignias on their collars, they looked like monsters from outer space. This was Hitler's elite Totenkopf Brigade, the S.S. Death's Head unit.

Behind the row of tanks trudged hundreds of foot soldiers in brown and green-spotted overalls, like a huge invasion of crawling frogs.

The entire convoy turned into the Lange Voorhout, a double tree-lined avenue flanked by stately patrician houses, it was the Embassy Row of The Hague. From far away I saw more and more vehicles snaking around the corner of the Kneuterdyk, joining the mass of black, brown, and green, and finally screeching to a halt in front of the Hotel des Indes at the end of the avenue.

For generations this had been the meeting place for foreign dignitaries and the site of The Hague's most prominent social events. Just a week earlier, my friends and I had been blissfully dancing and laughing at a tea-dance here. But we would never be young and carefree again. The fun was over and the springtime of our life was gone forever.

In between throngs of silent people I stood at the corner and surveyed the scene in utter amazement, never having seen so many different military vehicles. When they stopped I tried to reach the Government Bureau of Food Distribution, where I recently had started to work.

"Halt! Zurück, zurück!!" a tall Nazi policeman suddenly stepped in front of me and motioned me back. I was jolted for a moment. Then I glared at him. What! I couldn't pass! This was my town!

"Ich muss dort sein," I said in my best school German, pointing to where I was going and resolutely walking on to our building. The officer, surprised at my positive action, lamely waved me through. When I had the courage to peek back, he was still watching me, scratching his head, apparently not realizing that Germans were unwelcome and that the Dutch were not going to receive them with open arms.

At our office everyone crowded around the open door or in front of the windows. Although I was extremely upset and my eyes were getting moist, I still wanted to see what was happening. Arm in arm with my office friends I watched the Nazis unload. One of the girls put her head on my shoulder and sobbed quietly. She had not heard from her fiance' and didn't know if he was dead or alive. While we comforted her, we heard a few shrill whistles and barked commands. The soldiers were allowed out of their vehicles, and before we knew what was happening, they barged into our office, roughly pushing us aside. Without a word they took over the bathrooms. Some washed in the tiny hall-bowl, used for cleaning the marble corridors and the stoop outside. We stood around watching as a soldier shaped his eyebrows with a miniscule fold-up razor and mirror. It seemed ridiculous at that moment, and I laughed between my tears. What was he thinking? Was he primping for the girls?

A few seconds later our attention was drawn to two high ranking Nazis arriving in their shiny black Mercedes, emblazoned with swastika pennants. Stepping out, stiffly erect, they clicked their heels, and gave the straight-arm Nazi salute. They then entered the Secretary of Defense building next to us. We could not believe our eyes. Somehow none of us thought this fancy footwork routine was for real.

"For chrissakes, look at those clowns with their goose-step," I heard someone say. "They look like they have swallowed a stick."

"You mean they have a stick up their arse," someone else added. We all laughed nervously.

In the afternoon we watched Dutch soldiers march by to surrender their weapons, tossing them on a pile at the end of the avenue.

The night before, some guns had been burned to keep them out of enemy hands. From my home I could see the huge fire on the parade ground of the Malieveld. Father had run down to throw his anti-Nazi books into the flames. He watched while our motorized cavalry drove their bikes into a big heap. After throwing in more guns, they poured gasoline over the weapon pyre. As flames started to lick their way around the mound, the commander reverently put the regiment's banner on the pile, rather than handing it over to the enemy. It was a heartbreaking moment and many a soldier brushed away his tears.

Elsewhere, fearful families emptied out their wine, afraid that German soldiers would get drunk and become abusive. Though Father considered this possibility, he did not have the heart to take such a drastic measure and he hid the wine instead.

A few months earlier the Dutch army had marched by our house. I had many friends in the army and so stood on the sidewalk waving them on. Discipline was not the greatest in Holland and, behind the back of the sergeant, many soldiers turned and waved. I loved them for that! We were not a fighting nation! We were not aggressive. We were peaceful, happy, a little fat, a little complacent, and most of all, extremely small. We were like children playing with tin soldiers and toy cars.

Now as they dropped their arms on the pile, I saw that the tin soldiers had grown into men, who had fought hard and been beaten. They turned and marched off, heads high, and I felt with them the unspoken pledge to remain forever Dutch.

Everyone went home after that. We followed a seemingly endless convoy of German army vehicles west to Scheveningen on their way to install heavy artillery on the beach. Nazi officers began to move into the resort hotels.

It was still light outside. The weather was pleasantly warm. I inhaled the perfect spring air and let it flow out of my lungs with a sigh. The ducks in the canals were still quacking, sitting on their cone-shaped straw nests provided by the city. The tulips in the park were still blooming, some of them trampled, but although crushed, they still added color to the gloom. I thought of the bulb fields behind the dunes. They were in full bloom, too. Large squares of vivid colors stretched out as far as one could see. Most had been destroyed by the jackboots of the parachutists. Would they ever bloom again? Suddenly I felt a lump in my throat and holding back my tears I ran into the safety of our home.

Father called a family conference. He asked my sister to stop declaring her independence, leave her dingy apartment and come home. Our four-storied house was on the Nassauplein in The Hague. The "garden city" was the seat of the government, with beautiful homes, wide avenues, and a center of medieval buildings surrounding a square man-made lake, the Hofvyver. In this location my father's medical office was combined with living quarters. It was an old patrician house with oak paneling, green velvet wallpaper and leaded glass windows. Two blocks south we could see the tower of the Peace Palace. This permanent Court of International Justice was built in 1913 with money given by the American steel king, Andrew Carnegie. Unfortunately, with a madman like Hitler, the Peace Palace did not do us much good.

On the ground floor of our home were my father's offices and a patients' waiting room with a small dispensary. At the end of the hall was a large kitchen where Gretchen, our German maid, ruled. A Dutch girl came in daily to clean and open the door for the patients. Gretchen, who stayed with us almost ten years, saw my sister and me grow up. She often listened patiently to my stories as I chatted with her in the kitchen, perched on a little stool.

When the war came, Gretchen was in a quandary. After so many years in Holland, she felt very Dutch. But after the Germans took over she was besieged with letters carrying large swastikas on the envelope, asking her to join a Nazi women's group. Polite requests soon turned into threats. Gretchen became frightened and finally joined. She was now gone more than she was home, and we knew she was forced to spy on us. It became very difficult to live in the same house with her since we were all engaged in some form of underground activity.

In the summer of 1942 we moved to a smaller home without a maid's room and it was a relief to see Gretchen go. We had arrived at the point where we barely spoke to her. I felt very bad about it because we never heard from her again.

A week after Holland surrendered, Hitler installed Dr. Arthur Seyss-Inquart, an ardent Nazi, as "Reichskommissar" of the Netherlands. He was a native Austrian (as was Hitler) who had played an important part in arranging the annexation of Austria in 1938 by Nazi Germany. A man with a slight limp and thick dark-rimmed glasses, he brought his own Nazi police force, and settled in the historic government buildings on the Binnenhof in The Hague. From the spot where Queen Wilhelmina used to open Parliament, he made his first proclamation:

"Today I accepted the highest government authority of all civil affairs in the Netherlands. Thanks to the generosity of Der Führer and the power of the German Wehrmacht, order has been established only a few days after the disaster caused by the previous ruler of Holland."

We had to understand, he said, that the German people were fighting to win the war, a fight which the enemy — the British — had forced onto them, and that the Germans had to invade us in order to thwart a British attack on Europe. For now, he said, he would let the Dutch authorities run their own affairs and let the Dutch laws prevail. The speech went on and on, one lie after another, and concluded with a loud triple "Sieg Heil." For the first time we heard the Horst Wessel song, the Nazi national anthem, which would be our music from now on.

Hearing him talk was bad enough, but when the born Austrian said we were "blood relations of the same Germanic race," we were really upset. We had never felt any kinship with the Germans, nor did we want any. We are different in every way. Militarism is ingrained in the German people, while the Dutch are not militaristic at all. They hate regimentation and always try to ignore as many rules as possible. A Dutchman is a fierce individualist who does not want anyone, and certainly not a stranger, telling him what to do. His life is simple and unpretentious, and that's the way he wants it. Our family was brought up to act and feel the same way.

Unfortunately Seyss-Inquart knew as little about us as Hitler did, and he underestimated us in every way. The words "blood relation" were ill chosen, making us even more hostile. Geography had placed the Germans on our border, but it was a grand delusion that a common border gave us a common outlook on life. Although many Dutch conducted business with the Germans, spent vacations in their mountains, and appreciated their art, music, and science, we resented their extreme arrogance after they had embraced the Nazi doctrine.

Over the centuries Holland, situated at the mouths of the big rivers, had given shelter to so many European refugees that we learned to be tolerant and, even more important, to shun repression and value freedom.

Now, in five devastating days, we not only had lost our freedom, but nearly three thousand soldiers had been killed, and many civilians had died in air-raids. Families grieving over lost relatives and friends were still in a state of shock.

But life went on and damaged cities were rebuilt. New bridges replaced the ones that had been destroyed. Rotterdam filled its canals with the rubble of the bombardment and started an innovative plan to reconstruct the inner city. Trains, trams, and buses were soon running again. However, there was an ominous sign that some food already had to be rationed.

Our government in London advised us, through our daily quarter-hour of Dutch information on Radio Orange, to stay calm and return to work. Most people did, but as more German troops crossed our borders, our mood darkened. With disdain we watched the soldiers constantly shuttled around in buses and cars, thronging our sidewalk cafes, filling our hotels, laughing and drinking on our terraces, sunning on our beaches. German souvenir stands sprung up like toadstools after a rain, occupying shops from which Jewish owners had fled. Hundreds of wooden shoes and Dutch dolls were sold to the soldiers, eventually to be sent to families in Germany. All this was very hard to stomach.

At first the regular German army behaved decently. There were few cases of rape or looting. The officers billeted with my relatives were courteous. Some didn't realize we loathed them for condoning the cruelty and ruthlessness of their Nazi system, and for worshipping their deceitful Führer, who solemnly promised to respect our neutrality while secretly preparing for the invasion of Holland.

Although the Germans were trained in almost everything, they knew surprisingly little about us. Some didn't know we understood their language and purposely gave them wrong directions.

"They found the road to Holland, they can damn well find their way now!" the angry Dutch reasoned while happily watching them turn into the wrong road. A bus driver would not stop when a German waited on the street, cheered on by his passengers. Children mimicked Seyss-Inquart, calling him "Six-and-a-quart." They giggled and limped, peering through a circle of sticky fingers. One time I watched an old lady sitting in the park. She joyfully tripped a stiff strutting Nazi officer as he passed, sticking out her cane!

At first we were more confused than frightened by the different uniforms appearing in mass formation around town. We recognized only the double-SS in a lightning-bolt design, the emblem of the Waffen S.S., a hard core of vicious and fanatical Nazis. Day and night endless columns came marching by. Their heavy jackboots hitting the bricks made a terrible racket which resounded through the streets. This symphony on stone, combined with their loud singing with the abrupt halt after each sentence, jarred our senses, kept us awake at night, and drove us crazy. I started to detest their songs. Lili Marlene was their most popular one. We heard it constantly and were shocked to find that the American soldiers had adopted the same Lili Marlene as their theme song!

One day a woman's army, in sweeping grey capes, marched by our house. I watched in amazement and called my mother.

"Mom, come quick and have a look! What do you think they're doing here?"

Mother made a face. "They're Blitzmädel, girls of the Blitz war," she said. "They're here to keep their Nazi officers happy." She was probably right. The Nazis were organized in all ways, although I heard the women were telephone operators during the day.

The Dutch labeled them "Grey Mice." Later some of our *Dutch girls* cozied up to the enemy. We were disgusted to see them flirting with the Nazi officers and called them "field-mattresses," adding "They were lying under everything except the tram!" After the war they would be tarred and feathered, we promised.

"Die rot meiden, worse than alley-cats," I complained to my mother. It bothered me more than anything that some of my own sex had absolutely no scruples.

"I cannot believe they do this just for a fun time. The stigma of sleeping with the enemy will haunt them forever. Everybody will know and won't forget." I was thoroughly annoyed.

Mother was unperturbed. "They don't think that far ahead," she said calmly. "Besides, they don't care!"

The Germans were billeted all over town, here and there confiscating a house over the loud protests of the owners. Our family was proud of our great-aunt Cato who, when the soldiers came, glared down from the top of her steep dark stairs and shouted:

"I'm nearly one hundred years old! Don't you *dare* to come up. You're not invited and I'll shoot!"

The Germans knew that only two old ladies lived in the four-story home and had come to confiscate it for offices. But they had not counted on our spunky Cato, all ninety-nine years of her, still as spry as a sparrow. Fortunately for our dignified and feisty aunt, the soldiers had been told to tread lightly in the beginning, and so they retreated, disgruntled. Two years later our dear aunt peacefully died in her own home.

I was much impressed with Cato's defiance.

"How come she was so strong and lived so long?" I asked my father once, expecting him to give me some medical explanation. His eyes fell on a bottle of Dutch gin from Cato's family-owned factory, the well-known Rynbende gin. I followed his stare and I saw it coming. Father always laughed hardest at his own jokes. The corners of his eyes crinkled, he started to grin, and when he couldn't suppress his glee any longer, he burst out, "She probably was pickled in her own gin!" We both laughed. Father always kept his sense of humor. It became so important during the following years. A smile or a laugh, even in the worst of times, helped us keep our sanity.

3

The concept of Holland under Nazi control was a fact that we never got used to, and never accepted. It was a whole new experience, and for the time being, we took a wait-and-see approach to the matter, while we watched our invaders with contempt. At first we actually looked "through" them, acting as if they were not there. But after a few confrontations with the Nazis, the Dutch people started to commit themselves — some became active, some passive, and some Dutch became our enemy from within, our most despised group, the collaborators.

The vast majority of Dutch, though, were anti-Nazi. Part of these formed the basis of the underground movement. The other part was made up of those people who were basically also anti-Nazi, but only passively resisted the invaders. Some of them had German connections and could not make up their minds in the beginning. The irony was that, although these people took less risk, in later years they were in just as much danger of being sent to jail, picked up for labor in Germany, or shot as hostages. I presume they realized then that there had been no advantage in staying "neutral" as the Nazis did not trust any Dutchman.

A few young men managed to escape to join the fighting forces in England, while others decided to stay in Holland to help a future Allied invasion. They were the ones who started the Resistance.

Since we had been spared a war, or even a civil war for generations, it took many months for a Resistance movement to start. But after a while various loose-knit groups came into being. These secret groups started in offices, schools, universities, laboratories, hospitals, railway stations, government bureaus, little cafés, and even in churches. The first attempts at sabotage were generally the cutting of German military phone lines, the puncturing of the well-worn tires of their armored cars, and the writing of anti-Nazi slogans on walls and billboards around town. This was the beginning and it didn't take the experienced German counter-intelligence long to break up those little groups which had much courage but little experience.

I always felt that the Germans themselves contributed largely to the making of the real underground. In their arrogant way they went after the small-fry with far-too-heavy guns. Their viciousness not only made many neutral people eventually hate them, but it made us more determined to retaliate.

Aside from the few collaborators, men and women of all ages and all walks of life showed their patriotism in any way they could. How much they did depended only on how brave or how ingenious they were. We all became amateur saboteurs and it was a dangerous game. Children caught on immediately. They found out quickly how their parents felt and were delighted to play a secret part. Some sneaked out at night to remove the manhole covers in the street, hoping that when an unwary Nazi marched along, he would fall into the open hole.

Every obstructive thing we did kept up our morale and it restored part of our self-esteem which had been shattered after the surrender. We were not willing to submit to the Nazi regime. We wanted to get rid of these miserable intruders. We were ready to fight against all odds to defend our home, our family, and our way of life.

In the meantime, contact with England was established and expert advice came into our country by clandestine radio. Intelligence officers dropped into Holland at night, bringing arms, cameras, and transmitters. Everyone involved in illegal activities needed a hiding place. Some of them were Dutchmen who had escaped from Holland earlier. Helped by their friends they returned as secret agents to start an intelligence network.

After a while it was difficult to tell whether it was harder to escape from Holland, or to hide inside it. The country is mostly flat. Its wide open vistas with some trees and only a farm here and there has few natural places to hide. Lacking mountains, a rocky coast, or dense woods, we could not build up a movement such as the French Maquis. We also had no neutral neighbor. The treacherous North Sea on our north and our west was alive with German submarines and destroyers, Belgium on our south was occupied by Germans, and on our eastern border was Nazi Germany itself.

We soon figured out that the best cover was a job, the more normal-looking the better. As a result many people led a double life and nobody knew what else his neighbor was doing.

Eventually our sabotage became more sophisticated. Wireless sets were built at home and hidden into the smallest containers of normal household articles. A two-way radio contact with London was established. The underground was now undertaking many extremely dangerous tasks: returning British pilots who had bailed out over Holland, assisting hundreds of people to escape or to disappear in our own country, forging of documents and the printing of illegal papers.

At the same time human errors, lack of experience, and infiltration of traitors collected their price. This dangerous game was not a game anymore. When traitors slipped into the ranks and, if they were not found out in time, a complete group was often executed. ·

The enemy from within, most of them misfits in one way or another, was a serious threat we had to deal with. Nothing dismayed us more than seeing these pro-Nazi Dutchmen, even if there were only a few of them, cater to our enemy. I had never noticed them much before. They were mainly members of the Nationaal Socialistische Beweging, National Socialist Movement, an organization of about 30,000 members. Called "N.S.B." for short, it had been created before the war. Now we saw these Nazi clones march through the city in black uniforms. They copied the goose-step, greeted each other with straight-arm salutes, and shouted "Houzee" (straight ahead) instead of Sieg Heil. After watching the actions of these turncoats, we branded them *quislings*. Some were died-in-the-wool Nazis and others were just opportunists. They helped the Nazis for their own advantage, betrayed their countrymen, exposed Jews, and some actually fought with the Waffen S.S. in Russia.

With the support of the Nazis, N.S.B. members led a good life and were exempt from most regulations, which upset us even more.

Heading the N.S.B. party was Anton A. Mussert, a short, heavyset, balding man. Before the war he had worked as a civil engineer for the government. Although he skirmished with other Dutch pro-Nazis, he managed to stay on top of the party. He visited Hitler in Berlin, trying to be named official leader of the Netherlands, just as Vidkun Quisling, whose name became a synonym for a traitor, became leader of Norway. Hitler put him off by promising him power only if he could get the people's support. To this end Mussert started the Weermacht Afdeling (W.A.), a police action group patterned after the Nazi system. The W.A. became increasingly more provocative and, as patriotic activity increased, many street fights erupted between its members and the loyal Dutch citizens. When the W.A. brazenly marched through the tough harbor district of Rotterdam, angry citizens threw flowerpots, roof tiles, and even the contents of chamberpots down on their heads!

We laughed reading this in the papers, but the unpleasant fact was that the Dutch Nazis became more powerful through the years as the Germans used them to do their dirty work.

Despite Mussert's obvious devotion to the Nazi cause, Seyss-Inquart jealously guarded his own authority and never allowed him full power to run the government.

In 1942 Mussert again visited Hitler and offered him 10,000 disciplined W.A. Dutchmen to fight with the Waffen S.S. in Russia. Hitler finally agreed to appoint him head of Holland. Despite this appointment, our country was still ruled by Seyss-Inquart and the tough Hans Albin Rauter, who was chief of the complicated Nazi police system. During the post-war trial, Mussert was found guilty of treason by the Netherlands' Courts. He went to his execution in 1946 still complaining that he had tried his best for Holland, but he didn't get a fair chance.

I always wondered if the plodding German soldiers knew what was happening in Holland. Every area had different experiences. In the country I heard that some Germans were not as strict in enforcing regulations. But in the cities they were a different breed. Most of the troops that were sent to The Hague were dedicated Nazis with a singleness of purpose. Anyone who stood in their way would be destroyed without hesitation.

4

On the surface, life in Holland seemed to go on as usual. People worked during the week and relaxed or participated in some sport on the weekends. On the first warm day in June, I went to meet my friends on the beach in Scheveningen, knowing that, even though I had lost track of them since the invasion, they'd be at the beach club as usual.

The Luxe Bad was an ideal gathering place. I caught the tram to the Kurhaus, a sumptuous hotel on the boulevard. From there I ran down to the club, jumping two steps at a time to get down to the sand. The Germans were quartered in all the hotels of this seaside town, but they had not yet invaded our private club. Geys, the bathmaster, still ruled over the cabins. Born and bred in Scheveningen, he was a good friend and a true Dutchman. He now greeted me warmly with a bear hug. I felt at home.

There on the beach, war or no war, I saw our unique stationary Dutch beach cabins, chicken-coop size. They were still standing, and arranged in a square as comforting as the sight of Geys. Six or more of us would rent them for a year, changing clothes between heaps of shoes and wet bathing suits. In the middle of the square you could sunbathe and not be bothered by the wind. Outside was the wide, yellow, sandy beach. Waves of the North Sea pounded the coast, but the water was reasonably warm due to the Caribbean current passing through the English Channel.

I used to enjoy the beach thoroughly, but today I felt uneasy about this reunion. So much had changed in the last month. Most of the familiar faces of my friends, boys and girls in their twenties, were there and I immediately spotted Erik, who looked healthy, tanned, and extremely attractive. He seemed so mature all of a sudden. Perhaps the war had made us all look older.

Erik's normally smiling eyes were full of sorrow when he told us that two of our friends, Evert and Joop, had been killed the very first day of the war. They were in the army, and had been sent to defend the Ypenburg Airport. When they tried to cross the highway, they were shot. They had not realized that the innocent-looking farmers standing on the other side were German parachutists.

I was shattered after hearing this terrible news and I would have liked to ask Erik some more questions, but the others were crowding around him. Extremely upset, I turned away, laid my beach towel on the sand, and stretched out on it. Looking pensively at the sky with the ever-present grey clouds, I started to reminisce and didn't hear my friends anymore. All I could think of was Evert and Joop tricked to their death by German soldiers in farmers' clothes.

I remembered that some years ago I had actually seen this cunning, deceitful Nazi Führer, this monster, Hitler, who had ordered the merciless killing of so many innocent people.

I was only fourteen when my parents sent me to Godesberg-am-Rhein for German studies. My mother felt that an educated young woman should speak German, French, and English, and she arranged for me to go to Germany first, together with my girlfriend Carry.

On a bright summer day the two of us arrived at Godesberg, "City of Roses," one of Hitler's favorite places. We stayed as paying guests with a German family. Because the father was a teacher, we could visit the local high school to see what German children learned. When we arrived that day in 1933, everyone was excited about the upcoming visit of the Reichschancellor. We knew little of Hitler and had only seen him in the newsreels. All I knew came from my father who often said, "That little creep with the moustache is a dangerous man."

He really wasn't that little, as I found out later, but that's the way we all talked about him, as he looked deceptively unimpressive.

Hitler did not show up that day. Instead, two uniformed leaders of the newly formed Nazi Youth Movement appeared on the scene with a barrage of propaganda. They promised a longer summer vacation and the use of a horse or motorcycle to all boys who would join the Hitler Jugend. Their blandishments were irresistible and the boys joined up by the dozen. Only much later did I learn that everyone who didn't join that day was eventually forced to join later.

The next evening Hitler arrived for a more or less informal youth rally in the Sports Center. The hundreds of flags and torches were an impressive sight. When Hitler entered, the crowd's roaring never seemed to stop. I thought this little man with his narrow black moustache was ridiculous, standing there looking nervous in his dark blue suit. Although I knew German well, it was hard to understand him. It was unbelievable that, as loudly as he started each topic, he could get louder still, his voice finally rising to a hysterical pitch. It seemed that everyone believed what he said. The Germans were completely under his spell and loved him. After every important statement the boys and girls screamed, "Sieg Heil!" It was great fun even for us to yell along at the top of our lungs. At age fourteen who knew what it really meant?

Hitler passed close to me as he left the rally and I noticed his penetrating eyes. It was incomprehensible to me then that he would someday rule nearly all of Europe.

During the few months there, Carry and I made some German friends, who at seventeen seemed much more adult than us. One day, after we swam together in the new municipal pool, Kurt and Heinrich asked us to a dance that night. We went, properly chaperoned. Although we had a good time, the conversation always returned to the Hitler Youth Movement. It bored Carry and me silly. In their fancy swastika armbands and short black pants, the two boys practiced the goose-step, and tried to teach us.

"Keep your legs straight and kick high," they said. They looked so absurd that Carry and I fell over laughing. However, the boys were very serious. Within a few weeks, they were on police duty at a Nazi rally in a neigboring town. They felt important and became extremely cocky, secure in their numbers. It was amazing how they changed! Blindly, they followed the strict Nazi commands of not to hear, not to see, not to question. As an independent Dutch girl, I wondered how they could have such unswerving obedience. Irritated at my questions, they told us that they were making a better Germany, while getting free travel and free lodging. With a smugness that really bothered me, they added, that in uniform the "plain people" would allow them to do what they pleased.

None of their military affectation appealed to me and our friendships died quickly. How could they lap up that crazy propaganda? And why would they hate the Jews so much?

Carry and I, involved in school and new friendships, soon forgot them. Two years later, Interpol, the international police, came to our home in Holland, asking if we had hidden Heinrich. He had apparently disappeared, motorcycle and all. My surprised father shook his head sadly, predicting that these boys would mean trouble later. He was right. One day after the Nazis invaded Holland I stared in horror when I saw Kurt the perfect Nazi, tall, blond, crew-cut, and stiffly erect, striding at the head of a column of S.S. men. Disciplined to look straight ahead, he probably didn't see me, but I imagined that, for an instant, I saw his cold grey eyes turn my way.

The shrill blast of the beach horn, a warning for swimmers to stay close to shore, jarred me back to the present. I slowly got up and, joining the others, found they were in a heated argument.

Rolf, a longtime friend, was surprisingly aggressive. As I stood rubbing my eyes, he suddenly turned to me and asked,

"And who are you fighting for? For yourself, the Dutch, or the Queen, who left us?" He paused a moment, then added, "Why not stop thinking about resistance and join the Nazis?"

I gasped, "What do you mean? Are you crazy?"

I imagined Evert's lifeless young face, bloody in the dirt, shot to death.

"Are you serious?" I said, "I'm fighting for myself, for my friend, for the whole country."

By now I was really upset. "Do you think I want to be run by a half-wit Führer, a madman, who yells, and screams, and throws himself on the floor chewing on the carpet? I want to be free, not run by anybody. I want to live my own life, a decent life, and hon-est life! I want to be married and have kids, and bring them up in my own way. I don't want my babies born with a swastika stamped on their little bottoms! Besides, do you have any idea what those people are doing to the Jews?"

I stopped to catch my breath, while I looked at Rolf, shaking my head. Robby, standing next to me, listened intently to our con-versation, his large brown eyes looking sadder by the minute. He smiled at me and said,

"Thanks, Babes. You know my grandmother is Jewish. None of you has any idea what they're doing to the Jews, and you never cared to know either."

"If so, I'm sorry," I said, "but now we *do* know and we *do* care."

Rolf kept up his attack. "You talk about being Dutch and want-ing to be free. If the British had invaded, you would've welcomed them with open arms, even helped them!"

"Of course, if they came to beat the Krauts. Besides, the British are different. They're not Nazi. They don't torture the Jews. Tell me, would you, a normal human being, do that to any other race?"

Rolf shrugged his shoulders. "Well, it happens all over the

world."

"That might be," Frits answered for me, "But the Dutch aren't killing the Jews. For a hell of a long time, we accepted refugees from everywhere who were persecuted for any reason."

There was a silence. We had never been aware of the difference in race or religion among our group of friends. With the German occupation we suddenly became conscious of Jewish people.

"You're crazy, all of you." Rolf continued. "it's easier to work with the Nazis, now that they're here. Their ideas aren't that bad. They cleaned up their own country, after the last war."

His cool approach, knowing Nazis had killed our own friends, was infuriating.

"That's fine. They should've stayed in their own cleaned-up country," I said. "What are you, a Mof?"

Now Erik exploded, "For chrissakes, listen to him! He talks like a goddamn Nazi already!"

For a moment there was a silence. We looked at each other. A lot had changed in the last few weeks. With an uneasy feeling we left for home that day.

Slowly, but surely, differences crept into the attitudes of life-long friends. Some, like Rolf, became openly pro-Nazi and joined the Dutch Nazi Party. They drifted away until one day we saw them march by in a black uniform. Another friend went to Germany as a stud. When the Nazis asked for volunteers of pure Aryan blood to perfect and promulgate the master race, he signed up. Tall, blond and handsome, his picture appeared on posters all over other occupied countries, to the mortification of his family.

During the next year, our group of friends shrank. Some tried to study for degrees, but when they demonstrated against the removal of Jewish professors, the Germans closed the universities. Most looked for a job or joined the Resistance. Occasionally, we saw each other, but I never knew for sure whom to trust. An old friend could have become a traitor. Each conversation began superficially and no names were mentioned until the loyalty of the other person was established.

Some fell in love with a pro-Nazi and changed completely, often betraying their old friends. Others were fence-sitters. All were dangerous. Our friendships, which had been so strong for many years, became unpredictable. We still acted as if we were friends, but we were extremely careful. A traitor could have you executed, best friend or not.

My friends and I could only guess what the consequences

would be of committing ourselves that day on the beach. But I was sure there was no other choice for me. I would fight any intruder who forced me to be different, and who tried to enslave our whole country. *I never knew what democracy and freedom was until it was taken away from me.*

5

Being a sports-minded people in the best of times, the Dutch more than ever needed a physical outlet. On summer weekends we flocked to the beaches and lakes for water sports. After a year, the Germans declared most lakes and waterways off limits. The Dutch underground had been using them for escape routes. By the time they imposed new restrictions, our boat was dry-docked. This cut-back caused me to concentrate more on tennis.

When I was invited to play in the annual International Tennis Tournament in Noordwyk, I was ecstatic. Having a chance to play in this tournament was also a momentary relief from the harsh reality of war, although it was no longer international. In previous years top American players like Donald Budge participated, and the French were represented by "The Four Musketeers": Lacoste, Brugnon, Borotra and Cochet, who delighted all spectators with their brilliant play. Now there were only Dutch players.

I arrived in Noordwyk by bus and walked to the club. Some players were already practicing on the gravel courts. Others were milling around the tournament desk, reading the paper and nervously talking together. I wondered what the commotion was all about until I saw the headlines: There it was "Van Swol Shuns Davis Cup Partner."

Hans van Swol, our best player, flatly refused to play with his doubles partner, an admitted Nazi sympathizer. The Dutch Lawn Tennis Association was in a quandary when the N.S.B. threatened to cancel the tournament. Finally one entrant reluctantly agreed to play with the Dutch Nazi to keep the event going.

In the afternoon I played my match and lost, so I was out of the tournament the very first day. I was sad, but I now could enjoy the parties at night. I had a wonderful time at a dance at the club-house and wandered back to my housing at one in the morning. There I found the owners had left and another player was sleeping in my bed. When I asked him to leave, he said a few nasty things, but did not move. Extremely annoyed, I settled myself on the floor in the living room with pillows from the couch.

A little later, another tennis player, Piejan, short for Pieter-Jan, arrived. He looked at me on the floor and asked what was happening. I explained and laughed at his astonishment. He stomped into the other rooms only to find out that all the other beds had been taken, too.

"How come the owners have gone?" Piejan asked while settling himself next to me on the floor.

"I have no idea." I watched Piejan tossing and turning. After a few minutes he told me he couldn't sleep. By then neither could I. We started talking and after a while he confided that he had bought two big cans of white paint, and planned to write anti-German slogans on the walls of the town that night.

"You know those Krauts still think we like them," Piejan shook his head and pushed a recalcitrant blond lock from his forehead.

"Yeah, I can't believe it either," I agreed. "They really expected us to love being part of their so-called Third Reich, whatever that means. How could they be so darn conceited. I don't know what the other two 'Reichs' are, do you?"

"Nope, I don't care either. I'm just going to make sure they know we don't want those Nazi farts here."

Then Piejan, as if on second thought, looked at me and suddenly asked, "Would you like to help me paint, or shall we make love?"

I glanced at him and tried not to smile at this bold question. Of course he was joking. Teasingly, I was quiet for a moment, as if in a quandary about the unusual offer. After a few seconds, I looked up and said cheerfully, "Let's paint."

Piejan flashed me a brilliant smile and grabbed for the pails. Juggling pails, brushes, and flashlight, we started off into the black night, feeling our way in the beginning, but finally getting used to the darkness. It was hard to find bare walls which did not belong to private homes. We walked through the quiet streets, skirting the beach area, which was full of Germans, until we came to the inner village.

In the center of Noordwyk, at the town square, we found the bare walls we were looking for. I painted "Oranje Boven" hailing the House of Orange, on my first try. Piejan simply wrote, "Go home dirty Moffen." We admired each other's work, gaining confidence as we went along, splashing garden walls and public buildings.

We became so engrossed in our work, we nearly forgot about the Germans. Suddenly footsteps rang in the quiet street. A Nazi patrol. We scooted around the corner, through a back alley, and hid in a recessed back doorway of a restaurant, holding our breaths.

"Just one more street and we can hide in the church," I whispered. Piejan nodded in agreement. We crept out, walking on our toes toward the church. Groping around in the dark, we found the back door open and we slipped inside. I grabbed Piejan's arm, as he pulled me along toward the altar. There, we kneeled and bowed our heads, momentarily, then quickly hid in a nearby corridor. When everything was again quiet outside, we left our sanctuary to paint even more boldly, really getting into the spirit of things. With my last swab, I wrote in giant letters: "Hitler is a rotvent," expressing my feeling that the Führer was a bum.

We returned to our overcrowded housing thinking that our evening had indeed been well spent. I never saw a German reaction but the next morning I was scared. In daylight, our painting spree looked a lot more startling. We really had been carried away and were lucky not to have been caught.

Feeling guilty about defacing the buildings, I walked back to the small church, said a little prayer, and put some money in the box. Then I felt it was safe to leave town and go home to The Hague.

While I was gone, Father acquired a special stove to fuel his English Morris. It filled the trunk of the car. Gasoline was rationed, and since the amount was insufficient for him to visit the hospital and his patients, he made this conversion for about fifteen hundred guilders, a lot of money in those days. Wood or coal fueled this strange-looking contraption. It took our calm and helpful chauffeur, Strien, about thirty minutes every morning to light the fire, which eventually produced enough energy to drive the car. Every time my father stopped at a patient's home, Strien shoveled more anthracite on the fire. Without gasoline, Holland's transportation was a serious problem and became a challenge to the most inventive. Some taxi companies had huge gas balloons on top of their cars, and it looked as if the whole cab would fly away in a storm. Many kinds of electric cars were invented — small ones with three wheels, one in front, two in the back, with the driver inside, or sometimes outside the cab.

The most frequently used transportation in Holland was still the bicycle. Young and old, rich or poor, all Dutch rode their bicycles to school, to work, to church, and to the beach, everywhere.

A favorite pastime of the Dutch is people-watching and making loud, if not always complimentary remarks, from a sidewalk café. We used to watch the bike riders with just as much interest as the tourists. We would laugh at the conglomeration of people riding their iron steeds. It was wonderful how they managed to swerve through traffic with two children on the back, a dog in front and groceries somewhere in between! While pedaling they talked to each other, even while standing eight abreast at the intersection, waiting for the light to turn. Sometimes, it was a businessman in a dark coat tipping his hat in a formal greeting to a friend, or a priest in habit, a group of giggling girls, a chubby baker with a cart attached in front of the bike, a curly-haired butcher-boy with his wicker basket full of meat. We smiled as a pretty young girl rode past, slapping the mischievous hands of her boyfriend sitting behind her, while she steered furiously to avoid a crash.

When rubber tires became rare, the riders didn't give up. Wooden ones were invented, strips of hardwood bound together with wire. They were terribly noisy and they gave you a headache, bouncing over the cobblestones, even though we padded our seats with pieces of felt!

Finally the Germans just took our bikes. First, they asked, and, when we didn't bring them in, they came and got them. Hundreds of them! One moment you were riding, next minute a Nazi soldier stopped you and no more bike! From then on, we walked to work on shoes with wooden soles, leather by then being nonexistent. I learned to walk in clogs, and even to run, without losing them. It was better than standing in the overcrowded trams, jammed into so many unwashed people, soap being another luxury gone with our freedom. This was really shocking for the ultra-clean Dutch who used to scrub even the sidewalks with soap and water!

Although the Germans took a percentage of horses, there were still a few left in The Hague. They pulled wedding and funeral carriages. I heard that somewhere in Wassenaar there was a horse-drawn bus. For a while our vegetable man still came to the door with his old nag, Nellie, pulling his huge wagon, though it was only half-filled with produce. Nellie was my friend from childhood. She knew each customer's house, pawed her hoof on the sidewalk and knocked on the door with her nose while she waited for her master to catch up, knowing that the knocking would produce a lump of sugar. Sometimes, four or five little kids wobbled on Nellie's sturdy back, squealing with delight and holding on for dear life. The heavy wagon would sway behind, surrounded by a flock of saucy English sparrows, waiting to retrieve seeds from the droppings. That time passed, too, and soon the horse could not feed the birds because there was not enough food to feed the horse. By the start of 1944 when even potato peelings were listed "for human consumption," it was very sad to notice that our special horse-meat stores were doing a brisk business.

6

Many people in Holland were resigned to a few unpleasant changes as the consequence of defeat, and thought that the war would soon be over. Deep in our hearts we were certain that good would conquer evil, and this prevented us from having a realistic understanding of the situation.

Listening to any foreign broadcast was verboten, so we listened in secret to the B.B.C. on our hidden radio. Every day this station started the newscast with the same fetching Morse code signal, the V for Victory, which is the four opening bars of Beethoven's Fifth Symphony. It ended with Vera Lynn singing, "We'll Meet Again." It brought tears to our eyes. The news was our lifeline to the outer world, and was one of the most important events of the day. We all had learned English in school and could follow the broadcasts quite well. We loved hearing Winston Churchill's speeches, giving us such heart, particularly his address to the House of Commons after the miraculous escape at Dunkirk. His vibrant and infectious voice renewed our courage when he said they would fight on the beaches, on the landing grounds, fight in the fields, in the street and in the hills. "We will never surrender!"

In the following months new undercover activities started. Previous Dutch intelligence officers secretly organized, my future husband among them. They became an effective Resistance. Various escapes to England were planned.

Most plans were still in the talking stage when three students went to the beach in Noordwyk, a few miles north of Scheveningen, openly loaded a dinghy with provisions and crawled on board. German officers, drinking on the terrace of the Huis ter Duin Hotel on the dunes, stared in disbelief as the boat headed westward. Hurrying down the stairs to the beach, they started shooting, but they were too late. The little boat, hidden in the big waves, saucily made its way to freedom. After a week, Radio Orange made a coded announcement that the "Bebek," the Indonesian word for 'duck,' had landed in England. Rumors about other daring escapes were rampant and we believed them all, because in our despairing frame of mind, anything was possible. Hidden in a steamer to Sweden, mustered on fishing boats, and even alone by canoe, young "Englandvaarders" tried to get across the extremely treacherous North Sea. As the ocean seldom gives up its secrets, no one knows how many tried or how many failed.

Some of my friends did get across and joined the British Royal Air Force, those tall and lanky young men with their breezy manners and their independent ways. They became our heroes.

Slowly and subtly our life changed. We had a strict black-out regulation and the streets were dark in winter. In summer, when it was still light until eleven o'clock, we biked to Scheveningen, relaxed in tiny cafés on the boulevard or strolled on the beach, watching the sun go down. We ate croquettes sold in small tents on the Kurhaus Square. When the new herring arrived, we flocked around the colorful carts, holding the raw fish by the tail. We opened our mouths like chicks in a nest, and gobbled that delicacy! Afterwards we met our secret — and sometimes not-so-secret — lovers at the Palace bar, where a Hungarian violinist played his melancholy Magyar melodies. He knew every one of us. With his round face, his jet black hair, and smiling dark eyes, he would quickly notice a pair of lovers and make his violin softly cry next to their ears.

Soon after the invasion, we recognized Nazi informers in our sanctuary. With or without strangers, the walls seemed to have ears, and our old haunts were not the same anymore. Scheveningen with its beautiful beaches and luxurious hotels was put off limits, and our secret meetings took place in private homes. Dutch people like to belong to clubs or groups. We had a host of them: sportclubs, chess and bridge clubs, musical groups, political and religious organizations. We like to laugh at ourselves, saying, "When three Dutchmen get together, they immediately start a political party, a church, and a soccer club."

The Germans noticed the strength of the gatherings and banned them all. More than one hundred prohibited clubs were printed in the papers. Seyss-Inquart also ordered that all unions, professional, and cultural organizations be replaced by Nazi-oriented "chambers," headed by pro-Nazis. Anyone not belonging could not practice his profession. Many gave in, although most artists and writers refused. Art shows were held at home and books were printed underground.

Medical professionals realized that they were irreplaceable and did not cooperate. Eventually the Germans were provoked by a letter denouncing the new rules and inhuman treatment of prisoners.

Several hundred physicians were ordered to Vught concentration camp in Holland. They were released after six months and looked shockingly different with their bald heads, as their hair had been shaved off.

The churches, which strongly opposed National Socialism, kept a firm stand. They openly prayed for the Queen, although they were sometimes forced to grant equal time for the Nazi rulers. They always were a powerful influence in Holland with the Protestants mainly in the North and the Catholics in the South of our country. Ads for employment often stated the preferred religion.

Not only churches, but also schools, labor unions, newspapers, and political parties were organized, according to religion. During the war we did not worry about our differences and we joined in our fight against the intruder.

My first birthday during the occupation came five months later. I celebrated with a small supper party of family and friends of all age groups. My office sent flowers which my mother arranged in festive bouquets. The Germans had recently instigated a curfew from ten at night to four in the morning, so the guests arrived early in order to be home by ten. Among my many presents was the new American bestseller, "Gone with the Wind," forbidden in occupied Europe, and only sold underground.

It was a happy evening. We listened to French records, popular at that time, until someone said that a new Nazi ruling would soon be announced prohibiting any public dancing. Hearing this miserable prospect, we decided to dance the night away at our favorite restaurant, Chateau Bleu, since it would be our last chance for who knew how long.

Just before ten, I said goodbye to my older guests. Laughing and shouting, six of us younger merrymakers piled into my friend Jan's small car, two in front and four in the rumble seat, sitting on each other's laps, on our way to more fun.

We arrived just before ten and settled in to stay until four in the morning when the curfew would be lifted. The restaurant was crowded with other friends who also were planing to dance the night away. Some had recently come home from the front. They were the first soldiers released after surrendering at the end of our five-day war. The Germans called it a "long furlough," and it was later revoked.

Entering the bar, we received a joyous reception. Everyone was in a crazy mood to celebrate. They all toasted my birthday, and we became quite rambunctious. Our party grew as other friends joined us, singing, dancing, and flirting, or just sitting dreamily together on the couches.

Suddenly the party was interrupted by the sound of a droning airplane motor. We peered into the dark sky and saw a British reconnaissance plane drop a light bomb, which descended on its parachute, brightly illuminating the area for at least three minutes.

Our romantic hour was shattered. German flak went into action. Like hundreds of multi-colored Christmas lights the fiery tiny balls shot into the air. Searchlights nervously scanned the sky. We watched, mesmerized, until the cone of one beam suddenly caught the glint of the plane. Immediately the other beams zeroed in; all of them fused into one big circle of light following the flight of the lonely plane. A thunderous burst of bullets followed.

"Oh, no, don't let it happen! Please, let this brave little plane be spared!" I silently prayed.

We watched, holding on to each other, barely breathing. Gradually the plane seemed to fly even higher, and just as I thought the anti-aircraft couldn't reach it anymore, a sudden explosion — poof — a blue flame — the plane was gone!

I never forgot my 21st birthday.

7

How could we have known what it would mean to live under a Nazi regime? How could we have even imagined that they would be so evil? Unfortunately we soon found out.

The first open clash came on Prince Bernard's birthday, June 29. We always celebrated the Royal birthdays and this time everyone wore white carnations, as did our "Prince Benno," as we affectionately called him. I had forgotten my flower and seeing the others in the office wearing one, I rushed to the corner flower stand to buy one of my own. Outside there was a lot of commotion as irritated N.S.B. members tried to pull the blooms from peoples' coats. Some angry and brave souls then decided to slip razor blades in between the petals. Many fist fights started and soon Nazi squad cars appeared on the scene. The unlucky ones among us were caught and hauled off to jail. However, the Dutch, with a new outburst of loyalty for the crown, were not going to give up this happy occasion. Who were these Nazis, telling us not to celebrate?

At my lunch hour I saw people filing by the Royal Palace. Thinking this was a nice idea, I joined them. As usual, bunches of flowers were left on the steps by prettily dressed little girls.

Entire families trooped inside to sign the birthday register. Our dignified mayor, S.J.R. de Monchy, also signed with all of us. His courtly gesture was not appreciated by the Nazis, who promptly removed him from office.

This simple birthday celebration caused immediate big reactions. Troops came running into the area, planes buzzed the Palace, a dragnet was set up and quickly closed in. I returned to the office just in time to avoid arrest. I was scared, but still glad to have participated.

Now the Germans were touching the heart and soul of the Dutch. The grim reality of being run by a Nazi system started to dawn on us. Regardless of their earlier promises, we now knew that

this was a totalitarian state, a government for a few, run by a ruthless few. Seyss-Inquart's efforts to Nazify us only made us hate him
more.

In the following days German regulations were posted which
were intended to weaken the hold of the Royal Family. No orange
flowers, carnations, or the sentimental forget-me-nots were to be
sold or worn. A baby could not be named after anyone of the Royal
House or any person at war with the Reich, including Winston and
Dwight. Street names, stamps, and coins with the Queen's portrait
or name were to be changed. The last order was that Dutch flags
could not be flown; instead the swastika emblazoned many
buildings.

Our radio and newspapers were now heavily censored. Some
editors were replaced, others were told what to write. We heard
only of the successes of the German forces on their various fronts.
Immediately illegal presses went into action, and we had many.
Hiding in attics and basements, moving constantly to ward off sus-
picion, dozens of papers appeared. At first they were just mimeo-
graphed sheets urging us to resist. Later they were printed and had
some foreign news. We understood that this information gathered
in a hurry was probably not always reliable either, but it raised our
spirits.

It was mostly young girls and women who helped distribute
the papers. Frits asked me one day if I would secretly type a few
stencils at our office. Without much thought I agreed, and suddenly
I, too, was involved in distributing the papers after work. I picked
them up across the street from Oda's home in the Riouwstraat.
After a secret knock I descended into the cellar where my friends
worked in semi-darkness; only a single light bulb hanging on a cord
over the mimeograph machine gave a faint light. A few young men
were stacking the bundles and I watched their large shadows moving across the wall, giving me an eerie feeling. But I acted brave
enough and patiently stood in line with Oda and the other women
to pick up my bundle. We never said much to each other, and disappeared quickly, after carefully looking up and down the street. I
hid the papers under my groceries in the leather shopping bags
strapped across the back of my bike, and took them across town,
hiding secret notices in my hair. There I handed them to another
courier, never asking what happened to them after that, as it was
best not to know.

When one of the girls was caught and sent to jail, the press
was moved to another location and I quit working for awhile, wor-

ried that she would betray us. She never said a word and was released after a month. The papers kept on going week after week
and only stopped for a short time when a bomb fell on the house.
Miraculously my friends escaped unhurt, and started all over again
somewhere else.

When the Dutch in England heard that we had to hand in all
our radios, they started a small newspaper, aptly called "De Vlie-
gende Hollander." We saw British and much later American planes
drop millions of leaflets of this "Flying Dutchman" over our cities
every month. We heard after the war that they were led by Lt. Col.
Earl J. Aber, a brave American of the 8th Air Force. The pilots flew
breathtakingly low to pinpoint their drops. For the first time I saw
a picture of Churchill, holding up his two fingers in a V-for-Victory
sign. Unfortunately some planes were hit by German flak and later
Aber himself, just 24 years old, was shot down. We were never able
to give him our gratitude.

The Germans acted insanely when they saw the leaflets whirl
down, shooting at us instantly if we picked them up. We got them
anyway, retrieving them from roofs, balconies, and from the fields,
desperately wanting to know what was really happening.

Although we were restricted, our family life was still more or
less the same. I saw less of my friends. They were either busy or in
hiding. My sister Julie fell in love, and after a happy cross-country
courtship, she married Henk Thomassen and moved to Gorssel,
near Deventer, where he managed the family-owned can company.
After the wedding luncheon they drove off in a taxi with a gas
blimp on the roof, now adorned with gaily-colored serpentine paper
tossed over the top of the balloon, making the car look even more
ludicrous. With an old shoe and cans tied to the bumper for good
luck, all rattling along behind the car, it was a happy send-off.

A few months later they invited me for a visit. When my underground friends heard that I was going to be in the eastern part
of our country, they asked me to take a couple of handguns to a
connection in that area. With the Germans guarding the Yssel
river, it was difficult to get anything across. "They probably won't
search a girl on the train," my friends said hopefully.

I thought about it awhile. Being caught with guns would mean
concentration camp or probably worse. But millions of people were
jeopardizing their lives, also for us. Besides, I despised the Nazis. I
made up my mind.

I hid the two small guns under my full skirt with an elastic belt, and tied them around my waist in thin cotton bags. I had sewn the sacks myself, afraid to let anyone else know my secret. We had decided on a password to use when I met Remmert, my contact at the station in Deventer. I didn't know him very well, but I would recognize him anyway.

After a hug, a kiss, and a "be careful, dear," from my parents, who were unaware of my mission, I biked to the station and boarded the train, choosing a separate compartment with eight seats and a door at each end. Only a farmer and his wife were inside. They nodded a friendly hello and I relaxed. Two stations further the door opened and an S.S. officer, tall, Teutonic, with an ugly dueling scar, stepped in. I watched him, hiding my nervousness, and he peered at me like all Nazis did, trying to stare me down. It certainly worked. I immediately looked the other way.

"Wie geht's?" His steely eyes focused on me. I smiled and shrugged my shoulders as if I didn't understand. Too flustered to talk, I certainly wasn't about to have a conversation with him. He glared at me, then started to read, once in a while glancing suspiciously at me over his paper. The couple whispered to each other, watching the officer apprehensively.

In Utrecht I had to transfer to another train, but had time enough to do it leisurely. When I saw the Nazi officer transfer too, I decided to hide in the bathroom of my next train until the following stop. When I looked for it, two young men followed me, obviously with the same idea. In a hurry, the three of us pushed through the door at the same time, and there I was, jammed between two strangers in a tiny train toilet. We eyed each other in the silence common to fugitives.

It was only a short time to Amersfoort, our next stop, where I had to transfer again, this time across to the other side of the platform, Though it was a short distance, there was not much time. I was happy that I had lost 'Scarface' as I ran to the other side, pressing my hand on my stomach, holding on to my valuable package. In my haste I accidentally bumped into a German soldier and nearly fell down. Panting heavily I made it into a seat just as the train pulled out.

In Deventer I walked out behind a group of German soldiers, acting as if I belonged to them, thus able to keep an eye on their movements. The station was crowded. I looked around, anxiously scanning the crowd, but I didn't see a blond, curly-haired Remmert. Where was he? Had anything happened?

Slowly I shuffled along with the throngs of people until suddenly someone pushed me. I gasped and my heart skipped a beat.

"Sorry," a voice said softly. I looked up and saw a mop of dark brown hair. Was this Remmert? For a moment I stared at him, my eyes big as saucers.

"Hello, Babes," I heard him whisper while he put his arm through mine and pulled me along.

I smiled when I recognized the slight French accent. We two needed no password. While hundreds of passengers hustled by, we kept moving close together. I retrieved the two packages from my skirt and handed them over, fearing to look at him. For a minute he kept on walking next to me. I felt a gentle squeeze on my arm and heard a whispered, "Au revoir, ma cherie, bonne chance," as he wished me good luck. Then he slid away, disappearing into the crowd.

It all happened very fast, without any apparent danger, but I was still shaking when I saw my sister. In a daze I followed her out of the station and climbed into the horse-and-carriage sent by her husband, as there was no gas for the car anymore. Relaxing in the black leather seats, I slowly calmed down. What blissful luxury after my train trip, to now be clopping along through the peaceful countryside to their lovely estate "De Buitenkamp."

While I was with the family it was hard to act like nothing had happened just an hour earlier. Besides, I was thinking of Remmert all the time. I couldn't get him out of my mind. What dangerous thing was he involved in?

Nevertheless I had a good weekend in the country. For once I had enough to eat, as the family grew their own vegetables and could always get butter and eggs from the farmers close by. I returned home, relieved to be able to report that the guns had been delivered.

My next missions became easier with experience, and I found myself looking forward to seeing that handsome agent at the end of the line.

A year later I heard Remmert was picked up. I never saw him again. He died in a concentration camp.

8

That first year passed quickly. The occupation kept us busy and kept our blood pressure up. What would this new year of 1941 bring? Would we be liberated? Would we have peace? How badly England was scarred by Hitler's midnight bombings, we couldn't tell. We knew their supplies were at an all-time low. We wondered what the United States would do. Would they get into the war? Would they help us in our desperation? The United States seemed so far away, this huge and strong nation about which we knew so little. We had faith in President Roosevelt and felt a kinship with him because he had a Dutch background.

Just before the new year Roosevelt spoke over the B.B.C. Our family sat close to the illegal radio, turned down so low that it was hardly audible. Roosevelt talked about a letter he had received from Churchill which did not give an optimistic picture for England.

"There is danger ahead," Roosevelt said. "Danger which we must prepare for. If Britain should go down, all of us in all the Americas would be living at the point of a gun. We must help. We must be the great arsenal of democracy." In March 1941 Roosevelt signed the Lend-Lease Act and Western Europe got a new chance for life. The act gave Great Britain the military and financial aid to be able to fight on. It gave the Dutch renewed hope again.

We soon found out what the next year would bring: more restrictions, more persecutions, and less food.

The new regulations were designed to make a distinction between the Jew and non-Jew. They started with identity cards, and declared that Jews were required to have a large letter "J" stamped across their cards. One was considered a Jew if one had one or more Jewish grandparents. Exceptions often took strange and illogical forms: my Portugese Jewish friends were exempt from retribution for a while. Another woman friend, married to a Gen-

tile, received exemption by agreeing to sterilization, which infuriated the Catholic church. German Jews who had fled to Holland a
few years earlier, warned the others not to register. Some committed suicide, realizing that the agony of persecution was about to
begin all over again. Others immediately started an underground,
and another group managed to escape by boat to Sweden. Some
just stood still. True pacifists, who like the rest of us, couldn't imagine that Hitler's declaration to annihilate them would actually be
carried out. They still hoped they would be safe in Holland. With
pitiful resignation most of the 140,000 Jews in Holland stood in line
to receive the dreaded "J" on their card.

After the "J" the Jews were forced to wear the Star of David
as an even more public symbol of their precarious existence, and
eventually they were deported. The yellow, six-pointed star was
easily seen a block away, as it had to be worn on their coats. Once
registered, we saw that the Nazis, eagerly helped by the N.S.B., began to persecute them. To show solidarity with Jewish friends with
whom we had gone to school some of my Gentile friends also wore
a yellow star. It was a noble gesture, which unfortunately made the
Nazis even more vicious.

From my family in Amsterdam I heard that the action group of
the N.S.B., the W.A., was now bursting with new confidence because of Nazi support, and began to harass the Jews. Incited by the
inflammatory movie, "Der Ewige Jude," (Forever a Jew) an anti-
Jewish propaganda movie, they marched into the Jewish neighbor-
hoods to taunt and insult them. At the same time, they forced res-
taurants to exclude Jews and literally threw them off their bicycles
and trams. But this did not go unchallenged. A group of young Jews
and Gentiles banded together, formed a defense group and waited.
When in February a group of forty W.A. members returned to Amsterdam's Jewish quarter, the Jews were ready. With clubs, steel
pipes, wrenches, and any other lethal weapons they could find,
they attacked their antagonists, stabbed them and clubbed them,
even bit them. When the fight was over, one W.A., Hendrik Koot,
lay in the street, reportedly "unrecognizably mutilated." When he
died a few days later, the newspaper announced that a Jew had
jumped on his back and bitten into his jugular vein. This was un-
true, but was still enough to provoke brutal Nazi retaliation. Several hundred Jews were taken from their homes, beaten with rifle
butts until near death and then pitched into trucks headed for Westerbork, a pass-through camp in eastern Holland. There they were
sent to Austria as workers in the stone quarry of Mauthausen. Only

one of them returned alive.

We were horrified. How could this happen in our country where freedom was our most coveted trademark? It was completely against our religious and moral conscience and we started to rebel.

It wasn't in the papers, but through the grapevine we heard that Amsterdam, its neighbor city Zaandam, and a few nearby smaller communities went on a general strike. It was hard to organize this protest, we were told, because there was little communication, but on the day the tram workers left their jobs, everyone sensed the strike was on and did not report for work. The one tram which tried to move, couldn't go very far because a few loyal Dutch laid on the tracks.

The Germans retaliated in full force. General Friedrich Christiansen, previous Chief of the Luftwaffe, now commander of all German forces in our country, declared a state of emergency. Nazi Police Chief Hans Albin Rauter, an evil-looking Austrian, sent his ruthless troops into town. Rauter, more brutal and more feared than Seyss-Inquart, was the man who signed all execution orders. He lived close to us and seeing him driving around in his gleaming black Mercedes made my hair stand on end.

It was ironic and extremely sad that these Nazi Austrians who were ordering the executions of people in Holland were some of the children the Dutch so lovingly took into their homes after the Great War. When in 1918 families were starving in war-torn Austria, the Dutch took in many of the children, fed them, and loved them, until they could go home healthy. Of course it upset us greatly to think that this was their thanks.

By the end of the day we heard that more than a thousand arrested strikers were sent to concentration camps. They were kicked and beaten mercilessly. Many were wounded and some killed. The newspaper reported that fifteen were executed for many different reasons, adding that Amsterdam was punished with a fine of fifteen million guilders, to be paid in taxes. Zaandam and the other towns had a lesser fine, while the mayors of all striking cities were swiftly replaced by Dutch Nazis.

The Nazi Police displayed such an awesome strength in crushing the strike that we concluded it would be foolish to start any kind of uprising again. Nevertheless, for the first time we found out who our friends were. We also learned that there were not that many pro-Nazis in our country, although they were powerful. This gave us courage. We buried ourselves deeper in the underground, fighting the silent, desperate fight.

In the fall of 1941 Jewish restrictions multiplied. Nearly every day more repressive laws were printed in the papers. Jews had the first dusk-to-dawn curfew. They were banned from all public places and could use neither public transportation nor their own cars or bicycles. They were even forbidden to use telephones. The Jews had to report their money. Some of it was confiscated and later used to pay off the same Dutch Nazis who betrayed their hiding places. Soon their homes were appropriated and eventually they were forced into ghettos, mainly in Amsterdam. Their children were sent to separate Jewish schools. At that point, most of my Jewish friends went into hiding. They were rarely out in the open. As they were not even allowed to talk to Gentiles, we had to act as if we didn't know each other when we did meet.

Even my friend Robby bent over and hid his face behind his turned-up coat collar, showing no sign of recognition. One time he whispered when he passed, "It's better. It just jeopardizes both our lives." I was heartbroken.

The evils of a Nazi occupation were now aggravated, as it finally dawned on us that Hitler was indeed trying to wipe out all the Jews in our country.

"Destroy all Jews and create a Super Race," we heard this madman shout over the radio. At last we heard of "The Final Solution," total annihilation of the Jews. To implement this unthinkable plan, he established over three hundred camps in isolated parts of Poland, Germany, Austria, and other countries. In Holland old army barracks were being used as concentration camps. Vught, Amersfoort, Westerbork and Ommen were the most widely feared. In them not only Jews but later Dutch people of all persuasions were tortured, killed, or deported to other camps. The twisted master of this plan was Heinrich Himmler, the S.S. Reichsführer. We saw his picture in the paper the day he announced that he preferred an "orderly" mass murder of the Jews. It still was hard to believe. It came clear what he meant in the day and night pogroms conducted throughout the next two years. Thousands of terrified Jewish citizens were herded together and crammed into cattle cars to ride to their death in horror camps. Auschwitz, Treblinka, Dachau, Buchenwald, Ravensbrück, Bergen-Belsen and many others; names we had never heard before, but which to this day send chills down my spine.

For a long time we did not know what atrocities were committed in these faraway places. By the time the grizzly stories came trickling through underground channels, we didn't believe them.

Hitler's satanic plan to exterminate a whole race of innocent men, women, and children was something which couldn't happen in a civilized world, we thought, and we hoped it wasn't true. But eventually, in 1944, we did get eyewitness accounts of escaped prisoners. The stories were worse than the imaginary tortures of hell, and we, virtually prisoners ourselves, could not do anything.

9

Because they needed a tremendous amount of raw material for their war effort, the Germans started an organized plunder of our country's textile, coal, and gasoline, leaving us without enough to lead a normal life.

Although we carefully stockpiled before the British blockade, we watched while our much-needed supplies were carted across the border to Germany. We were not organized enough to prevent it.

Fortunately we did better with our food provisions. Hoping not to repeat the famine of the previous war, our government appointed Dr. Stefanus L. Louwes to Director-General of the Bureau of Food Supply long before the invasion. Louwes, a forceful and intelligent man, realized that we could again be isolated in case of war, and would not have enough to feed the population. He started to build reserves and drafted a rationing program, which used a "Master Card." A few months before the German attack, he tested his program with the rationing of sugar. It worked acceptably, and when the Germans invaded a year later, a well-designed plan was ready to go.

Extra coupons for laborers, sick people, babies, expectant mothers, and even a special rice allotment for the many Orientals in our country, were not forgotten. Farmers were pursuaded to plant more wheat, utilizing every plot of land. Even some tulip fields were plowed for wheat and potatoes. Raising pigs and chickens was limited drastically in order to provide enough grain for people.

We all received a folded Master Card. Inside were numbered squares. Whenever the newspaper announced the available food for the week, we took our sheets of stamps with all the main commodities, and hoped that some would still be available. Separate cards offered textiles, shoes, candy, fuel, tobacco, and bicycle tires, items which were soon sold on the black market. Finding cigarettes was like discovering a treasure. Most were made of heather, peat moss or even seaweed, and smelled delightfully dreadful! On the textile card you could get a coat only if you turned another one in. Leather shoes were soon not available. A pair of sandals with wooden soles was about all you could buy.

Occasionally there was an extra food ration and we rushed to the stores to stand in line for hours. Through the years the price of food doubled, and many people who could not afford to use all their coupons sold them to buy bread. In addition Louwes started central kitchens, some stationary and some mobile, where for twenty cents and a potato coupon you could get two big ladles of soup, which at first was pretty good and nutritious.

On the whole the food distribution system worked well and became a respected and powerful organization.

At this moment we in the main office were still wondering what to do about the strike in Amsterdam. Louwes called a meeting of department heads, informing them that our government in London had asked us not to strike. "Our time has not come yet," he said. We had to realize the terrible consequences of a strike. People would start plundering, and the Nazis would just love to put machine guns on plundering Dutchmen. And, he pointed out, the Germans would replace us with Dutch Nazi sympathizers, which would help no one. We listened intently, then gave Louwes a complete vote of confidence. We returned to work confident of our moral decision, but our hearts and prayers were still with the strikers.

Louwes was misunderstood for his stand, but the office defended him. We recognized his decision as being unpopular. But we knew the importance of providing food at all cost, a stand that saved many people's lives.

Years later I found out that my future husband, Paul, was at the same meeting. He admired Louwes and felt he was very perceptive. A strike would have been suicide with no benefits at all. "Besides," Paul added, "that way we could use our communication and transportation network for the underground, as well as keep young men from the claws of the Nazis."

Whenever we faltered, we remembered what Louwes had said:

"The only thing between our people and hunger is a well-run organization and a strict discipline to resist black market trade." Experience proved him right.

A few weeks later our beautiful 18th-century office building on the Lange Voorhout was in flames. Although it was not proven, we thought the fire was set. The arsonist, upset by Louwes' decision not to strike, intended to hurt us and the Nazis next door, we reasoned. Unfortunately the Dutch were hurt by it most as our building and most of our files were destroyed.

It was a major project to find another office in the overcrowded city. Finally the Germans gave Louwes permission to move into the old Hotel Zeerust, overlooking the Atlantic Wall, which the Germans were building on the wide, yellow beach at Scheveningen. We were given special passes to enter this forbidden military territory, on the written and signed condition that no photos of the fortifications would be taken. In fact we were not even allowed to look out of the windows.

Before moving into the office, I had a chance to survey the rooms, to decide what furniture we needed. I was alone and noticed the perfect view of the German bunkers. Ignoring the serious warning, I climbed onto the flat roof. Hiding behind the chimney, I took a few pictures, delighted at the easy opportunity to help my friends in the underground. They developed the negatives themselves, and gave me copies, while the originals found their way to London.

No sooner were we settled in our new office than two uniformed N.S.B. men walked in. We stiffened. Seeing them made my skin crawl. They stopped in front of my desk and ordered us to remove the Queen's portrait from our office. We firmly objected. For a second they stared at us, surprised at our defiance. They then turned around and walked out, muttering that it was acceptable as long as the picture was not seen from the outside.

Because Scheveningen is a village whose fishermen have resisted change for centuries, it was an unusual experience for all of us to be there. There were two parts to the town: the old fishing village and the new resort. The old portion was the original town with two large harbors to shelter the herring fleet. The seaside resort was a luxurious hotel area with the Kurhaus hotel dominating the site.

The Germans working on the Atlantic Defense Wall were billeted all over town. Only the Scheveningers were still allowed to live there. They still wore their traditional clothes, the men in huge, baggy trousers, a black jacket, and a fisherman's cap; the women quite buxom in their voluminous skirts of thick black wool with a red lined cape from the same material. Low on their hair they had sparkling white bonnets neatly starched, and held by intricate gold ornaments. Often they wore "klompen," the Dutch wooded shoes, hollowed by hand from a piece of willow. These clogs were very practical. Filled with straw or newspaper, and worn with woolen socks, they were waterproof and perfect footwear for those working in wet sand, soggy soil, or for cleaning the sidewalk. The "klompen" were always left outside upon entering the house. Spotting the big ones, the small ones, and the very tiny ones on the stoop gave you a warm feeling of togetherness.

These Scheveningen families lived their own strict lives and clung to their customs, a strange contrast to the Nazis patrolling their beach. The hardy fishermen chose to ignore the Nazis and their regulations. Some helped Resistance men to escape by hiding them in their trawlers. But the Nazis caught on quickly and soon ordered two German soldiers to be stationed on every outgoing fishing boat.

A year or so later, when the area became completely off limits, local families too had to move. Our offices were also evacuated again, and we now settled in the recently finished Shell building on a tree-lined avenue back in The Hague.

After the strike in Amsterdam, the Jewish persecution became more severe. Seyss-Inquart now gave the N.S.B., those hated Dutch Nazi puppets, free reign to treat the Jews any way they wished. With that, these traitors taunted them unmercifully. In downtown The Hague I saw them break the windows and bash down the door of a small Jewish store in the Spuistraat, dragging the petrified owners out. They shoved them and beat them and kicked them, until their victims dropped onto the pavement, bleeding profusely. I just stood there, not able to escape as the narrow street was barricaded. In shock I looked at the other bystanders, wondering if together we could stop these tormentors. But I knew we had no chance, as there were too many of them. I realized more than ever that, if caught by the Nazis for whatever reason, you were desperately alone and no one could save you.

Once, I saw a brave young Dutchman lunge at the N.S.B. bullies, swinging his arms wildly, hitting them as hard as he could. Two other Dutchmen ran to help but were quickly overpowered. There was a shrill whistle, and a minute later Nazi police rushed in, grabbing the men and throwing them into a squad car. In the melee I managed to slip away, following others who also fled the scene. We scattered, fleeing like rabbits into a store and out the back door. It was a ghastly scene, but now I had seen it for myself. It was etched indelibly into my mind.

Our family tried to do as much as we could for our Jewish friends. Hitler's fanatical persecution was not only insane but completely unjustified. When he condemned innocent lives, our normal humane instincts compelled us to help, despite the risk. And the risk was high. To hide Jews not only jeopardized your own life, but that of the entire family as well. If caught, the sentence would be very severe for parents and children alike. Besides, hiding them was not enough; they needed new identity cards, ration cards and money. Some sympathetic banks cooperated by dispensing secret funds, hoping they would later be compensated by the government. Unfortunately, by the time we were better organized many Jewish families in hiding had already been discovered.

Jewish children were easier to conceal. Loving Gentile families, often living on farms or in small communities, took them into their own homes, giving them new names and new identity cards. Those extremely brave families saved the children from being murdered by Hitler's minions.

Sometimes, to treat someone who was seriously ill, my father had to crawl into a hiding place. Mother and I worried because Father loathed the Nazis, and we were afraid he would get into some kind of serious confrontation. He was not one to back off easily. Sure enough, a problem soon came up.

My father leased a small villa in Wassenaar, which he had owned for a long time, to a Jewish widow. She never registered as a Jew and carried an identity card without the dreaded letter, feeling relatively safe about it all. Father didn't know she had been discovered until the Gestapo came to our home, demanding to speak to him. I heard them yell, and curse, and carry on, because he had rented to a Jew. After this diatribe they forced him along to their headquarters. There he learned that the widow had swallowed cyanide and had died a horrible death on the sidewalk as the Gestapo pulled her out of her house. Although it was extremely tough, my father remained silent when the Nazis threatened and insulted him, feeling it was futile to fight back. At the end of the day they released him with the parting statement that the S.S. would take over his little house.

Luck was with him that time. As a physician, he was immune from harassment for a while, but that, too, changed in later years.

The Nazis did not enjoy my father's house for very long. One of their own bombs accidentally fell next to it, demolishing the building like a house of cards. The four walls collapsed towards the middle, pulling the large Dutch roof with its wide overhanging eaves on top of everything, covering the rubble. Five S.S. officers died inside.

We stared at it in amazement. It looked like a huge hand had lifted the roof to squash it down and crush everything inside as a violent act of revenge.

The Nazis battered us consistently with one new regulation after another, a non-stop show of power. We did not see them as people anymore. They were like robots — disciplined, unbending, inhuman. I wondered, where were those "just drafted" doughboys stationed like in other nations, those soldiers in fatigues who were just waiting for it all to be over?

When a new order was issued, directing us to hand in our silver coins for zinc ones, only five percent of our precious metal was exchanged, the rest was hidden. Some coins bearing the Queen's portrait were made into spoons, rings, or bracelets, and secretly sold to help finance the Resistance. The change to zinc money caused people in the Resistance some terrifying moments. Allied agents, dropped into Holland and carrying the old silver money, were not always able to discover their mistake in time to evade capture!

The coins were just the beginning. Soon we were ordered to hand in anything made of metal. Even churchbells were not spared. It was heartbreaking to see German soldiers throwing a bronze bell from the steeple to the yard below while the clergy watched in despair. Today it was a piece of metal, but by tomorrow it would be melted down and made into guns. Of course we reacted to this order, too. Father and our neighbor dug a large hole in our yard to hide our precious metals. Into the ground went our brass fireplace tools, the copper kettle, the pewter ashtrays, boxes and beer mugs, the bronze statue of the Chinese symbol of Happiness, and my father's Oriental knife collection. We stood downcast around the open grave, burying our belongings with sighs and sad farewells, a feeling which worsened when we returned to our barren rooms.

After the war the two families stood again in the yard. The long-awaited moment had come. The men dug and we watched for the first treasure breathlessly. Alas! We stared at the large hole, now completely empty. We looked at each other dumbfounded and, for the briefest moment, suspiciously. Our neighbor leaned on his shovel, tired and disgusted. My father shook his head. In a resigned voice he philosophized, "At least the Krauts didn't get it for their cannons!"

Or did they?

10

The European winter of '41-'42 was exceptionally severe and the Dutch suffered greatly from the cold. Our mines in Limburg were forced to send large shipments to Germany, leaving little coal for Holland. We nearly turned blue from the cold, warmed only by the knowledge that our hated enemy was at the same time freezing at the Russian front.

On the way to the office one wintry morning, I noticed that as far as I could see, the North Sea was frozen over. Amazed, I stared at the glacial waves of blue-grey ice. England seemed closer and I was suddenly confident that one could walk all the way to London and be free! As if the Germans could read my thoughts, the guards were doubled on their patrols the next day.

Whenever the temperature dropped below freezing for more than a week, we followed the weather predictions hourly and measured the ice daily. Finally it was strong enough to stand on. The schools gave a three-day skating vacation and most offices closed for one day. During this unusual winter, a thick layer of ice formed early. Young and old swarmed to the canals and ponds within the city. We were determined to enjoy the sport we had learned when young, Nazis or no Nazis.

No matter how tired, cold, or hungry, people tied on their "doorlopers," the long wooden skates with the cotton or leather straps, and glided until they were too tired to stand. The Germans were amazed and startled to see all those bundled-up, determined skaters, their cold noses sticking out from under a colorful assortment of caps.

Holding on to a long pole, a row of three, four, or sometimes six people skated at great speed along the glassy surface. Their legs struck out strongly, in unison, left-right, left-right, stepping one foot over the other to turn corners. Small tents on the ice served as places to rest, to sip hot chocolate, or to savor Holland's famous pea-soup. In normal times it was thick enough to hold a spoon upright, but that winter it resembled dishwater.

The sub-zero weather lasted for more than five months, an unusually long time. It froze all the canals and rivers. Even the Zuiderzee, a stormy bay in the north of nearly a million acres of thrashing water which had recently been dammed by a 20-mile long dike, was frozen solid. Our ever-curious family decided to have a look at this phenomenon which might happen only once in a lifetime. With hundreds of other spectators we traveled by special train to Volendam, a picturesque fishing village with peaked roofs rising over rows of green and white painted houses. We stopped at the dike and stared at the island of Marken. Usually this tiny island stuck out from the choppy waters; now it was surrounded by a carpet of ice that had silenced the eternal waves. We blinked in surprise at the enchanting scene in front of us, a Breughel-like setting of wooden fishing boats, dirty and weather-beaten, stuck in the ice; the whir-whar of scrambling skaters, and against a solid grey sky, a windmill, a silent sentry in the background.

The women of Volendam, clothed in a five-colored striped skirt and a black apron with flowered border, looked charming. The traditional clothes of their town were topped by a pointed lace bonnet on their blonde hair. A necklace of red coral beads completed the costume. The men, also in their Sunday best, ambled along, hands deep in the pockets of their large, baggy pants; a massive silver button and chain across their jacket. Small boys and girls, who were all dressed like girls up to the age of five, were running and sliding, the tiny ones being pushed along in wooden sleds. All those bright colors splashing on the ice created such a pleasurable winter scene that for a moment I forgot the evil behind me.

As we walked along a well-used path over the ice, we watched an ice-boat glide by at a tremendous speed, its large blades scraping against the frozen sea. The sailor in his small seat held on to the billowing sail. Like a large bird the boat turned and swooped by us, driven by the blustering wind. Further on, a fisherman squatted on an old beer crate, jigging for eel and peering intently at the hole he had chopped in the ice. The entire scene was one of contentment marred only by two Nazi cars driving beside us on the ice. We all had to scurry off the path to make room for them.

"Bloody irritating," my father growled, the familiar furrow creasing his brow.

After the wonderful days of skating, it was hard to return to the office and face reality again. The frost had stopped all shipping from our fertile north-eastern provinces to the large cities in the west. I was now working in the Department of Sugar, which handled such diverse products as babyfood and food for cattle. Attending many staff meetings I understood the situation in Holland was getting worse each day.

Every morning a stream of farmers, businessmen or factory owners came in with their tales of woe. The directors often had to make decisions which were highly criticized by the censored press. Many times I went home heartsick after hearing the agony and suffering of so many people. The Nazis took three of the five milk cows from a small farmer and also one of his two horses; he needed both horses to pull his plow! Aside from the deprivation and monetary loss, the farmer was also deeply attached to his animals.

"Like losing a child," his wife sobbed in the office, recalling the moment their favorite horse had been led away.

One day we received a call for help from the distraught mayor of a small community in the south of Holland. He explained that saboteurs of the Resistance had cut a German communication cable outside his town. The S.S. punished the town by making all male villagers stand guard at the cable in four-hour shifts, day and night. This meant that in four days the first one had to start again. If the cable was tampered with, the person on guard was held responsible and shot. Since the entire village was guarding in shifts, there were not enough men to harvest the sugar beets.

"If the beets are not dug up this week, they'll rot in the ground," the mayor mourned.

When I told my boss the problem he shook his head sadly and quickly phoned the German Agricultural Commander, who in turn promised to talk to the S.S. Sometimes we would get results, as the agricultural chief was sensitive to our problems, but we seldom got any help from the S.S. who had no sympathy for our troubles.

It was a vicious circle, shared by every department through the years. We all wanted to quit many times. But then what? People who quit their jobs would be sent to Germany; more families uprooted, more men and women killed. So we all plugged on, trying to do the best for the people and the country, while the complaints hit us from all sides, Dutch and German alike.

The sugar beet farmers complained that half of their workers were in hiding or had been sent to Germany. In either case we had no solution for them. The factories did not have enough coal to keep running. Consequently, the biscuit, candy, and chocolate plants, including many pastry and baby food manufacturers, did not have enough sugar to continue. There were also hundreds of one-man ice cream vendors, with little pushcarts and tinkling bells usually a common sight in the streets of Holland, with no wares to sell. None of them would have a livelihood if we could not distribute sugar to them. The Germans would then label them "unnecessary." Anytime a group was deemed *not* "necessary," its workers were shipped to German war plants. Our office therefore divided the sugar democratically to keep all alive and in Holland.

In the middle of our severe winter we suddenly heard that Pearl Harbor had been savagely bombed by the Japanese. Three days later, Japan, Germany and Italy declared war on the United States. After our initial shock was over, we were selfishly pleased that the United States was now our ally. This, we felt, was the beginning of our salvation.

But the war in the Pacific gave the Dutch another worry. There were thousands of Dutchmen living in the Orient, mainly in the Dutch East Indies, which had been a long time colony of the Netherlands. Because I had been born there, I felt it was my second homeland. My two brothers and their families were living there, having left Holland a few years earlier. Of course, we were always thinking of them, wondering if they were safe, and if they knew about us. But we had little contact, only through a printed card of the Red Cross once in a while. Would they now be thinking of us, too?

One day we realized that some distant Dutch did know of our plight, when they tried to cheer us up. Suddenly we saw two British Wellingtons fly daringly low over the city. While we curiously watched, thousands of tiny bags dropped from their silver bellies, fluttered down through the barking German flak and landed in our streets. When we spotted the red, white and blue tags on the packages we ran to gather them. To our big surprise the bags were filled with precious orange pekoe tea, a gift from the Free Netherland Indies where teaplants grow on the hills of beautiful tropical islands. I shook with emotion when I read the tags with the encouraging words, "The Netherlands will rise again. Keep up the spirit!"

People came running from all sides to pick up the tea, scurrying on their roofs to search for more. Though the Germans warned they would shoot anyone touching the bags, we grabbed them anyway. It was a minor incident, taken in the context of the war, but it lifted our spirits at the right time.

All this occurred before the Dutch Archipelago was attacked by Japan. After heroic resistance, the Dutch East Indies surrendered on March 8, 1942. The Japanese occupying forces arrived and our families were herded into camps and incarcerated for the duration of the war. Only after the war did we hear how they suffered. Many of them didn't survive.

11

As the Japanese piled up victory after victory in the Far East, the Germans advanced on the Russian front, albeit slowly. They had forgotten the lesson of Napoleon, and the Russian winter. The turning point came in January '43 at Stalingrad, where the Russians stood firm. The German army was beaten by severe cold, Russian determination and new rocket launchers. Thousands perished in the sub-zero weather.

Intent on building up his forces and supplies, Hitler turned to occupied nations for factory workers to release his soldiers for battle. The Dutch had caused a lot of trouble, harassing his troops, which called for a large occupation force. Hitler now ordered a draft of furloughed members of the Dutch Army starting with the officers. When it became clear that some of these 300,000 ex-soldiers would have to work in war factories, many "dove under," a new term for going into hiding. Only 8000 showed up.

Students, too, were included in this roundup, especially after many refused to sign a pledge "to refrain from any act against the Third Reich." The Nazis now closed all universities. Night after night we saw the Grüne Polizei, so-called because of their green uniforms, cruise by with flashlights and lists of names to rout hapless students out of bed. Four hundred were captured and a week later I saw them marching along, guarded by Germans riding in cars. They headed toward the train station boldly singing, "It's a Long Way to Tipperary," the old World War I song.

From the safety of my room I watched them, hardly able to contain my emotions. Finally I grew brave enough to lean from our second story window and hold up two fingers for the victory sign shouting, "Long live Holland!" The men looked up and waved. A German soldier raised his gun. I quickly dropped behind the ledge and did not reappear until they had passed; then I closed the window and wept.

Frits dropped by our house a few days later, and told me that Jan, one of our friends, had been picked up and sent to Germany. Jan, a born comic, who often had us in stitches with his hilarious stories, had the misfortune of being arrested as a defiant student. Frits and I discussed the situation, realizing the Nazis had little sense of humor and Jan didn't have much chance of getting out alive.

But we were wrong. Jan not only survived, but returned home after only a few weeks, a bit pale, but otherwise unhurt. We bombarded him with questions. In his nonchalant way he told us that he worked in a munitions factory close to our border. The men ahead of him on the assembly line built medium sized airplane bombs. He, the last in the line, was to place them horizontally, point first, on a conveyer. From there the empty shells, positioned peacefully end to end on the running belt, guided themselves through a small tunnel opening to another part of the factory.

As soon as he arrived, Jan pondered how to slow down the operation. What would happen if he put one shell the other way, the blunt end first? He tried it and was disappointed when outwardly nothing appeared to change. But, once inside the tunnel, the shells began to pile up. One by one they crowded in, pushing and sliding on top of each other. Suddenly there was an enormous crunch. The whole assembly line tore apart, the tunnel collapsed and falling brick flattened Jan against the opposite wall. By the time he came to in the emergency ward, the Nazis had discovered that he was responsible and had thrown him in jail. Not having enough spare parts, the assembly line was out of commission for a long time. After two days Jan was interrogated, kicked, and beaten. All the time he acted extremely dumb and finally the Germans put him on a train to Holland, yelling that he was too stupid to work in their plants, firmly advising him to "go louse up your own country!"

Jan was not the only one who was returned to Holland. The Germans wrote in our papers that they were sending some Dutch workers back as they were extremely disappointed in them. Instead of being the good workers they were known to be in Holland, now in Hitler's Reich they were just lazy slobs! I could not believe their crazy reaction. What did they expect from slave labor forced to work under miserable conditions in a foreign country?

Soon the Germans were not so benevolent anymore and few men came out of the labor camps alive.

When the weather changed for the better, the Allies started regular bomb attacks on both Germany and Holland. The strafing of our own shipyards and military installations unfortunately also killed some Dutch, even though it was mostly done on Sundays, when fewer workers would be there. Nazi propaganda played the bombings up to the hilt and thought it would turn the Dutch against the Allies, but it never did. After all, we daily saw the Allies make tremendous sacrifices to free us. Our Queen Wilhelmina also played a large part in our anti-Nazi feeling with her frank talks on Radio Orange. An overwhelming number of people still remained loyal to our government in exile. We believed in our Queen and while she encouraged us she became a symbol of strength. She worked hard in London and represented us well. We knew she really cared. During the last years of the occupation, we were never more united. Hitler's Nazi propaganda fell on deaf ears. But that, of course, made our life even more precarious.

After the German defeat at Stalingrad we were more confused and frightened every day. German attitudes changed for the worse with their losses. We all came to dread the psychological campaign which preceded any new Nazi regulation. It always started with a rumor heard on the streets. Then when a news story denied it, we knew that the denied rumor was about to become a newspaper announcement, headed: BEKENDMAKING. This scary procedure crawled towards us like an oozing mass. But at least it gave us time to plan.

Simultaneous to the recall of the ex-military and the draft of students, the Germans announced that 150,000 other Dutchmen would also be called up for the Arbeitseinsatz, German forced labor, before the end of 1943. They increased the numbers the following years until eventually every man between the ages of 18 and 60 was called for work in Germany, except those who had an exemption ticket. Most men, knowing they would live in barracks, be without their families and often under Allied bombardments, refused to go, even if they did not have jobs at home. This enraged the Nazis who now desperately needed foreign workers to free their own men for fighting.

When the various drafts were announced, the overburdened workers protested and went on strike. The action was contagious and went from plant to plant, province to province, big plants and little plants. As the strike was mainly in the rural areas, we in The Hague did not notice much, and only a few days later understood its magnitude. In the two years since the Amsterdam strike, Nazi indignities had become unbearable and more people were determined to make a public stand regardless of reprisals. And Seyss-

Inquart certainly had them. He instituted summary justice, which was viciously enforced.

From a memo circulating in our office I knew that Nazi Police Chief Rauter had sent his henchmen to the potato-flour plant "De Woudbloem" in Drente, demanding the employee list. After two warnings they went to some of the still absent workers' homes and picked them up. I wondered why these men just sat there and did not try to escape Nazi vengeance. But most were from rural areas, which had not yet experienced the Nazi ferocity. Some didn't know where to hide, some felt righteous, and others were so paralyzed with fear that they delayed any action. The Nazi Police dragged them back to the plant where they were publicly shot. The following day a few men from the huge Philips Electrical works in Eindhoven were executed in the same ruthless way.

The strike went on, and once again we in the Food Distribution faced Louwes with the question of two years earlier: Should we continue working or join the others so willing to risk their lives?

Louwes gave us the same answer: "Be true to yourself. Everyone defines his own limits, but when you decide it's time to quit, base your action not only on what's best for you, but also on what's best for the country."

Louwes not only forced us to make our own strike decision but forced me to ponder a lot of other problems needing answers.

As far as the strike was concerned I decided to follow Louwes' advice. I trusted his judgement and since he went on working, I felt I should do the same. Fortunately all the "right" Dutch, as we called ourselves, decided to stick together and no one left. But I had another decision to make. I had fallen in love and my feelings were very confused. Would it be better if I didn't have any emotional involvements? Should I lead a normal life, marry and have children, or would I be in a man's way? Would he be less daring in the Resistance because he feared reprisal against me?

With these thoughts spinning in my head I followed everyone else out of the building and headed home for the day. We glared at the few pro-Nazis in our office, who were still sitting at their desks and acting unconcerned, which irritated the rest of us no end.

The strike was suppressed in one short week, but not before Holland was in complete turmoil. It was estimated that about 100,000 persons were in hiding, a staggering figure. For so many to disappear was a feat that jeopardized the lives of at least a like number. But we knew that withholding workers from German war plants would bring an Allied victory sooner. It not only saved our workers, but the Germans, afraid of being stabbed in the back, were forced to keep a large occupation army in Holland — soldiers who otherwise could have been used in battle.

During this strike the rural areas were really involved and the farmers helped to hide "underdivers," as they were called. They hired them to work in the fields where they could disappear quickly whenever the creaking of trucks and stomping of boots was heard. Other underdivers preferred the city and did not leave the shelter of the crowd. In four-story brick houses they hid in the attic, the basement, and closets in between. These thousands required not only hiding places, but also money and food stamps. The Landelijke Organisatie (L.O.), that part of the Resistance responsible for rural activity, became a huge organization able to cope with every emergency. They were so ingenious, that you could get a fake Nazi signature of the commander of any area to validate your papers. This catalogue of counterfeit signatures became our secret weapon, saving many a Dutchman in trouble. The cards themselves were taken from small distribution offices in the countryside, robbed with guns stolen from police stations, or dropped from Allied planes by night at pre-arranged spots.

After a few months the Nazis realized that an organized draft would not work and began a round-up system of young men, just as they previously had rounded up all Jews. It was called the "razzia," after an Arabic concept for capturing slaves. Starting with Rotterdam, the Grüne Polizei unit surrounded the city at night and barricaded its entrances. In the early morning, before anyone knew what was happening, the green uniformed Nazi police swarmed over town in open trucks. Closing in, they shot in the air and banged on doors. They shouted through bull horns and ordered all young men outside, in front of their house. Any house with no one on the stoop was searched thoroughly. The police often shot through doors, not even bothering to open them.

There was no time to run or hide. Terror-stricken families held on to each other watching the Nazi police grab a struggling young man, regardless of age, and push him into the waiting truck. Stuffed into box cars they were sent to German munition plants to become slave laborers.

Now the wrath of the Nazis fell on every Dutchman, and we experienced what the Jews had before us. All hell broke loose, and we were now the hunted. Holland had been combed empty of thousands of Jews, who were viciously massacred in cold blood. Next 12,000 Dutch non-Jews, picked up in the razzias, died a slow death of hard labor, beatings, freezing, and starvation in the German labor camps.

The Gestapo, helped by the N.S.B., began actively hunting down the "underdivers," secret agents, and the many Dutch Resistance groups. The German military counterespionage played a bigger game. Only after the war did I hear of the sensational espionage case, the "England-Spiel." It was a cat-and-mouse game against England in which the clever Germans caught a British agent dropped in Holland, and forced him to transmit planted information to the unwary British intelligence. In addition, the German counterespionage in Holland employed their captured agent to contact subsequently dropped undercover men, who then also were arrested. The "Spiel," the game, was successfully kept up for more than two years without the British catching on. Unfortunately this slip-up cost many young Dutchmen their lives.

Unaware of the intelligence scheme played around me, I only saw the roll call of the dead printed in the paper. To read the names of my friends who were executed every week was a terrible shock. I tried to keep my emotions under control, tried not to think too deeply about it, to maintain enough strength to go on myself. But I wanted to keep their memories fresh, so I took these lists of friends, putting them with paste and tears into my diary.

Whenever more violent resistance occurred, we could never guess how the Nazis would react. After the sabotage of a railroad, a fruitless hunt for the culprits made them stoop to the lowest kind of retaliation, the taking of hostages!

Heads of major companies or other influential people were taken from their homes at night and thrown into jail, their names and positions printed in the paper with the threat that they would be shot if the culprit was not found or did not surrender within a week.

A shock wave rocked the country, but the underground men made the awesome decision to sit tight, and no one came forward. On August 15, 1942, Willem Ruys, internationally-known president of the Rotterdam Lloyd Steamship Company, Count E.O.G. van Limburg Stirum and Baron Alexander Schimmelpennink van der Oye, both members of the Dutch nobility, Robert Baelde, attorney in Rotterdam, and Christoffel Bennekers, past Police Chief of Rotterdam, were executed. We were sick with grief, but still the underground fight went on, now more determined than ever.

Through the years more executions followed. Some were held in the middle of the city or village square, the bodies left slumped on the pavement. Most of my friends, when caught, were prisoners of the "Orange Hotel," as we called the jail in Scheveningen, which housed the loyal Dutch. Despite the efforts of their distraught families, who even bribed the guards, many of the men were marched across the road into the lonely dunes to be executed. We would cringe in our homes at the sound of shots ringing out in the quiet night. As the reverberations lingered in the awesome silence, we would renew our vow never to give up, never, never, ever.

In the meantime, as more loyal Dutchmen were betrayed by our quislings, to be brutally murdered by the Nazi police, the Resistance started to develop its own list of executions. Heading it was General Seyffardt, the retired Dutch Army general, who became a Nazi and organized the Dutch Nazi Legion, which fought with the Waffen S.S. in Russia. He was shot when answering his doorbell one night, and died the next day. A few other high officials who openly supported the Nazis were also done in by the underground. In reprisal the Germans swiftly executed three young Dutchmen and sent many others living in the area of Seyffardt's house to concentration camps.

One of my new friends, Paul, lived in Seyffardt's vicinity. Just before the German invasion he had returned from India where he lived. He was literally "a man of the world" and I was fascinated by him. In the next few months he would become very important to me. The night Seyffardt was shot he knocked at our door, our secret knock, and I hurriedly let him in.

"They killed the old bastard," he blurted out, quickly closing the door behind him.

"Seyffardt?"

He gravely nodded, "Yep, somebody finally got him."

"Oh my God!" I worried. "What happened? Why are you here? You didn't shoot him, did you?"

"No," he said slowly shaking his head, "they're picking up guys all around the neighborhood. Can I stay here tonight? Tomorrow I'll find another place."

"Good heavens Paul, my parents are asleep." I was alarmed.

"So much the better, then they won't know and won't worry. It's only for a few hours."

I looked at him in the dim light and saw the tight lines around the corners of his mouth. I didn't mean to sound unsympathetic, but I tried to convey my concern to him. At the same time I wanted to help him. Hoping my parents would understand, I found a blanket and watched Paul settle himself on the couch in the living room. I sat down beside him and we started to talk, never mentioning Seyffardt again. I knew better than to ask dangerous questions. I felt I could trust Paul as he seemed to know what he was doing. After talking for an hour or so I went up to my bedroom, satisfied that I had been of help.

Early the next morning Paul left for his grandmother's attic hide-out near Leyden. He warned me to stay off the streets for a while, as they were beginning to pick up women.

"If things get rough in The Hague, you too can come to my grandmother's home," he offered just before leaving. "It's quiet there, very few Krauts. My grandmother is quite feeble and doesn't know what's going on, but I'll ask the housekeeper to let you in, if you come after dark."

He left quickly while I was still thinking about it. I wanted to go with him but I decided not to.

I didn't feel comfortable about the underground doing their own killings. But, when Madelein, a much older friend of mine, told me what had happened to her in the concentration camp at Vught, from which she had just been released, I understood why they wanted revenge.

Her story of the bunker incident at Vught was an account of cruelty and callousness that haunted me for years.

She was one of 91 women who helped cut off the long braids of a roommate who had betrayed them by fraternizing with the camp guards. The Nazi camp commander had them all punished. Seventy-four frightened women were pushed and kicked screaming into one small cell of a concrete bunker, completely filling the tiny space. The remaining ones were dragged to the next cell. Packed upright together with little air, and no food or water, the first group could not move and barely breathe. When the lights went out, panic set in. While shrieking in terror, some women started to claw and bite; others tore off their clothes to find relief from the unbearable heat.

As the oxygen disappeared, the women in the middle fainted and slipped to the ground with others falling over them. Madelein was fortunate to stand against the wall next to a friend, holding on to each other. The sweating bodies of the others pressed them against the side of the cell and kept them upright so they could not slump down and be trampled.

After fifteen hours, the cell was quiet. Finally the guards entered and found death inside. One woman on the bottom of the heap had suffocated. Others had fainted. The lack of oxygen to the brain caused one of them to go insane, never to be normal again.

It became a "cause célèbre" and Seyss-Inquart was forced to react. This cruelty was even too much for him. Besides, everybody knew about it. His solution was to send the camp commander to the Russian front. The woman who had betrayed the others was shot and killed by the guards when she tried to escape.

Babes before the war, 1940

Open trenches in our street. The Hague, 1940.

The Dutch army marching past my home a few weeks before the German invasion.

Rotterdam bombed by the Germans, May, 1940.

*Air raid shelter dug into the ground in our yard in January, 1940.
The structure was ordered from the United States.*

The arrival of German parachutists into Holland, May 10, 1940.

Germans arriving in Holland, May 15, 1940.

"The Big Ones"
Allied planning conference, 1943

Left to right: Anthony Eden, Sir Alan Brooke, Air Chief Marshal Tedder, Admiral Sir Andrew Cunningham, General Alexander, General Marshall USA, General Eisenhower USA. The Prime Minister, Winston Churchill, is seen in the center.

Our chauffeur Strien, lighting the coal driven Morris-car.

My sister, Julie, departing for her honeymoon in taxi with gas balloon.

Anti-tank moat built by Germans through the middle of The Hague and Scheveningen. All homes and buildings that were there were bulldozed down, even the new Red Cross hospital.

Photo I took of fortifications of the Atlantic Wall. If caught taking pictures of military fortifications I would be severely punished.

Our wedding day. Arriving via pedicab, June 11, 1943.

The beginning of our honeymoon, The Hague, 1943.

Nazi Police barricades in Amsterdam, 1943. The beginning of a raid on young Dutch men.

Gestapo picking up a young man for work in German war plants.

The bombed Kleikamp home in The Hague where the Nazis kept the statistics of every person in Holland. It contained the names of men slated for work in Germany. In a daring raid, two RAF planes dropped incendiary bombs on the house, destroying the files.

12

On the other side of the world in 1939, Paul van Dillen was working in Rangoon, never suspecting that one year later he would be living down the street from my house and seeking shelter in the night. He was a slim athletic man, just over six feet tall, with a handsome face, intense blue eyes, and a distinctive white streak through his dark hair. He had an air of confidence and a forthright approach to life, winning him staunch friends as well as enemies. But he carried no grudges, was interested in everything, adventurous and intensely loyal. When I met him, I thought he was the most exciting man in the world, and I called him "the last of the Buccaneers."

Like all young men born in Holland, Paul was drafted into the Dutch army when he was eighteen. After a year of duty, he became a sergeant in the Royal Grenadiers, and was chosen to be a member of the Queen's guard. Like most of his young friends, he admired and respected the Royal Family. After his army year, the Depression had reached its height in Europe and Paul looked for employment elsewhere. His first stop was Casablanca, where his father had bauxite mining interests. There he learned the import and export trade, learned to speak French and Arabic, and qualified for a pilot's license. After three years in 'Casa,' he was off to Rangoon as a trader for a British commodities firm.

In this new job he learned English and Hindustani within six months, and in somewhat less time, to drink the refreshing shandy. Not only did he speak seven languages by then but also had discovered the intriguing life of Burma, and the strict social rules of the British in the colonies. His free time was spent at the country club where he played a good game of tennis in the early morning, cricket after four, and in a white mess jacket escorted lovely women through elegant tropical evenings.

When Hitler invaded Poland, the Dutch mobilized and over-

seas citizens were recalled. Paul, just 24, was one of the last to join
the Dutch battalion of expatriates. What they lacked in military
knowledge, they made up for in loyalty and enthusiasm. Having
lived abroad for some years made Paul appreciate his country
more. He, and many like him, returned to defend it and some died
in its service.

After five hard days of battling the paratroopers around the
airports, they finally suffered defeat. Paul and other army personnel were sent home on a "long furlough." He took a job with the
Food Distribution in The Hague and later joined a firm of potato
buyers associated with the Dutch Government. His job with the
V.B.N.A., as it was called by its initials, was to oversee the buying,
selling, shipping and storing of potatoes in Holland. It included the
scheduling of train transportation and distribution. This made it
possible for him to become a major link in the secret escape route
of Allied pilots shot down over northern Germany and Holland.
Pilots downed during the big raids on the Ruhr industrial area
knew they could escape via Holland. Many made it across our borders into the hands of friendly Dutch farmers and Resistance workers. They hid the flyers and gave them civilian clothes and
identification cards forged or stolen from the distribution offices.
Dressed like Dutch burghers, the Allied pilots were escorted from
their first hiding place to a safe point in the city. From there they
waited to be smuggled onto a train, hidden under sacks of potatoes.
The unscheduled trains carried them to the Belgium border. At
that point, they could hide in the two hundred miles of underground tunnels, the mines of St. Pietersberg in the province of Limburg. I was told no German dared to enter these mines, afraid of
being swallowed up by the dark labyrinth, or ambushed by underground fighters. By the end of the war, not only pilots but thousands of other fugitives were hiding there. Holland's world-famous
paintings, among them Rembrandt's "Nightwatch," were also kept
safely in the underground caverns.

Many fugitives waited there for the Belgian Resistance to
transport them further into Belgium, and from there to France.
Once on French soil, they would head south and by foot across the
treacherous Pyrenees Mountains into Spain and finally to Lisbon,
Portugal. From there the British Consulate would fly them back to
England. The RAF received hundreds of returned pilots in this
way. Through the years other escape routes were started, some
through Switzerland. The Gestapo was incensed about the Dutch
aid to downed British airmen. Any person who helped an Allied

pilot, either by hiding or transporting him, was immediately executed. Occasionally German secret agents managed to infiltrate the
escape lines, resulting in the capture of some pilots and Dutchmen.
The Allied airmen were treated as prisoners of war, but the brave
Dutch underground workers were shot, or worse, tortured and sent
to die in German camps.

For a long time, my friends in the office had described Paul
van Dillen and had told me that I should meet him as "we would be
perfect together," they said. Paul worked in a building nearby and,
although he visited our office often, we somehow kept missing each
other. One day he walked into my room requesting some trivial information. For a moment we just stared at each other. Paul's eyes
were fixed on mine as I watched him curiously. His blue eyes had
an unusual brightness and fascination and the natural white streak
through his dark hair was the envy of many girls. I continued to
stare at him, as he sat down and calmy talked about his exciting
life in faraway countries.

Because he gave most of his money and clothes to the underground, there was not much left to take me to the movies or out to
dinner. That was fine with me, for those places were always filled
with Germans. One freezing day I asked him why he wasn't wearing
a winter coat.

"I gave my coat away," he said simply.

"To a pilot?" I asked.

He didn't answer. He just looked at me, slitting his eyes, while
he thoughtfully lit a cigarette. That night I kept dreaming of his
coat walking around London.

We saw each other quite often and I enjoyed being with him.
Sometimes, during the day, I found an excuse to join him on a secret "business" call in the country. My boss never believed the little white lies I told him, but he trusted me to make up my time.
Sometimes after work, Paul and I left the office together for a
game of tennis or squash. Occasionally he joined my parents at our
house and we talked for hours. Then, sometimes he would come by
in the middle of the night, looking a little shaken, say "Hi," and
leave quickly to avoid being caught during curfew.

The more I saw him, the more I liked him. He shared my de-
sire to live a normal life, to be close to another human being, to
love, and be understood. In spite of all the miseries and all the
horrors of the war, our love became more important than anything

else in the world.

Even more than I knew, Paul was deeply involved in the intelligence part of the Resistance. Aside from his Rangoon experiences in this field, he had renewed his acquaintance with a chief of prewar Dutch counterintelligence. This trusted army friend asked him to help organize an underground group.

One day I felt I was being followed. When I questioned Paul, he said, "You're being checked out. My friends just want to be sure you're all right."

Indeed, his friends in the Resistance were not happy that Paul had fallen in love. They felt women caused complications.

"Perhaps you should slow down?" I asked, already nervous about it.

"I'm all right," he assured me. "I know what I'm doing. When we're married, I won't take the dangerous jobs. Please trust me, and also for your protection, never ask me what I am doing."

I trusted him; I trusted his wisdom; I trusted everything he did, feeling safe with him. Whatever might happen to me, I was sure he would get me out. He would fight dragons for me. I was in love! He then taught me some simple words in Hindustani and Arabic, so that we could have a secret language over the office phone.

After a few days I saw him again. In an off-hand way he started to talk about getting married. Although I was very much in love, I said lamely: "Don't you think we should wait? We really don't know each other that long."

Paul stared at me, "Wait? Wait for what? We might be dead by then! How long d'you want to wait?"

Three months later he respectfully asked my father for my hand in marriage. We were married in June 1943 at the City Hall in The Hague. It was a tumultuous wedding attended by so many family and friends that some had to wait outside. During the ceremony a squadron of Allied bombers flew over on their way to raid Cologne. German antiaircraft blasted away, making such a racket that we could not hear the portly wedding official solemnly describe the responsibility of love and loyalty.

Mother, extremely nervous, laughed and cried at the same time. My father and my uncle looked uneasy; they felt out of place in their cutaway coats and top hats. But Paul and I saw only each other. We just nodded at the questions and signed the official wedding register. I was extremely happy in my pink lace dress, cut down from an old evening gown, with three carnations in my hair. Paul looked dashing in the cutaway jacket and striped pants he borrowed from a friend.

After the registrar's nice speech, Paul tenderly took the gold wedding band from my left-hand finger and placed it on my right hand. We looked at each other for a moment, our eyes full of love. As I repeated the ritual with his gold ring, I glowed with happiness.

A small reception with soup, sandwiches and wine — a veritable feast in those times — followed at my parents' home. Halfway through the festivities we left for the honeymoon, starting our trip to the train in an Electrotax, a newly invented electric taxi.

We sat in the small cab in front, while the driver guided the vehicle from an outside seat in the back. It looked like a big, three-wheel enclosed bicycle built for two.

By train we rode to the eastern part of Holland, where Paul knew of a small hotel, the Gouden Karper in Hummelo, which was not yet occupied by the Germans. This country lodge still had some pretty good food, according to my sister, who lived in the area. Arriving in Doetinchem, we still had to ride our bicycles a long way to get to this remote village. My parents had given us their hidden tires as a wedding present, but within half an hour we both had flats. The inner tubes' rubber was just too old and had disintegrated. We repaired them ourselves, sitting on the side of the road.

Soon after we had another flat. It became hilarious and we sat down in the grass convulsed with laughter. What did it matter, we were in love! Deciding not to repair my bike, I rode the rest of the way on the crossbar of Paul's bicycle, holding on to mine with the flat tire. To make matters worse, it started to rain and we arrived soaking wet. Our destination turned out to be a charming country inn. My sister had been right about the food. I can still taste the "coq au vin," although the roosters were scrawny. It was a heavenly meal at the time.

Our honeymoon lasted two happy days. It ended when the office phoned Paul, telling him that the recall of furloughed members of the patriotic Dutch army had begun in earnest. He was needed. As an ex-military man, Paul received the dreaded summons, too. We had to hurry back to The Hague to see how he and his friends could get an Ausweis, a German exemption certificate from the draft, so they would not end up in a German P.O.W. camp.

On our way back we passed a large farm. This was our golden chance to buy some butter. We stepped off our bikes and walked through a vegetable garden to the low farmhouse where tall covered milk cans stood near the door. We could see that at least they had milk.

Before we knocked the farmer's wife opened the door, wiped her hands on her blue striped apron and gave us a big warm smile.

"Goede morgen, Mevrouw," I said, wishing her good morning and returning her smile, "Is there any chance we can buy some butter?"

"Kom maar binnen, hoor," she invited us in, "I'll have to ask my husband."

The man came in from the fields and looked at us suspiciously. We repeated our request and he told us how they were besieged by city people who came to get food. Hordes would come by train, by bicycle, or on foot. He and the other farmers couldn't possibly help them all, even though it was hard to turn anyone down. Not saying very much, we just stood there and chatted for a while about the Nazis and the war.

The farmer softened a little and invited us to sit down. After his wife gave us a cup of coffee, neatly served on a tray with a lace doily, the farmer looked at Paul in anguish and told us what was really on his mind. They had lost their only son who had been about Paul's age. Tears came to his eyes as he described how their son had hidden a helpless and wounded British pilot.

"It was the only humane thing to do, but the Krauts picked him up and shot him. They killed him, they killed my son!" he cried. I had tears in my eyes, too. Trembling, I looked at Paul and found his widened and sorrowing eyes looking at me. We both shuddered. I ached for this nice couple who had gone through this terrible ordeal. Instinctively I knew we could trust each other. They seemed to be happy to have people to talk to who were the same age as their son. It was hard to leave this affectionate couple, but we had to get home to our own problems.

Just before I stepped onto my bike, I felt a package being pushed under my arm. It was a pound of butter and a big wedge of Gouda cheese. We were speechless. These two strangers had become very close to us. We embraced.

"Please be careful," the farmer's wife said, hugging Paul.

We left and waved goodbye for a long time, looking back at them still standing there, a forlorn couple in the fields of war.

Our mood had changed as heavy-hearted we returned to the realities ahead. Quietly we pedaled on. Cycling through a wooded area, we stopped for a minute to walk through the brush and look for chanterelles, the yellow edible mushrooms which look like a rooster's comb. Between the pine needles, often close to a tree trunk, we found their yellow heads sticking out of the ground, waving at us. The mushrooms were a delicious, vitamin-filled supplement to our meager food rations. We carefully picked them and put them in our bicycle bags, feeling close to nature. The walk through the woods calmed our nerves. Although we were both loathe to admit it, we were still very upset about the farmer's son. It had really hit home. After sitting for a while with our arms around each other, we remounted and biked to the train. Within two hours we were in The Hague, looking at, and being depressed by, a hoard of heel-clicking Nazis.

We stood in front of our home as an S.S. platoon marched by and Paul stiffened, eyes narrowed, clenching his teeth. Suddenly I realized that my new husband was a man of emotion and commitment. He could put himself in such peril that I would have to be the calming influence, if we were to survive together for a better day.

"Paul, be calm," I whispered.

He turned abruptly and opened the front door for me. It was not the romantic moment I had dreamed about. I found myself recalling my mother's words, "Marriage is not a fairy tale and certainly not in these times."

Inside I turned towards him. "Darling, please relax. I hate them just as much as you do. But don't let them spoil this moment. We can't do anything about it."

Paul looked at me. He drew me close, and I felt his strength that was going to sustain me for the rest of my life. We hugged and he kissed me, nuzzling my neck, but we could not really relax. It was no use pretending that the poor farmer's son was out of our minds. We sat on the couch, our arms around each other.

"I hope you're not involved in anything more, are you?" Paul looked straight into my eyes.

"I'm not." I said, feeling uneasy by his gaze.

"To take guns across the Yssel was crazy," he continued, still holding me and kissing me.

I wriggled, "How d'you know?"

"I also know you were a courier." Another kiss. "And please, Babesje, please, don't do it anymore. Believe me, a year ago was one thing! But God, the Krauts are cruel. It doesn't matter that you're a woman. They'll send you straight to jail, or to Germany, or God knows where! And you wouldn't last a week!"

"I know, I know," I said nervously, "but I wanted to do it."

"Babes, the underground is really a man's job. You'll do plenty just keeping us alive. Besides, it's too tough for me to worry about you. I don't want to find my wife dead in the street somewhere."

I understood his feeling. Being married suddenly made me feel different about a lot of things, made me more cautious. The Germans were getting rough, and I wasn't so sure that I could handle it any more. When Paul started to lecture me further, I kissed him to shut him up. I didn't want to worry. Not now, not today. At this moment I just wanted to love and be loved.

Within a few days I began to know what it meant to be married to a man like Paul. His mind went in 20 directions. As soon as he returned to the office from our honeymoon, he persuaded the German Agricultural group to give our Food Distribution workers an exemption from the draft. The Germans were willing to sign Paul's newly designed passes but warned that, to make them legal, they still had to be stamped by the German Draft Board, located in Amersfoort. All we could do was hope for the best. A few days later a contingent from our office, including a few underground friends who secretly joined us, took their passes by train to Amersfoort. I went along, for I was not going to let Paul confront the Nazis again without me. A sad group, representing vital community functions, was already waiting in front of the Nazi recruiting office, which was guarded by the S.S. with helmets and fixed bayonets. While we nervously discussed who would be the first guinea pig to test the passes, Paul resolutely stepped forward and told the guards he wanted to go in. Aghast, I watched my brand-new husband being led away and the iron gate close behind him. The locked gate blurred while I stared at it. Someone, seeing my distress, put his arm around me.

"Paul didn't even say good-bye!" I wailed, brushing away my tears, and wondering if I would ever see him again. The others were silent. The tension mounted. Paul's boss arrived along with a few other friends of the department. More onlookers gathered. As for the guards, they just glared at us. Waiting, and more waiting. Finally, after about an hour, Paul appeared, waving his stamped card.

"What took you so long?" I asked, holding myself back until he merged into the group.

He had a strained look on his face. "I had to explain our food distribution. They're all Austrians."

Austrians! Not Austrians again! I thought back on our many ski trips in the Austrian alps a few years ago: Zürs, Lech, Kitzbühel! What a great time! What great people! We skied during the day and drank beer at night, singing with them, swaying arm in arm, clutching overflowing steins of beer. What was the matter with the Austrians? How could these people, whom I had really liked, change so drastically?

The others surrounded us, listening to Paul's every word. When they had the courage to troop in, they too came out with the coveted stamp. Finally, in the afternoon the Draft Board had had enough of exemptions and, capriciously, shipped some of the Dutch workers off to Germany without even letting them get their clothes from home. We felt very badly that some of our friends were caught and Paul complained to the German Agricultural group, saying that he needed his men for the food distribution. Eventually the Germans did release four of them.

In the office in The Hague, Paul was involved in all kinds of things like the passes. Aside from organizing the distribution of po-tatoes, he worked very hard trying to keep food and personnel in Holland, while secretly helping those who were in hiding.

Once in a while he could get a government car to inspect po-tato growers. This gave him a wonderful opportunity to meet with underground contacts in Maastricht, enabling him to give them the much-needed ration cards. Paul called these "business" trips, but I knew differently.

Just before our marriage, he had come to our house needing a doctor. It was in the middle of the night and he was bleeding pro-fusely. He had tangled with an unexpected German roadblock and had driven through the barricades at full speed to get away. Father removed a dozen pieces of windshield glass from his face. We could only guess why the Germans had erected an obstruction there. As he was being repaired, Paul asked Father to hide a slip of paper in one of his medical books. In case Paul was ever caught, my Dad was to alert others that their lives were in danger. Father was pleased that Paul trusted him that much.

Paul kept his promise to avoid dangerous jobs in the Resist-ance for only a short time, perhaps only the two days of our honey-moon. He became extremely nervous. His increased smoking caused a lot of coughing as well as stained fingers, which were hard to clean without any decent soap products. Cigarettes were impos-sible to get and most people bought straight tobacco and rolled their own. All paper products were extremely rare. Black marke-teers not only made a lot of money selling the tobacco, but they also sold the thin Indian paper on which bibles were printed. In batches of one hundred, the pages of this sacred book were sold to roll cigarettes with.

Soon I sensed that my brave husband was involved in very dangerous projects. He told me once that he had acquired a detailed map showing all the German gasoline dumps in Holland. He didn't volunteer more information. After the war, he told me that on this particular project, the guards were bribed to "accidentally" leave the front door of the building open in the evening. Paul, with an expert locksmith, opened the inner closet, rummaged through the papers, and photographed the requested map. This picture was then transmitted to London.

Although I did not know exactly what he was doing, I knew enough. Every time I heard footsteps in the street, my heartbeat quickened to match the tempo out there in the dark. Each time he came home a little late, I nearly went out of my mind, but I learned not to mention names and never to talk, never to ask many questions and never to say anything about him to anyone.

13

As soon as the Nazis had conquered Western Europe they began to defend it, building a steel and concrete wall of fortifications along the whole west coast, known as the Atlantic Wall. These series of bunkers, gun emplacements and pillboxes were intended to block the path of any Allied invaders.

Todt, the German public works bureau entrusted with the task, first relied on German workers. Later many nationals of occupied countries were forced to work for them. In addition, there were collaborators, mainly contractors, who volunteered for the Nazis, earning millions. A notable exception was a patriotic French housepainter, whose daring laid the groundwork for victory at the Normandy landing. He stole a German coastal defense map and passed it on to the British, we heard through the grapevine.

After a year, the defense of the Dutch coast was completely built and a second defense line, further inland, was begun. We were dismayed to see part of our city being leveled to make room for a 15-meter wide anti-tank moat. A strip of land running straight through The Hague and Scheveningen was completely flattened by bulldozers to make room for the moat. I cried when I saw my friends' beautiful homes, office buildings, and even our modern Red Cross hospital demolished. Eventually the ditch filled up with rainwater and barbed wire barricades were built on either side.

My parents lived within the horseshoe-shaped area between the moat and the ocean. For the time being, they were allowed to stay there. But when Father retired, they were forced to move to the country, as persons without work couldn't stay in the city. Just married, Paul and I were happy to rent their home. It was a three-story house on the van Alkemadelaan, a thoroughfare linking the city of The Hague with Scheveningen. Military transports were constantly driving back and forth to the Atlantic Wall.

Since there was a shortage of living space, we had to share our home with other people. We occupied the ground floor with the kitchen and the garden. The second floor was rented to the Dinger family and their two teen-age daughters, both tall and slender with pretty blond hair and flirtatious eyes.

"What legs! Like long-stemmed vases!" Paul, using a Dutch expression, watched the girls appreciatively when they walked by in the hall. I grunted. As a newlywed, I was not too happy about this intrusion.

"How come that with hundreds of families looking for a home, we're getting one with these two gorgeous creatures?" I asked, looking suspiciously at my grinning husband. "You chose them, didn't you?"

Paul stopped smiling and drew me close, "Would you believe I rented the house to the parents. I never even saw the girls."

I still felt very dejected. Paul sensed it and pulled me towards him, "Aw, c'mon, I've been all over the world. I've seen a lot of beautiful girls. Blonde ones and dark ones. Sure, they were attractive. But dearest, when I finally came home, I saw you!"

The Dingers moved in and we soon became friends. They converted the bathroom into a kitchen. Four gas burners on top of a chest of drawers served as their stove. A board covered the bathtub on which their kitchenware was stored. Once a week we could use their bath, after first removing the board with all the pots and pans. The clanging heard all over the house, made us remark dryly that at least one of us would be clean!

A longtime family friend, Mrs. Zuur, rented the third floor and we arranged cooking facilities for her in a large closet. She didn't have a job in the city, but we were sorry for her and hoped that her presence would not be discovered. Her daughter, Sabine, had been picked up by the Gestapo, and with her daughter gone, Mrs. Zuur had nobody to help her. It was difficult for older people to cope with ration stamps and new regulations. We became her substitute family.

We spent many happy evenings with the Dinger family, listening to their stories. Mrs. Dinger was extremely quiet. While her exuberant daughters made fun of some of the petty Nazi regulations, she seemed scared. She lived in Belgium during the Great War, and having already gone through one war, she knew that the situation would only get worse. In the next two years I came to know what she meant by never, "ever" feeling completely safe again.

After a few months the Germans were satisfied with the defense wall. Field Marshall Erwin Rommel came to inspect it. They called it "Sperrgebiet," and proceeded to surround this restricted area with barbed wire. The Dutch were given passes, but they were revoked after a few sabotage attempts. This meant that our families and friends could not visit us. I never felt more alone.

Knowing this, Paul surprised me one day coming home early holding a tiny wiggling wire-haired terrier puppy in his arms. I couldn't believe my eyes. My parents had taken all our pets to the country with them and I loved having a dog again. I reached for the pup, holding him up and inspecting him from all sides.

He was a pretty dog with black symmetrical spots on his ears, ending in brown as they encircled his eyes. He had a white body with one black spot on his back. The puppy squirmed, trying to lick my face as I cuddled him against my neck. Paul beamed. My reaction was even happier than he had hoped. Stroking the dog and touching his pert little nose, shiny black like a licorice button, he said, "It's an early birthday present. Think of a good name."

"Terry, let's call him Terry!" I couldn't know that a year later his name would be heard by millions of people over BBC as part of our secret code.

Terry proved to be smart. He adjusted quickly. It was as if he knew we were in danger and, like us, had to learn fast to survive. He traveled with me everywhere, walking or running, or perched in a basket on my bike, in crowded trams, hiding under the seat. He shared our happy and sometimes scary days. In our worst moments, the puppy cheered us by being bright-eyed and full of trust, and wagging his tail so enthusiastically that his whole body wagged with it.

Living within the confines of the Sperrgebiet became so uncomfortable that we were relieved when the Germans finally ordered us out. Within three months the 80,000 people residing there had to find homes elsewhere. These people were to be absorbed by families living in the outlying areas. We were allowed two months to find our own housing, or the government would assign us a place. Paul and I wanted to stay with the Dingers, but it was impossible to find a home for all of us. Mrs. Zuur was invited to move in with a friend.

We had to find our own. Since my parents had moved to the country and my friends had their own family, we had no one to take us. Thus we decided to ring doorbells in the suburbs, hoping to find someone who would like us at first sight. We reasoned that perhaps some family would be willing to take a chance on us, rather than wait for pro-Nazi officials to send them perhaps some miserable characters.

We started looking in Wassenaar, a suburb of The Hague, a wooded area that would give needed protection if necessary. It also was a little further from the coast. After a few tries, we found a delightful childless couple, with a full-time maid, two dogs and four chickens. Their names were Ysbrand and Hanneke Hiddes Galema, a Frisian name from the northern province of Friesland. Great People! Their home was a square villa on the Wittenburgerweg. A garden full of flowers surrounded the house, overlooking lush green meadows dotted with black and white cows, lazily chewing the grass.

Ysbrand and Hanneke also seemed happy to have found us. The men set out to conform to the Nazi regulations for a certain square footage per person. They plotted that with a little luck, they could prove that each had a right to an office at home. If that were accepted by the city officials, the Galemas would not have to house a third family. The following day Paul and Ysbrand went to the government office to tell them that they were set. When the inspector came out, he still felt our living space was too big for two families, but the persuasive Paul and the persistent Ysbrand convinced him that all requirements had been met.

The day we rang the Galemas' bell was a lucky one for us. We came to love these strangers, bound to us in a time of terror. When it was time to actually move, I was too numb to care. Paul fumed. In organized fury, he did not leave a single thing for the Germans, dismantling even the washbasins and the toilets. The house looked as forlorn as we felt.

We borrowed a horse and potato wagon, loaded with our furniture, and set out for our new home in Wassenaar. Hanneke and Ysbrand stood at the door waiting to help us. Seeing all our belongings shocked them and they wondered how we would put it all in our two rooms and a balcony. But it all fit, a little crowded perhaps, but reasonably cozy.

Of course, everything felt very strange in the beginning, but pretty soon we got used to our new surroundings.

The head of the family, Ysbrand Galema, was a small man in his late thirties, who had once wanted to be a jockey. He still exercised the horses at the nearby race track after managing his own beer brewery. The couple was very well read and had a great sense of humor. We had interesting talks in the evenings during the winter blackouts spent in the only room that was heated.

Hanneke was slender and elegant, showing the grace and beauty that had won her fame as prima ballerina of the Viennese State Opera. This was an enormous feat for a Dutch girl. The couple, such an unlikely combination, had an unusually happy marriage, and Paul and I benefitted greatly from this pleasant atmosphere.

Janie, the maid, was a country girl. She was sincere and willing, with only one problem; she was extremely nervous. Many times our local priest came over to talk to her and she seemed more relaxed after a while.

The Galemas' two small dogs, a West Highland terrier and a Dachshund, became friends with our Terry. They ran up and down the stairs and rolled over each other on the landings, Terry yipping and yapping as only a puppy can. When they were exhausted they flopped down on the cool tiles of the entrance hall, panting heavily. With his shaggy hind legs stretched out behind him, Terry looked like a soft fluffy toy.

The four chickens were a prime target for burglars. Their cackling informed everybody where they roosted. Many times when we were hungry we wanted to eat them ourselves, but the eggs they laid so faithfully made them more valuable alive. I always wondered how they did it, those lovely leghorns. Their food was just crumbs from the table, certainly not a well-balanced chicken diet. Two were stolen out of the backyard, and one died, but we kept the last one for years. She became an important household member and lived with us in the kitchen at night, because we were afraid she would be stolen if left outside.

Her name was "Kip," the Dutch word for chicken. One day when she had an obstruction in her throat, we had to do a delicate operation. Kip, slightly chloroformed, sat on the kitchen table, while Paul read instructions from a book and Ysbrand wielded a razor blade as a scalpel. Our textbook surgery saved her life. She died years later, a little old lady.

After putting everything in place in our rooms, we were exhausted and gratefully accepted the Galemas' invitation to dinner that night. Afterwards, sitting around the fireplace, Paul and I became very quiet remembering the events of the day. We had left our lovely home behind and were starting out with a completely strange family. Ysbrand, sensing our depression, suddenly left the room and returned with a glass almost big enough to hold an entire bottle of champagne.

He smiled at us kindly and said, "On our honeymoon we had this glass made for us in Venice. I was told that anyone who drinks from it will have a happy marriage."

He offered Paul the Veuve Cliquot, holding the glass delicately by the stem. "We want you to have the first sip. Here's to your health and happiness!"

We were thrilled by their graciousness. Together, holding the enormous glass high and admiring the sparkling golden liquid, we toasted our host and hostess, took a sip and savored it for a moment. By Dutch custom we raised the glass again, not saying a word, then returned the glass to them as they did the same.

Although it was a happy moment, Paul appeared distressed. He finally admitted that he couldn't help me unpack, as he had to go to the office the next morning. The Germans had suddenly demanded 300,000 tons of our potatoes for the heavily bombed Ruhr area. Paul could sometimes negotiate the tonnage down, or send less than Berlin demanded without being discovered. Still, he realized that no matter how we cheated, we were driving slowly towards starvation.

I sighed when I saw Paul leave early the next morning after giving me a fleeting kiss. His mind was already on the unpleasant encounter with the Germans.

While our life was reasonably good because of the Galemas, we had many problems. Hanneke and I were busy, not only with normal household chores, but with the pursuing of rationed items such as clothing and food. All textiles were scarce and only available on special cards. Besides, one had to exchange an old coat to get a new one. The price was still outrageous. Father gave me his blue suit which I had made into a suit for myself. Paul's shirt cuffs and collars were turned and even his suits were turned inside out, the facing reversed and worn again. We unraveled old sweaters, washing the wrinkles away to knit new ones, Hanneke and I swapping colors with each other.

Together we spent many an evening in front of the fireplace. The less food we had, the more we talked about "the way it was," the delicacies we all had liked the most during times of plenty. We daydreamed of Dutch poffertjes, a plate of dollar-size pancakes with sugar and a gob of butter; or my favorite birthday dinner, a juicy beefsteak, a tasty salad, pommes-frites and a hazelnut-mocha cake for dessert. Wow! We remembered eating as much as we wanted and the thought made us smile and lick our lips. We could even taste it! As our life together began to take on a pattern we fell into a feeling of false security.

Then one day, it happened. It was just a slip up. Perhaps just one word or one gesture heard or seen by the wrong people. One morning in the spring of '44 when the war was four years old, the doorbell rang and Bob, Paul's assistant, stood outside. Bob had never come to the house before and I was half-curious and half-afraid of his mission. Before I could ask, he blurted out: "Paul was picked up by the Gestapo and might now be in jail somewhere!"

I screamed in anguish, "Die rot Moffen!" remembering Hitler's statement that people would be picked up, not tried or shot, but would just disappear. *People would vanish without a trace!* I knew Paul was strong, but how strong can a man be? How much torture can one endure? I saw the whole scene in front of my eyes. I knew what had happened. God knows I had heard it often enough from others, but nevertheless I asked, "What happened?"

"Two Gestapos with drawn guns barged into our office," Bob said. They went straight to Paul's desk and made him get up and follow them. Paul tried to stall. Thinking fast, he said he had to tell his boss that he was leaving. The Germans consented. Although they kept the door open, they didn't follow Paul into the main office. Instead they searched Paul's desk and took his French and English dictionary. While walking towards Bouman, Paul quickly dug his small notebook out of his pocket and flung it into the wastebasket.

"They're picking me up," he said and stared intensely at Bouman, spelling out the word basket under his breath, "I have no idea what they want."

As soon as the Gestapo had gone Bouman ran to inform Louwes, then he went to the German Bureau of Agriculture next door. Woltheim, one of the Germans who knew Paul, seemed to be genuinely upset. He liked Paul and had been as fair as possible in dealing with the potatoes appropriated by the German Army. He promised to find out where Paul was.

Nobody saw Paul toss the little notebook into the basket, and Bouman could not catch the words Paul was trying to mouth. Fortunately, the office rule insisted that the wastebaskets be checked each day for incriminating papers. Through sad experience, we had found that traitors were everywhere. Some had gone through the garbage cans outside and sold the used carbons to the Gestapo.

Later that afternoon they found Paul's booklet. Bouman immediately called Paul's contact to tell him what had happened.

Bob meanwhile tried to assure me that the office would get him out, but I was frantic and went with him to the department. Only a few older men were still sitting at their desks. The young ones, afraid they might be next, had gone into hiding. Louwes promised he would do whatever he could.

I waited two weeks, not knowing where my husband was, who was helping him, or why he had been seized in the first place. I cried my heart out. I couldn't sleep, I couldn't eat. I just sat with the dog on my lap thinking of how to get him home. During this time 20 young Dutchmen were executed, and their names appeared in a boxed column, with the heading "Bekendmaking," on the front page of the paper. I knew four of them. I nearly fainted reading those familiar names.

What would I do if Paul never came back? We had spent so little time together, had had such a short time to love. Wasn't there a God for lovers? God helps the ones who help themselves, my father often said. I knew I had to shape up, to help myself and help Paul to get home. Shortly before he was picked up, we had talked about what to do if one of us were caught by the Gestapo. We argued back and forth and I finally opted, "Of course, there is always one thing a woman can trade."

Paul looked at me and his eyes darkened.

"For heaven's sake, Babes, don't ever say that! I would rather die, rather be shot!" In a tight voice he added, "If it were *your* life. If you could save your *own* life, but not mine!"

Now, the Gestapo had taken him. Would Paul still think the same way? Yes, I was sure he would. But I thought there must be some way to convince the Gestapo that Paul was indispensable for the food distribution!

A month went by, and then another week. They were weeks of worry and sadness, compounded by the fear of an Allied invasion while Paul was in jail. The Nazis would kill him and everybody else in the face of the advancing Allies. We felt sure that would be the last nasty gesture in a nasty war.

Finally, people at the office found out Paul was held in the Orange Hotel. It was the most dreaded jail in Holland. I went down to Scheveningen to see the high brick walls rising there in the outskirts of town. I imagined the long, dank corridors turning into darkness between rows of cells. I looked at the heavy wooden door,

large enough for trucks to pass through. It was flanked by two
smaller doors guarded by S.S. soldiers. As I stood there feeling terribly helpess, a sleek-looking Nazi came out, riding crop in his hand.
Feeling ready to kill him, I knew I'd better go home instead. How
could I ever spirit Paul over the wall, or lure the guards away from
the gate. I went home more depressed than ever.

A few days later someone from the office called telling me they
had been in touch with the Gestapo and Paul would be released
soon. I didn't believe him. How soon is soon? Still distraught, I kept
my daily vigil, sitting on the balcony and peering down the road.
One day I noticed a frail man down the street. He could barely
walk, stumbling several times. I watched him, holding my breath, as
he began to look familiar.

Paul! I ran towards him and we fell into each other's arms. He
was so emaciated that I could feel every bone through his clothes.
His eyes were big black holes above grey and hollow cheeks. The
white streak in his hair now ran through his beard, too. It was plain
to see that he could not stand up much longer and I supported him
as we shuffled forward to the house. The Gestapo had tried to
starve him in those few weeks.

For days Paul could not talk about his experience, but finally
he told me a few things. I never heard it all, but I could see some of
what they did; his broken thumbs were still black and blue. He said
only that they had used thumb screws.

"They're barbarians. They're savages. They're the worst bastards in the world," he said. "The worst thing is to see other people
being tortured, especially women. One day, they grabbed me and
two other guys and made us stand against a wall to watch them beat
and kick an older woman. I knew they did it just to make us wild. It
sure did. All three of us jumped on the bastard and hit him as hard
as we could. I don't know what happened after that."

Paul just stared ahead and I wondered if he would go on. He
finally continued, "I was kicked unconscious and woke up in soli-
tary. I never saw the others again. The guards left me alone for — I
don't know how many days — throwing a crust of bread in the cell
once a day. At night I got a bowl of soup, just water and potatoes.
Once they let me go out to walk in the courtyard. I had no chance to
talk to other prisoners. Yes, I did see some friends.

"At night we knocked on pipes, trying to talk with each other.
I was quite isolated and I couldn't hear much through the walls. The
nights were the worst. Sometimes I heard screaming. I also tried to
read the writing on the walls. They were covered with messages,

prayers, names, even "Long live the Queen."

"Did you write anything on the walls?" I interrupted.

Paul looked at me intensely. Ever so slowly he said, "I started to scratch a letter to you. I wanted you to know how much I loved you in case I never came out." He sighed, and his eyes looked inward, not really seeing me. I hugged him and kissed him gently, afraid to hurt him.

Paul shivered, shook his head and went on talking. "They interrogated me all the time, asking over and over why I had an English and French dictionary in my desk. Was I in contact with England? I never admitted anything. They never found out. They hit me constantly, just for the pleasure of hitting, in my face, in my stomach, in my kidneys."

He stopped talking for a moment. Although they had hurt him seriously, I thanked God he had returned alive.

"Then," he continued haltingly, "suddenly, I guess it was this morning, I had to appear before the Kommandant. God, I stood in the office for a long time before he even looked up. When he finally saw me, he said I had expressed myself "deutschfeindlich," anti-German, while standing in line in a vegetable store. That was all. I could leave!"

Paul never found out the real reason for his arrest nor why he got out so suddenly. It was better not to ask, he decided. Sometimes he thought they let him go so they could follow him to ferret out the underground. Or perhaps the Germans thought he was indeed important enough to continue working on food problems.

It took a long time for Paul's strength to return. His weight never came back. He coughed constantly. The doctor diagnosed it as bronchitis, picked up in jail, where all kinds of lung diseases raged. He was given a permit for extra food rations and some pills.

14

As time went on, our lives changed again and all activity focused on survival. It bothered me at first to leave my job because I married, but it was a traditional Dutch feeling that a married woman should stay at home. Also, because of severe unemployment, men were given priority when a job opened up.

I soon found out I did not have time for a job anyway, because foraging for food took days. I started out on my food safari when the men went to work every morning. Every week the rations were announced in the papers and with our numbered cards we stood in line at the store, hoping there still would be food available. The only chance to get anything extra was to search and be lucky.

That winter the mobile soup kitchen began to include a stop at the far end of Wassenaar. Carrying my two tickets and one big pan, I walked half an hour to the designated spot. People were already waiting, looking worn out and dull-eyed, their cold faces warmed by woolen shawls. Some stood, others sat on the sidewalk, pots and pans spread on their lap. Men and women of all ages came on foot or on ramshackle bikes. I saw them, day after day, rain or shine, sleet or snow!

The kitchen truck, with the large steel barrels of food, was almost always late, except when I was late, and then, for sure, the truck came early. At those times I didn't know whether to curse or to cry, because I had missed out on an extra ration for our dinner that night.

One day I sat beside a woman who stared vacantly. She wore a black band around her arm and I wondered if she had just lost her husband to the Nazis. She looked extremely sad but kept her agony to herself. Although others in line chatted with each other and started friendships in their misery, she didn't seem interested in a conversation. I gave up trying, and instead I watched my friend Oda's dignified father arrive on a wood-tired bicycle. We heard him rattling from far away with his two large pans jammed into sacks on the back of his bike. He collected his share plus an extra portion for his sick mother, and wheeled away, his long black coat flying and his worn fedora flopping. I always wondered how he managed to get through traffic without spilling anything.

For many months I saw the woman with the black arm band waiting for the kitchen truck. In time she became a lot thinner, but then we all grew thinner as the rations were reduced drastically. Sometimes we sat next to each other on the sidewalk, our legs stretched across the gutter, but even when our shoulders touched, she was uncommunicative. Still, I felt close to her somehow.

Suddenly, one late day in November, I heard a ruckus behind me and I saw her collapsed in a heap. I ran toward her and helped put her head on my folded coat. When I asked for her name, she just gasped for air. She died right in my arms. When I lifted her, she felt as light and thin as a wafer. It was then I saw her bloated legs, a shocking sign of hunger edema.

It all happened so fast I didn't have time to think about it. Later, I couldn't forget seeing her lying there, so alone, so miserable, and nobody around her with enough strength to be of any help. Some kind of an unusual-looking ambulance had taken her away. Where to? We really didn't know what medical agencies were still functioning. I went to my room and burst into tears.

In the beginning the Central kitchen fare was pretty good. We received two ladles of stew one day, cereal the next. As time went on all we had was soup, grey water made from potatoes and occasionally something floating in it that looked like meat. This and some food from the store bought with coupons was not half enough to keep us healthy. We trudged through the fields trying to talk a farmer or two into selling us anything edible. At first the farmers were agreeable, but after too many city dwellers trampled their produce or stole their livestock, their attitude toward us hardened. Only with a lot of money could you buy food. Later even money got nothing. The farmers asked for sheets, blankets, or clothing in return for butter. Towards the end of 1944, the stakes went up until gradually we were bartering gold and diamonds for meat and any kind of fats or oils.

My parents in the country raised their own vegetables and gave them to us whenever possible. Mother sold all her jewelry for dairy products. When the Nazis forbade travel to anyone under the age of forty, we were no longer able to get to our parents. We became hungrier.

One day, to get extra fruit, vegetables, or fish, I decided to bike to The Hague, a ride of about twenty minutes. I bounced along on my bicycle with the wooden tires, clattering across bricks and cobblestones. It was always a tiresome and frustrating trip, made even worse this time because it was raining. On top of that, I was not very successful in finding food. On my way back I began to feel sick and decided to take the tram. With the help of the conductor I lifted the bicycle onto the tram's balcony and stepped inside. As always Terry was with me, leaning against my leg. I petted him, clutching my newspaper-wrapped sanddabs, the only reward for an active day of shopping.

There were not many people on the electric tram to Wassenaar, and I stared vaguely at the grazing cattle. They were Lakenvelders, a valuable breed, all with the same white saddle-shaped spot on their black backs. They looked pretty against the bright green grass. Terry sat quietly. I stroked his long, silky hair and wondered if he was the pure-bred terrier that Paul believed he bought.

Daydreaming, I did not notice the two German soldiers across from me until I saw them interested in the dog. After looking at both of us for a long time, one of them asked, "Fraülein, is that your dog?"

"Ja," I answered curtly and resumed staring out of the window, hoping the conversation would end right there.

"Where did you get him?"

I was annoyed and shrugged my shoulders, "I don't know; it was a present."

"It sure looks like the dog that was stolen from our commander," the soldier continued, unruffled.

"Well, this one is mine," I said positively, pulling Terry closer. The soldiers conversed in low tones, looking searchingly at me, and finally one said, "We'll have to take the dog with us. Our commander will decide if it's his dog or not."

"Over my dead body!"

I spoke loudly, hoping for help from passengers in the tram. It worked. Three men sitting toward the front came to see what was happening.

"These soldiers bothering you?"

They looked threateningly at the Germans, who stared back, apparently deciding to leave well enough alone for the moment.

When I left the tram ten minutes later, they followed me home. During the short walk to our house, I heard the ominous clicking of their boots behind me. I looked straight ahead and put the key in the lock. Now, they were right behind me and I heard them say with finality, "We'll be back tomorrow!"

I was angry, alarmed and filled with foreboding. I had just been bothered earlier by another trauma. The German army told all dog-owners to show up with their pets on the Malieveld in the center of The Hague. The wehrmacht asked for large dogs, German shepherds, Bouviers and Dobermans, saying they should be "donated" to the army where they would be used in police work, "to be returned well-trained after the war."

I breathed a sigh of relief when I heard that small dogs only had to be "registered." I wondered if I had to go with Terry, but Paul said the Germans surely had the list of dog-owners from our pre-war license bureau, and it would be safer to go now than "to have them come looking for us."

I went early, which was our habit in response to any German confrontation — they always became nastier as the day wore on. Terry and I joined at least 50 other distraught owners and their dogs on the tram which passed Wassenaar from Leyden to The Hague. Twice during the trip the sirens wailed. We had to leave the coach, dogs and all, and seek shelter in the field as Allied bombers passed on their way to Germany. We dropped flat to the ground, with yapping dogs around us, and then climbed back on to continue our unhappy mission.

The parade ground of the Malieveld was a total confusion of barking animals, shouting owners and tangled leashes. If it hadn't been so sad for everyone, it would have been funny. Even the normally organized Germans could make neither head nor tails of it. The soldiers pushed and shoved us to make a line. The Dutch, never good at standing in line, all tried to get to the registration table at the same time. I cringed when I saw the large dogs being taken away, slinking down with their tails between their legs. Their owners were upset, unprepared, and didn't know what to do.

When it was my turn to register Terry, a Prussian officer behind the desk eyed me coldly, then tried to make a date.

"I'm married," I said, scooping up my dog and running off even as I heard him say, "So what?"

His look frightened me and I kept on running. Around the corner the tram conductor slowed the tram for me and helping arms pulled me onto the step. Once inside I told my story and the sympathy of other passengers made me feel better.

"You know that those big dogs are used to clear the mine-fields, don't you?"

I looked into the eyes of the man talking and the truth was sickening, causing me to forget my own woes.

It was a bad afternoon, but I was glad I did go. The Galemas, on the other hand, had refused to take their two dogs. Within two days they were called to the army office and had to pay a fine. Just by the sheerest of luck, their pooches were not confiscated. The Germans were enraged, for out of the thousands of dogs in the city, only 500 showed up. With dire threats, they organized a second dog-registration day.

All this had happened a few weeks earlier. I had just gotten over it when these soldiers tried to get my dog again! I sank onto the couch, trying to think while my head was spinning.

"How I hated those Nazis! How I despised their high-handed mannerism, their boots, their crew-cuts, their voices! I became more and more emotional. How dare they want my dog! How dare they come around my home! I knew what they were going to do. They were going to pick up Terry and keep him. He would disappear, just like my human friends who never came back. You never saw them again. You never even knew what had happened to them. Not my dog, I thought. I'll kill them before I give in!

By the time Paul came home at six, I was quite hysterical. In tears I told him about it and vowed, "I'll kill them if they come to the door, Paul, you know I will!"

I took Paul's small army gun, the F.N., which he had kept after his discharge from the Dutch army, and without loading it, I hid behind the door and practiced aiming at a phantom intruder. Paul became worried. He knew I meant it and was all set to shoot it out. After so many years of seeing people disappear, I was ready to defend my dog with my life.

He watched me with concern, a furrow growing between his eyes as he urged me to be realistic. "You can't fight the whole German Army. You know what'll happen. Please be smart!" He looked into my eyes. "I've never seen you like this before! Please don't do anything foolish!"

I let him talk. He was often so right, but this time, I knew I had to follow my heart. Tears streamed down my face and, while sobbing in Paul's arms, I vowed never to give up our dog. It was a long time before I promised Paul that I would not use the gun. But if they took the dog, I said, I would go along to convince the commander that Terry was not his but mine. That night the puppy slept safely curled up in my arms.

Paul left early the next morning, kissing me goodbye with some reluctance and reminding me of my promise. He added that he would rather be with me, but he had important work to do.

"You're on your own," he said, sounding at the same time loving and matter-of-fact, "and I trust your judgment."

His good-bye left me with the feeling I had exaggerated the whole episode, and that the soldiers were looking for a date, only picking up the dog as a "come-on." He even implied that my aggressiveness made me more attractive to them.

He was soon proved wrong! After lunch the doorbell rang. One of the soldiers was outside demanding the dog. I argued but when he reached for his gun, I gave in but insisted on going along. I left a note to Paul and we silently walked to the tram stop. Terry and I boarded and the soldier followed, sitting across from me. I gave him a quick sideway glance. He seemed so young, younger than I. He looked terribly sad and was suffering from a bad cold. I decided he was a milder breed of German, just a poor guy picked up to fight Hitler's fight. When we stepped out and walked together toward headquarters, I summoned the courage to ask him, "What's wrong?"

His frankness almost made me like him. He was in love with a Dutch girl, he said, but just this morning, the army had decreed that German soldiers could no longer fraternize with the Dutch.

"That's a switch," I said. "I thought your Führer wanted us to be part of his Nazi kingdom! What happened?"

He took his handkerchief from his pocket, blew his nose, and suddenly looked forlorn and vulnerable to me.

"I don't know what happened," he answered, "This new order comes from something about a soldier who drowned. They believe his Dutch girlfriend pushed him into the canal last night."

I tried to act surprised, but I really wasn't. We all knew this was happening. Sometimes I watched the children on their way to school run to the bridge to see if any dead bodies were floating by.

He sighed. Then he told me he was assigned to the commander who lost the dog.

"Oh no! Your commander has no right to take my dog. He's mine!" I spouted out the words in half-baked German. Then I tried to calm down. I knew I had to keep my emotions under control. I sighed deeply. When he looked at me sympathetically, I became bolder and pleaded, "Bitte, would you help me?"

I saw friendship in his mournful eyes and I knew he would. My step was lighter as we neared the commander's headquarters. We were, after all, two helpless people, with our private grief. Although enemies, we passed each other just long enough to offer a moment of sympathy.

After walking about fifteen minutes more, we arrived at the estate the German area commander had chosen for himself. My escort opened the door for me and went over to whisper to the soldiers who eyed me curiously from behind their desks. As Terry and I walked up, several of them reached to pet him. Nervous Terry, however, answered their attentions by lifting his leg. It made me smile. Good for you, Terry, I thought, that's exactly how I feel.

The commander was away, so we waited and waited. It started to get dark. They told me to go home, insisting I leave the dog. I refused and sat on the same hard chair through the long night. Except for a few guards, everyone else left. I was allowed to get up and let the dog out, but that was all. I became extremely tired and close to tears, but I was determined to stick it out and get my dog home.

The commander arrived very early in the morning, ignored me, and went upstairs. While I waited I became curious what the Germans did all day. Whenever I was left alone for a second I tried to read the papers on their desks, but never found anything worthwhile. The soldiers finally told me that they had orders to find the stolen dog. To ingratiate themselves, every man grabbed puppies that looked even remotely like the lost terrier.

At last the commander came down. "Yes, that looks like my little Putzi!" he said. He snapped his fingers to get Terry's attention, then called him. In that tense moment, I sensed the support of the soldiers who had been with me throughout the night. Terry didn't move an inch. Instead he hugged closer to my leg, growling softly.

To my great surprise, I heard someone say, "I don't think this dog is yours, Herr Kommandant. Here's a black spot on his back and Putzi was all white."

The commander looked Terry over very carefully, brushing through the dog's fur to see if the black spot had been painted on.

After this inspection, he reluctantly agreed that this was not his dog and sent me away with Terry in my arms.

I strode away purposefully looking straight ahead toward the open door. Freedom was out there, but something compelled me to tarry a moment longer. I looked into the face of the sad soldier. Our glances met and his fleeting smile showed me he acknowledged the conspiracy that gave each of us a small victory over the system.

Once outside the building I remembered that my business education had taught me to get any important decision in writing. After thinking a split second, I resolutely returned to ask for a letter stating that this was my dog, Terry.

The commander looked at me in sheer disbelief, but he called his secretary for dictation. Paul later expressed the same astonishment and had difficulty believing the story.

Many times after that, as I walked the dog, German soldiers whispered, pointing at me. I wondered what they were saying to each other. Would they have fought for their pet? I was glad I had, and Terry, as my partner in this success, became more precious to me than ever.

15

In one explosive week of February 1944, thousands of USAF and RAF bombers permanently crippled the Luftwaffe. Churchill announced that air raids on Germany would increase. Day and night we heard large formations of Flying Fortresses fill the air with a continuous hum. Running outside, we would gaze into the clouds. Sometimes we spotted them only by a flash of light as a ray of sun hit their silver bodies. High up in the sky they soared steadily towards the east. These B-17's could accurately bomb from that altitude and were not bothered by German flak, nor by the Luftwaffe.

We looked in awe at this huge armada of silver-grey birds, winging past in perfect precision. We waved at them, cheering, and hoped that this was the beginning of the invasion of Holland. It was not. Instead, they flew on to drop thousands of tons of explosives on the major cities of Hitler's Thousand-Year Reich, avenging the massive blitz of London.

When our newspaper announced that England had stopped all travel for civilians, we knew that an invasion was imminent. Although one of the narrowest parts of the Channel was between England and Calais, we discounted that route as being too obvious. Because the area of Dieppe to the south of Calais had been probed a year earlier by the Allies, we were sure that this little scene would not be repeated. Since the port of Cherbourg was filled with German elite troops, we assumed the Allies wouldn't land there either. As time dragged on, we began asking not only "where?" but *"when?"*

Day after day we listened to the reports of poor weather around the North Sea, which the British call the Channel, especially treacherous in the spring. When the weather worsened, we were sure the Allies would wait till summer. While we speculated, the Nazis kept us increasingly busy. Eventually I paid no attention to the rumors at all. Our super traitor, Mussert, head of the N.S.B., was asked what he would do in case of an invasion.

"I would stay right here," he announced in the papers, "as I have just received my uniform as a volunteer soldier of the German army. That's what I will wear in case of an invasion."

I could not believe that he said this so nonchalantly, as if there were no death penalty for being a traitor!

Suddenly it was D-day, June 6th, an unforgettable day for millions of people. As part of the great deception, the Allies sent British torpedo boats toward Holland. While they were landing in Normandy, Germans in Holland snatched Dutchmen from the streets to dig trenches on the coast. Poor Ysbrand was caught and put to work digging, but somehow he managed to escape and came home, a nervous wreck. Prudently he went into hiding for a few days.

To frustrate possible glider landings, the Germans also planted hundreds of heavy iron stakes, called "Rommel aspergus" in the sand. Some of them were booby-trapped.

The papers no longer wrote glowing reports of German victories. Instead, German news told us that the situation was "confusing." We desperately wanted to believe that the Allies could easily overtake the Germans. We did not know that the situation during the landings was extremely precarious and could have become a disaster. We were full of hope and by the time we received reliable news, the situation was under control and the Allies were advancing through France.

I still could barely believe that the Allies were on European soil. As if they would be here any minute, I carefully packed an emergency suitcase and put it next to my bed. France was still far away, but it had just come a lot closer. In The Hague people were seeking further news in front of the Haagsche Courant, the local newspaper. An enterprising young man sold maps of Normandy, but only for a short time. The Nazis picked him up an hour later. Paul came home with more information. Our own battery radio had run out by then, but he had listened to the BBC at a friend's house. Churchill had told the House of Commons that "an enormous armada of more than four thousand warships, together with several thousand smaller craft, had crossed the Channel to land on the European continent, escorted by more than eleven thousand planes!"

In the spirit of the moment, I danced around Paul, singing well-known show tunes, my arms wrapped around his neck from pure happiness. Ysbrand and Hanneke joined us, dancing on the black and white tiles as the phonograph played American jazz. This release made us feel light-hearted and happy. Freedom seemed so close, just around the next fox trot.

During the next few days, the city's mood was elated. We were getting happier even if the Germans were getting tougher. Now there was hope! Warnings appeared, forbidding help to the Allies. Did the Nazis expect a second invasion, perhaps in Holland? Certainly it was what the Dutch hoped for, but after looking at secret pictures of demolished Normandy, it was clear we were lucky to have been spared the inevitable devastation of an invasion.

But other problems developed for us. "Corporal Hitler," as Churchill called de Führer, was counting on a surprise of his own to reverse events. Although I had read about it, I had never seriously thought about his "secret weapon." But suddenly, just a week after the Allied invasion, it made its deadly appearance, Hitler's V-1, the first of the V-weapons! We were told that the capital V was taken from the German word "Vergeltung," for vengeance!

It was an unusually beautiful and clear morning. I had opened all the windows as I was cleaning the rooms. The job was pretty hopeless as I had little soap to clean with and the vacuum cleaner was not working anymore.

When I finished I sat on our balcony overlooking Wittenburger Avenue, delighting in the green of Jochem's meadows with his precious cows. Everything seemed peaceful on this gorgeous day.

Paul had left for the office, and Hanneke and Ysbrand were out. Only Janie, the three dogs and I were home. As usual, Terry stood next to me, looking through the balustrade at the street. Suddenly I heard an unfamiliar sound. Terry's nose pushed against me and I could see that he, too, was puzzled. His ears pricked up and his head cocked sideways. Of the many sounds in three years of war, I had never heard this one before. I seemed to feel it as much as hear it. I looked down curiously to see what strange thing was coming down the road, but the street was bathed in a mass of sunlight and nothing moved.

Then I saw it! Something like a lead cigar was flying no higher than the top of my window. It was an unusual-looking plane with rudimentary wings, ungraceful stumps that added to its ominous silhouette in the sky. A jet exhaust puffed above the tail leaving a trail of smoke and a small flame. Concerned I remembered reading that the concussion of this flying bomb could pulverize everything. If this was really Hitler's secret weapon, why was it flying in the middle of a populated area? These new weapons should be in a war zone, not cruising among peaceful citizens. But there it was. The V-1, about 30 feet long, chucking close to the ground on the last leg of its destructive journey. It put-putted along, traversing the length of the meadow, lower and lower, nearly hitting the black and white cattle. The nervous animals scattered in panic, running in circles, desperately trying to hide.

It slid down and finally belly-landed behind the trees near the race track. By this time Janie had come to the window, looking pale and scared. We both stared at the spot where the strange thing had disappeared. I wondered if it would blow up or if it would be like the Trojan horse, crammed with hundreds of German soldiers who would unfold miraculously into a full-fledged army.

We stared and waited for a minute. Then I ran to the phone and called Paul. Everybody within five miles came to look at the "thing." Neighbors cautiously came out of their houses, staying close to their front doors, ready to dash back inside. It seemed a long time before a truck with a Dutch demolition squad arrived. They looked at the V-1 from a distance, not daring to go closer. One of our neighbors told me that it was a pilotless plane, a robot that was supposed to detonate over England as a massive bomb.

A Dutch air patrol had also spotted the V-1 and arrived in army vehicles. They, too, were uncertain about how to proceed. Having no experience with this "cigar," they did nothing. Finally the German Polizei came screeching around the corner in open trucks. As usual they made a lot of noise, barking and snarling at each other. We looked on from a safe distance, amused that the Germans obviously knew no more about it than we did.

Janie and I picked up the dogs, our chicken and my emergency suitcase to leave the area before it was closed off. That night Paul and I tried to sleep on the floor of a friend's house. The V-1 lay in bone-chilling silence in the meadow overnight and was dismantled the next day.

This was the first of many V-1's that were catapulted from a ski-jump-like ramp in the eastern part of our country. Most of the ones we saw were unable to make it to England. They blew up in the sky, their imperfect technology putting them far short of their

Bekendmaking

Aangezien ondanks de uiterst dringende uitnoodiging van den Wehrmachtsbefehlshaber — General der Flieger Christiansen — de daders van den springstofaanslag in Rotterdam te laf zijn geweest om zich aan te melden, zijn de volgende gijzelaars aangepakt en hedenmorgen doodgeschoten:

1. Ruys, Willem, directeur-generaal, Rotterdam;
2. Graaf E. O. G. van Limburg Stirum, Arnhem.
3. Mr. Baelde, Robert, Rotterdam.
4. Bennekers, Christoffel, vroeger hoofdinspecteur van politie, Rotterdam.

Baron Alexander Schimmelpennink van der Oye, Noordgouwe Zeeland.

Den Haag, 15 Augustus 1942.

De Höhere SS und Polizeiführer Nord-West
get. Rauter
SS-Gruppenführer en Generalleutnant d.P.

ANNOUNCEMENT

"In spite of the recent request of the German Air Force Commander, General Christiansen, the culprits of the bomb attack in Rotterdam were too cowardly to come forward and the following hostages were picked up and executed this morning."

BUREAU: *OV2*

No.: ▬ *14415*

BERICHT / VERVOLG OP SCHRIJVEN VAN:

BETREFFENDE:

BIJLAGE(N):

'S-GRAVENHAGE, 16 November 1944

Bezuidenhout 30
Tel. 720060 - G.

Gelieve bij beantwoording dagteekening,
Bureau en nummer aan te halen.

ERKLÄRUNG

Herr P. van Dillen, Adjunktdirektor des V.B.N.A. (Verein zur Förderung des niederländischen Kartoffelhandels) hat den Auftrag zu prüfen wieviel Kartoffeln in dem Gebiet zwischen den grossen Flüssen, östlich von Dordrecht - Ridderkerk für die Ernährung des Gebietes der Grossstädte verladen werden können und diese Verladung möglichst schnell durchzuführen.

Ich bitte jede deutsche oder niederländische Instanz ihm dabei soviel wie möglich Behilflich zu sein.

DER GENERALDIREKTOR
FÜR DIE ERNÄHRUNG,

VERKLARING

De Heer P. van Dillen, adjunct-directeur van de V.B.N.A. (Vereeniging ter Behartiging van den Nederlandschen Aardappelhandel) heeft opdracht om na te gaan hoeveel aardappelen in het gebied tusschen de groote rivieren, Oostelijk van Dordrecht - Ridderkerk voor de voorziening van het gebied der groote steden kunnen worden verzonden en dezen afvoer zoo snel mogelijk tot stand te brengen.

Iederen Duitschen of Nederlandschen autoriteit wordt verzocht hem daarbij zooveel mogelijk behulpzaam te zijn.

DE DIRECTEUR-GENERAAL
VAN DE VOEDSELVOORZIENING,

Department of Agriculture and Fishery
Bureau of Food Supply in War Time
'sGravenhage, November 16, 1944.

Mr. P. van Dillen, assistant-director of the VBNA has been authorized to inspect the available potatoes in the area between the big rivers, east of Dordrecht-Ridderkerk. If available these then should be used to supply the area of the large cities in the west. This transportation should be organized as soon as possible. We request all German and Dutch authorities to assist him in every way.

The director-general of the Food Supply Service
Signed: Louwes

Bekendmaking

De Dienststelle van den Wehrmachtsbefehlshaber in Nederland maakt bekend:

Een aantal Nederlandsche onderdanen is wegens begunstiging van den vijand en spionnage door een krijgsraad ter dood veroordeeld moeten worden Het vonnis is na onderzoek van de gratiekwestie met den kogel aan de volgende personen voltrokken:

Johan van Hattem, ingenieur, geboren 7-5-1914 te Soerabaja; Johannes Willem van Pienbroek, stud.-ingenieur, geboren 4-8-1917 te Middelburg; Cornelis „Cees" Wegerif, geboren 20-12-1919 te Dordrecht; Willem van Hattem, ingenieur, geboren 6-8-1916 te Soerabaja; Robert Blaauw, student in de rechten, geboren 6-2-1917 te Rotterdam; Kars Lucas Kamp, ingenieur, geboren 15-12-1912 te Valparaiso; Werner Heinrich van Doorninck, ingenieur geboren 27-11-1914 te Kruiningen; Gerard Abraham Tuyl, contrôleur, geboren 27-5-1908 te Alkmaar; Willem Hendrik Emil van den Borch tot Verwolde, geboren 17-5-1910 te Gorssel; Friedrich Alexander van Oven, doctor in de economie, geboren 3-1-1914 te den Haag; Jan Stenger, inspecteur spoorwegverkeer, geboren 10-1-1911 te Amsterdam, Adolf Snijders, geboren 14-1-1920 te Amsterdam; Willem Koimans, volontair, geboren 2-3-1923 te de Steeg; Jacob Strobos, geboren 26-1-1920 te Amsterdam; Franciscus Jacobus Brejart, luitenant beroepsmilitair, geboren 1-2-1917 te Breda; Cornelis Willem Sturm, blikslager, geboren 16-10-1909 te Westkapelle; Jacob Brasser, timmerman, geboren 11-3-1915 te Middelburg; Gerard de Paghter, timmerman geboren 11-3-1915 te Middelburg; Bartholomeus Marinus Christoph Braat luit. ter zee 2e klasse geboren 25-6-1912 te Samarinda; Johan Jacob Diederik ten Bosch, luitenant beroepsmilitair, geboren 8-10-1914 te Den Haag.

Bekendmaking

Het bureau van den Wehrmachtbefehlshaber in Nederland maakt bekend: Een aantal Nederlanders heeft zich — in het bijzonder ook met deelneming van voormalige Nederlandsche officieren — schuldig gemaakt aan begunstiging van den vijand, aan spionnage en sabotage en aan overtreding van het verbod tot het in bezit hebben van wapens. Zij zijn derhalve door een krijgsraad ter dood veroordeeld.

Het vonnis is, nadat de mogelijkheid van gratieverleening was onderzocht, aan de volgende personen door middel van den kogel voltrokken: 1. jhr Joan Schimmelpenninck, directeur, geb. 30 September 1887 te Rhenen; 2. Anton Willem Marie Abbenbroek, voormalig cadet en student, geb. 9 Dec. 1917 te Den Haag; 3. jhr Willem Theodore Cornelis van Doorn, reserve eerste luitenant, geb. 31 Mei 1911 te Den Haag; 4. Fritjof Dudok van Heel, student, geb. 19 April 1918 te Semarang N.-I.; 5. Christiaan van den Bergh, voormalig kapitein, geb. 27 Juli 1901 te Arnhem; 6. Willem Hendrik Hertly, gemeente-ambtenaar, geb. 2 Jan. 1891 te Engwierum; 7. Salomon Vaz Dias, journalist, geb. 1 Juni 1904 te Amsterdam; Rudolf Hartogs, textieltechnicus, geb. 3 Oct. 1918 te Berlijn; 9. Johannes van Straelen, vertegenwoordiger, geb. 26 Aug. 1915 te Bussum; 10. Abraham Wijnberg, lasscher, geb. 17 Oct. 1913 te Groningen; 11. Johan Frederik Henri de Jonge Melly, eerste luitenant, geb. 16 Oct. 1905 te Amsterdam; 12. Gerardus J. F. Vinkesteyn, binnenhuisarchitect, geb. 22 Maart 1907 te Schiedam; 13. Eduard Alexander Latuperisa, kapitein der infanterie, geb. 9 April 1902 te Coetoes; 14. Adrianus Aloysius Felix Althoff, journalist, geb. 12 Sept. 1904 te Haarlem; 15. Antonius C. van Rijen, groentehandelaar, geb. 2 April 1913 te Utrecht; 16. Willem Mulder, onderwijzer, geb. 20 Dec. 1888 te Amsterdam.

A somber page in my diary
August, 1943

The "Bekendmaking" (announcement) of the execution of a group of Dutchmen, students, members of the previous Dutch army, a journalist, a teacher, who were arrested because of alleged sabotage, espionage and carrying weapons.
(The ones underlined were my friends)

DER REICHSKOMMISSAR
FÜR DIE BESETZTEN NIEDERLANDISCHEN GEBIETE

DER REICHSKOMMISSAR
für die besetzten Niederländischen Gebiete

DER BEAUFTRAGTE
für die Provinz Südholland

Den Haag, den 12. Oktober 1944

Bescheinigung

Herr P. van Dillen ist in seiner Eigenschaft als Hauptabteilungs-
leiter der Vereeniging tot Behartiging van den Niederländschen
Aardappelhandel (V.B.N.A.) als der zuständigen niederländischen
Bewirtschaftungsstelle für Kartoffeln mit der Sicherstellung des
Existenzminimums an Kartoffeln für die niederländischen Zivilbe-
völkerung beauftragt. Er hat die notwendigen Regelungen auch
ausserhalb seines Wohnsitzes Den Haag zu treffen. Es wird gebeten,
ihn ungehindert passieren zu lassen und ihm erforderlichenfalls
Hilfe und Unterstützung zu gewähren.

Wehrmachtkommandantur
Den Haag

The State Commissioner for
the occupied Netherlands Territory
The Hague, October 12, 1944

Certificate

Mr. P. van Dillen, as department head of the VBNA (which is the
organisation for the administration, promotion and care of potatoes
in the Netherlands) is responsible for assuring that the civilian population of the Netherlands receive the minimum amount of potatoes
for their substance. Necessarily he has to travel outside his domi-
cile, The Hague. I hereby request to allow him to pass unhindered
and to give him assistance and support if needed. Signed, for the
Commander of the German Army in The Hague,

Signed: Rohde

The V-1, German robot-bomb, also called "The Buzzbomb" by the British.

V-1 diving over the rooftops, 1944.
IMPERIAL WAR MUSEUM, LONDON

German V-2 rocket ready for launching behind our house in Wasse-naar, 1944. IMPERIAL WAR MUSEUM, LONDON

Launching of the V-2.
IMPERIAL WAR MUSEUM, LONDON

A hungry little girl licking the lid from the empty soup-kitchen can.

Hungry children picking leftovers from the empty soup-kitchen can.

Terry with his bone, painted by BvDC, 1943.

Paul with Terry, left. The other dog is from my parents.

Tired and hungry, this picture of me was taken when we arrived in "Free Holland."

destination.

As we heard them coming from afar, we would anxiously listen to the distinctive putt-putt sound. We hoped and prayed the motor wouldn't stop over our heads, as it would then glide into a noiseless dive and explode on impact of buildings or ground. Unfortunately many of them fell in Holland, causing considerable loss of life and property.

Of course, we followed the progress of the Allies as closely as possible. Now short of batteries for the radio, we heard little information. Thus, when Paris was liberated we listened to a replay, two days later. An emotional Frenchman cried over radio Paris, that on August 19, 50,000 men of the Free French Army, armed with rifles, and thousands of others with pitchforks, sticks and hatchets, liberated Paris, taking the government buildings in the same way they had stormed the Bastille in 1789! Hurrah for the French! We became just as emotional; somehow Paris was important for us. We were grateful that the city had been spared. We celebrated with one of our last bottles of wine and lit a fire for this special occasion. Paul and Ysbrand started to boast about their escapades in the City of Light, happy in their memories. Hanneke and I heard hilarious stories of their youth, which they obviously had never told before. We all laughed until tears rolled down our faces.

In the meantime, General Patton's armies were sweeping across northern France, tearing into Belgium. The Germans were on the run. We heard exciting tales about Patton which caught the imagination of the Dutch. Many an impatient young man tried to escape Holland to join his forces. A short time later Brussels was liberated, and again we heard the exhilaration over the radio with the whirring and clanking of tanks in the background. This time Ysbrand brought out a crock of gin.

It was freezing during those few days and I came down with a nasty cold. Barely able to breathe, I stayed up anyway enjoying the evening to its fullest. When I finally went to bed I was unable to sleep after so much excitement. I kept looking out of the window, hoping to see an Allied tank come by and smiling soldiers waving at me. But nothing happened. Disappointed, I looked at the desolate avenue and finally fell into a restless sleep.

The next day, September 5th, will go down in history as *Mad Tuesday*. No Dutchman who was there will ever forget it. As I opened the curtains, there were still no Allied tanks. Instead I saw our two N.S.B. neighbors nervously conferring and then leaving town, lugging heavy suitcases. They were taking advantage of the N.S.B. arrangement to leave the West in case of invasion and go to Westerbork, once a Jewish concentration camp in eastern Holland. They could escape to Germany from there.

Paul came home for lunch with the latest news. Maastricht, our most southern city, had been liberated and now the Allies were already in Breda! I jumped out of bed, forgetting my cold and fever, feeling only euphoria. I was not going to miss the arrival of the Allies, this historic moment of our own liberation!

As soon as Paul left, I got dressed and caught the tram to The Hague. Strangely I was the only passenger. Everything seemed so quiet. But when I arrived at the inner city, I saw total chaos. People ran across the tracks without looking, and the tram had to stop several times to avoid hitting them. I saw both Nazi and N.S.B. families rushing to the station, trying to escape the jeering crowds of Dutchmen pressing them toward the waiting trains. With pushcarts, baby carriages and anything else they could commandeer, our tormentors fled in panic, pushing and clawing, even climbing through the windows of the slow-moving trains.

The mob was rambunctious finally being allowed their revenge. They loudly insulted the Huns, kicking and shoving them, delighted to get even with the "Master Race." The once high and mighty goose-steppers changed in an instant to frightened and fleeing cowards. Carefully the tram crawled toward the Plein, a large square in the center of town. There, masses of people ran and danced, bobbing up and down with the Dutch flag in hand, orange sashes flying from their waists. They gathered on the marble steps of our stately courthouse and squatted between the pillars of the Witte Societeit, the exclusive men's club, beaming at forbidden news played over forbidden radios. A men's clothing store quickly sold about two hundred Dutch flags, which had been hidden many years awaiting such an occasion. Two large department stores raised their long-absent flags of many nations, as we whooped and hollered and applauded loudly from the street. Our happiness knew no bounds.

While buying my own flag, I saw a noisy mob chase a fleeing Nazi four blocks to the train. He was plunged head first into an open compartment aided by a Dutch boot in the rear.

Later that afternoon, on the way home, I met other exhausted celebrators. They had spent the day waiting on the road to Rotterdam for the Allies to arrive, and were still clutching bunches of flowers, now wilted. Why weren't they here yet? Radio Orange said they were in Breda, only two hours away. Our concern grew. We feared silently but remained outwardly optimistic.

Street parties were in progress everywhere. Small children with tired little faces still waved their orange flags. As time passed, what had been unthinkable became reality: Radio Orange informed us that it was all a ghastly mistake!! The Allies had indeed briefly stepped over our border but were now marching, not toward us, but toward Antwerp!

We were stunned and disbelieving, staring at each other vacantly. We looked away into the distance, wondering what was out there, what would happen to us now. I tried to remember what I had said and done during the whole day. What would the Nazi reaction be? Would they get even with us?

The Germans recovered quickly. It was now clear that, in case of invasion, the Dutch would assist the Allies. Rauter was sure that the ready and waiting Dutch would revolt as had the Parisians. To stop any rebellion, he decided to simply execute three Dutchmen for each Nazi killed and started by declaring a state of emergency, issuing some frightening new orders.

All travel was verboten and so were gatherings of any kind. Groups of more than five people, or anyone on the streets during curfew, would be shot without warning. All over Holland the Wehrmacht grabbed men from the streets to dig trenches. The energy of their panic became a wind of vengeance. We knew that we had to stay out of their savage claws at all cost, and so we barely dared go outside. The Germans confiscated all cars, trucks, bicycles and even hand carts. Rumors ran wild, and it was impossible to know what was really happening.

16

A few days after Mad Tuesday Paul and I were in the kitchen discussing our food situation with the Galemas. My cold was worse and I felt wretched. It was hard to get over any illness with the bad weather outside and no heat inside. Ysbrand showed us a letter from the utilities company saying we were cut off for three days as we had used too much electricity!

"How do they know we have used too much?" Paul asked after swearing a couple of times.

Ysbrand shrug his shoulders, "How the hell do I know!"

Our life was getting tougher, our rations smaller and our provisions fewer. Gas and electricity were rationed to a few hours each day. There was no coal or wood for cooking or for heating. A hard winter, like a hungry wolf, was standing at our door. Paul and Ysbrand went out to scare up some wood. They secretly dug out a few wooden tram-ties, not needed anymore since only a few tram lines still operated, and triumphantly carried them home. We could cook for a few more nights. Although we bitterly complained, we knew that we were fortunate in comparison with other people who had even less. In desperation some of them trooped north towards Haarlem to find tulip bulbs to eat, one of the few things still available.

Depression set in as the cold surrounded us. One night Paul and I went upstairs to sit by ourselves in the freezing cold, wrapped in blankets. We talked for a while and read by candlelight. I was worried about my eyes. A few days earlier the church steeple at the end of our road had looked blurry, something I had never noticed before. Lack of Vitamin A, the doctor said, and he recommended raw carrots, to be taken with bread and butter. Paul promised me he would get me this diet, somehow. While fretting about it, I idly turned the pages of the book. But I was restless. I sensed an unusual feeling in the air and went to the window to watch the dark sky. It was quiet outside. A lone dog howled in the distance. I turned around and saw Paul reading with the blanket now draped over his head. He looked up at me and winked.

Suddenly, there was a rumbling, cracking, terrifying roar, then an ear-splitting blast. The earth rocked, the windows rattled, the house shook violently and a brilliant flash of light illuminated our room. I froze, holding on to the windowsill.

"For chrissakes, what the hell is that!" Paul cried out. "The whole damn world is blowing up!"

We rushed to the balcony. In front of us a flaming cone thundered straight up into the sky, so close that I feared the orange-red blaze would engulf us and burn us to a crisp. In that deafening moment we couldn't hear each other, though we did hear a hysterical voice outside scream, "Oh, my God, a burning torpedo!"

The missile's overpowering glow narrowed into a tail of smoke and fire. In awe we stared at the alarming sight. I grabbed Paul, holding on to him for dear life. With eyes large from fright we watched the hellish scene in front of us.

"It's a rocket, Babes!" Paul bent over and shouted into my ear. "They're launching the damn things right behind our house!"

Shivering uncontrollably, I just stared at the shimmering flame, weaving its terror in the dark.

"Now I know what those long trucks carried", Paul recalled. "I saw them a few days ago turn the corner of the Schouweg."

I just nodded. The noise diminished and for a few minutes the cone pushed its silver body straight up, higher and higher. One moment it was lost in the clouds, then we spotted its fiery tail again. When it reached the stratosphere, it suddenly seemed to stop. We watched breathlessly.

"Look! It's thinking!" I yelled in panic. Indeed, the missile seemed to stand still for a split second as if it were alive and had a brain. Then it resolutely turned westward. I later discovered its second stage was programmed to go west towards London, aimed at all those innocent people who would never know what hit them.

Ysbrand ran outside while Hanneke came upstairs. She was sobbing and asked if it would ever end. I hugged her. Hanneke had become very dear to me.

"Those goddamn Krauts!" was all Paul could say.

Before the night ended, one more rocket was launched. Needless to say, we couldn't sleep. The next day Hitler triumphantly announced the powerful V-2, his newest secret weapon!

Soon we not only worried about the rocket destroying us, but also that the Allies would look for it and start serious air attacks against it, which could be disastrous for us.

From then on two V-2's blasted off nearly every night. Some did not make it to England and fell short in Holland's cities and meadows. Because they traveled faster than the speed of sound, we didn't hear them coming. There was no time to run or hide before its 2200 pound warhead dropped. There was no defense against it and it killed more people with no more explosives than the V-1, packing a double punch with its combination of contact and tremendous air pressure.

The following afternoon we had a better chance to see how it looked. The rocket roared up into the blue. Its shiny body reflecting in the autumn sun was an awesome sight. Only a few hours later the first Allied reconnaissance plane buzzed overhead, searching for the launch-pad. The Germans, good at camouflaging, had hidden it between private homes in a small wooded area behind our house. The Allies, although they knew it was nearby, could not pinpoint it, a fact that worried us more than anything else at that time.

Paul, in the meantime, became very secretive. I knew he was acquiring details about the V-2. The Allies wanted to know if the V-weapons were guided from the ground or if they had the control unit in the body itself, Paul told me in simplified language. At night, strange men would come to the house for messages, disappearing quickly.

"Who is that little guy who comes to the door once in a while?" My tone of voice reflected my distrust.

"He's all right," Paul said. "He just looks different, that's all."

I shook my head, "I don't know, but somehow I don't trust him."

"Don't say that," he reassured me. "He's all right, I'm telling you. Don't worry about it!"

I still had my doubts, but after the war Paul told me that this man with the squinty eyes and funny hat was the bravest man he knew. What his name was, I would never know.

At the daytime launches we could easily judge if a V-2 was going to make it all the way to London. I discovered that if I could count to sixty-three and not hear it anymore, the rocket had made it to its second stage, putting it on its way. Once, a V-2 fired at noon acted abnormally. I could see something was seriously wrong. It never reached its second stage. Instead, it careened backward faster than it had been going forward and fell on its own firing table, killing the German ground crew. We felt the terrible blast, but the trees around the launch pad partially protected our street. For the next few days we had peace but the Germans repaired the damage in an amazingly short time. Once again the missiles were shot into the heavens. Unfortunately many fell in our country, because whenever the weather was bad they would detour.

"Only pig-headed Nazis would fire off one of those things when it's storming." I remarked.

"They're a strange breed," Paul muttered.

Nearly every morning a squadron of Spitfires would come over, dive down, and try to hit the launching pad. They flew the length of the avenue with tremendous speed and riddled the street with machine-gun fire. It certainly wasn't peaceful having a missile-launcher behind our home. Nevertheless, we were so busy just surviving that we had to ignore the danger. Ysbrand and Hanneke became fatalistic, believing that only bad luck would get us killed. They seldom went into the cellar when the Allied planes came over, but I was chicken and took no chances.

When we finally had some gas distributed to us, Hanneke and I took turns taking our first baths in months. No sooner was I in my lukewarm tub than the familiar humming filled the air. I jumped out dripping wet, threw a towel around myself and dove into the cellar.

The Galemas and Paul laughed when they saw me looking like a drowned cat. Ysbrand told me not to bathe anymore, for this seemed to provoke an Allied attack.

The lack of warm water for washing became a real problem and my complexion was soon as grey as my clothes. The only solace was that everyone was in the same boat and we did not notice it much anymore. We all tried to keep up a semblance of normalcy. I even ironed my dresses with a flat-iron, warmed on the wood stove, if some heat was left after cooking.

One day the beauty parlor, which was still going somehow, sold me a bottle of shampoo. I immediately went home and started washing my hair. Sure enough, while my hair was still full of soap a V-2 blasted off, its thundering sound waves shaking the whole house. I began my old routine of counting. I had only made it to fifty when the roaring stopped, and I knew something had gone haywire. Dropping the kettle of hot water I was just about to pour over my hair, I ran to the window. The sight out there was straight out of a science fiction story. Ever so slowly, the forty-six foot-long missile turned around as it lost its flaming tail, indicating that the fuel which had powered the rocket was spent. It came down nose first, falling like a leaf driven by the wind, heading in my direction.

I panicked. I tripped over the dog. I screamed at Janie to get out of the house. Where would we go, where would we hide? Not in the cellar to be buried alive! Racing around, I opened the windows in the living room before I ran outside into the meadow, Terry close at my heels. Janie and I dropped on our stomachs and according to instructions, put our thumbs in our ears and our little fingers against both nostrils to avoid pressure inside the sinus cavities. I shielded Terry, held my breath, and braced myself for the blow.

There it came! I quickly closed my eyes. With a tremendous blast the rocket slammed into trees half a mile away and exploded, throwing up a mass of debris while digging an enormous crater. A strong wind, like the lashing of a dragon's tail, tore our double garage doors from their hinges. Numb from fright, I watched them sail by, followed by red and grey roof tiles tossing around like confetti scattered in the air. Suddenly all was still, except for the sound of a few more tiles splattering onto the bricks of the avenue.

When it was over I shook for a long time. I rolled onto my back and stared dazedly at the empty sky. Terry's wet nose touched my arm, telling me we were still alive. I held him while I looked at Janie, on her knees, stunned and disbelieving.

"Are you all right, Janie?" I asked.

She nodded, crossed herself quickly and staggered up. Holding on to each other we slowly walked back to the house. The Galemas' two little dogs, cowering under the stairs, came out wagging their tails. It was a grand greeting. Kip, our chicken, had also survived the blast. She sat on her perch in a state of shock, her feathers ruffled, looking dolefully at us.

Rushing through the rooms we found that wherever we had opened the windows, everything had been thrown on the floor, but was still intact. In the other rooms windows had been blown out, frames and all; inside all was in a shamble. The houses in the next block were still standing, but a closer look showed that the entire insides were blown out. Considering the damage inflicted by this wrong-way missile, it was fortunate that most people were at work. We were extremely lucky that our own house survived in pretty good condition. Aside from the flying garage doors and some windows, only the chimney had to be replaced.

I called Paul, who had not yet heard anything. With no radio and the Germans never admitting a mishap, the news had not reached The Hague. He quickly came home and while I told him my horrendous story, yet another V-2 soared up. It fizzled too, but this time it was a real killer; dropping in the densely populated Laak district in the center of The Hague.

That night I woke up screaming as the gleaming torpedo came at me all over again. It was to be the first of many nightmares.

From then on the RAF not only searched for the firing site but also bombed the V-2 storage site where dozens of rockets were hidden. It was about twenty blocks from our home, in the Haagsche Bosch, a beautiful park with dense woods and scrub brush just within the city limits. The missiles were stowed under the spreading beech trees. It had become 'off limits,' but not before its purpose had been relayed to the Allies.

Unfortunately, no RAF mission ever succeeded. Sadly enough, however, on March 3, 1945 they mistakenly bombed the adjacent Bezuidenhout district, flattening the entire area. Hundreds were killed. Nobody knew exactly how many Dutch perished, nor how many underground families huddled together in the large four-story homes that became their coffins. One bomb fell on a filled Catholic church.

It was one of the most dreadful accidents of the war. We were told through the BBC that the plastic overleaf designating the target for the lead-bomber, slipped into the adjacent area on the map and thus misdirected the raid. But, even this terrible mistake failed to turn the Dutch against the Allies. We understood their explanation and accepted their apologies. After all, we were grateful for all they did for us, for the many times the courageous RAF flyers had helped us out.

In one instance the underground requested them to destroy the Kleykamp building in The Hague, which held the vital statistics of every person in Holland. It was situated across the open square from the Peace Palace, which made it easier to target from the air.

The astute Royal Air Force responded immediately. The following day we saw two Mosquito planes dive with tremendous speed through the clouds, and streak low over town. With pin-point precision they dropped delayed-action bombs right into the hundreds of files containing the names of men to be picked up for slave labor. The building blew up, shooting the half-burned papers into the air. This brave attack unfortunately cost a few lives, but it saved hundreds of others, men who would otherwise have died in Nazi labor camps.

With Allied bombings on railroads, stations, docks and factories becoming routine, it slowly dawned on us that in case of an invasion nobody would care about the civilians who had struggled so desperately to stay alive. We were suddenly pawns in a larger scheme and had become expendable. This realization was hard to take, when liberation was so close, but we had to swallow this bitter pill.

When the attacks on the V-2 became more frequent, the Germans ordered our side of Wassenaar to be evacuated within forty-eight hours. Even Jochem's cows had to go. The Nazis were delighted to tell us, "Your friends in London are deliberately shooting at the Dutch population. But we will show our compassion and allow you to move out of the area."

Paul and I decided we'd better leave fast. We were fortunate that so far there were a few bullet holes in the walls of our house, but none in us.

There was a mad scramble for everyone to hunt for another place and to move within the deadline. Since there was no organized transportation available, everyone had to find his or her own resources. No sooner was the announcement made than thugs and thieves, the real scum of our nation, showed up and began to plunder. This made us decide to take our furniture along, no matter what. But where would we go? Nobody had any room.

Ysbrand, for many years a board member of the Library of the Blind, received permission to move into the library building in The Hague. The two men decided to use the big wagons from Ysbrand's brewery to move our belongings. At four o'clock in the morning they hitched up two strong draft horses to a cart. Neither had ever led a horse and wagon before, let alone through narrow city streets, but the skill of the horses was exemplary and they made it to Wassenaar without a problem.

Hanneke and I were waiting. It was exciting to see these heavy-set Belgian steeds, with their flowing manes and white tufts covering their feet, coming down the avenue on this misty morning. I couldn't resist taking a few moments to pet them while they patiently stood there, snorting and vigorously nodding their heads. Paul watched for a moment, then told me to get going and we hurriedly loaded our furniture, some for the warehouse, and some for our destination. All our neighbors were up by then. The lucky ones had carts, but others loaded their clothes in baby carriages or on bicycles. The streets were full of sad people with their even sadder-looking possessions.

When daylight broke, the scavengers roamed in groups. They brazenly sauntered by, stealing things right in front of us. Paul and Ysbrand chased them, and helped by our neighbors, roughed them up when they caught them.

Hearing of our plight, Paul's sister Gerda and many of our friends came to help. They carried our things out and dumped them on the wagon. One stood on top organizing the load as best he could, while others stood guard. In the middle of this pandemonium the Germans launched another V-2, a block away from our house. Jan, who stood on top of one wagon, nearly fell off when he saw this fiery rocket's tail pass by so closely. He was petrified, as he had only seen this missile at a distance. Excusing himself ever so politely, he left in a hurry, cursing the Krauts loudly.

Since we were used to the rockets we paid little attention to them, and kept on loading, working like coolies, running back and forth. The front door was open, and while we rushed around, a looter ran in, grabbed something and dashed out. With our hands full, we could not move fast enough to get him. Paul ferociously yelled, "I'll clobber the next sonsabitch!"

He found a long lead pipe and planned to hit the next thief on the head or, preferably, on the collar bone, figuring that a broken collar bone would disable, but not kill. Unfortunately Paul's best friend was the next person who came to help. I was packing. Looking up in time to see Herman, I shouted, "Watch out!"

Too late! Paul, hearing footsteps on the walk, hid behind the door and swinging the pipe, he hit Herman with utmost precision on the shoulder.

"God almighty!" Paul shrieked to the chorus of Herman's curses, while the poor man clutched his collarbone. He tried to take it heroically knowing Paul would have a good reason for such an incredible welcome. A hockey player, his collarbone had been broken before and although it was painful, he knew it would heal by itself. He laid down on the grass while Hanneke and Ysbrand came rushing up to inquire what had happened.

They looked at the pale Herman while Paul told his story. Hanneke burst into a nervous laugh and pretty soon, we all laughed from pure tension and exhaustion. Even Herman grinned along painfully. Paul started loading again and I found our doctor who put a sling around Herman's shoulder.

Returning home, Herman was treated like a hero. He sat down on the grass again and gave everyone instructions on how to load.

He was soon joined by Picolien, my girlfriend since kindergarten. I had not seen her for a while as we lived too far apart, and I had missed her stories and optimistic outlook on life. Even in the worst of times her pretty face would still glow, and her smile became a charming giggle. A year earlier I had attended her wedding. In a simple ceremony at home she married Eef Duetz, who headed the central kitchens of the Food Distribution. I could still see her mother frantically hammering out the wedding march on the old piano. The newlyweds then moved nearer to us in the Marlot area and I was glad I could see her regularly again.

We talked and giggled for a minute like old times. Her sense of humor was still delightful and I loved to listen to her. But after a short while I got up to help Paul again. Pico followed me into the house. Her face suddenly turned serious and she told me she was pregnant.

I stared at her, shocked. This was something all of us worried about, as there were no contraceptives available. We all wanted a child sometime, but not now! With never having enough to eat, the terror of the Gestapo, bombs, gunfire and invasion possible anytime, this was a dreadful time to have a baby.

Pico watched my reaction and knew what I was thinking. I wanted to make her feel comfortable, so I hugged her and assured her that I would help, and that she would be fine.

"I hope so," she said, trembling a little.

I moved to help Paul, but my mind wasn't on the job anymore. Pico stayed for a while. When she started to leave, I waved, giving her the thumbs-up sign. I kept on thinking of her and envisioned how her life would be with a baby. Deep in my heart I had a mixed feeling of alarm and envy.

Would Paul and I ever live a normal life, have a place of our own, have children and pets, and no worries about being hunted by the Nazis, or killed by a bomb?

Herman was still sitting on the grass. He smiled at me, and seemed to know that I was troubled. Our eyes met in a quick exchange of genuine friendship and I felt a little better. He stayed to supervise for a while, then left for the tram. Paul helped him up the steps supporting his injured shoulder.

When everything was piled on the wagon, it looked like an Egyptian pyramid, held together with ropes. Just before leaving we threw two more carpets from our neighbors on top and started our journey towards The Hague. Paul and Ysbrand sat in the drivers' seats, Ysbrand holding his two dogs and Paul taking Terry and Kip. Hanneke and I followed on our bicycles which the Germans allowed us to use for this occasion.

We could have walked faster than we rode. The street to The Hague was jammed with overloaded carts. Some wagons lay on the side of the road with broken axels, others had just tipped over from their groaning burdens. Exhausted women and children sat next to their belongings, crying. Paul reached down to place one mother and a baby on his lap as they had no transportation at all. He was sad that he had no more space for others.

As we progressed, we heard another V-2 thunder into the air making the entire scene even more frightening. We were all so depressed and so tired that it did not matter anymore. This sad procession of exhausted people moved on for a whole day and night, followed by a pack of thieves, who took advantage of the easy opportunity to steal from these unfortunate people.

The Library of the Blind was located in the middle of the city on one of the canals. It was late afternoon when we arrived and we hurried to unload before dark. First we took the oak armoires. They were set up in the middle of the large library room, which was lined with bookcases filled with books in Braille. The armoires became the dividing wall between the two families. The rest of the furniture and cases were put in the middle of the room. Since the blind came to find their reading material twice a week, nothing could be placed against the walls lined with these books. I smiled as I thought about it. It was too ridiculous to think of us sitting in the middle of the room, or in our beds, while the blind were feeling around the bookcases.

Paul and I stayed in the library only one night for it became clear that the situation was impossible for two families. A cousin offered us his dining room and we moved again. Our faithful armoires again became the dividing line between their living room and our area. The rest of our furniture went into storage at the beer brewery.

Two days later the Germans announced that we could return to Wassenaar at our own risk, and we decided to take that chance. In reverse, we retraced our steps for the third time. The area was deserted during the day. Even the Germans had gone by now. They felt we were insane to return and left us alone.

The Dutch Civil Defense started a volunteer unit to guard the empty houses near by. Paul, Ysbrand, and some neighbors joined up. They received helmets, but had to bring their own defense weapons. Paul embellished his steel pipe with a knob. Ysbrand made a similar one. With the other neighbors they took turns patrolling the streets at night, for the looters were now stripping the houses bare. They took doors, washbasins, wire and pipes from the wall, staircases and anything that would sell in the black market. Paul and Ysbrand would return home late and tell us about the chases and fights that filled their evening. Hanneke and I were quite unhappy to be left alone with all this violence in the street and every strange noise made us cringe.

Other nights Paul would go out alone, while Ysbrand tried to barter for food. I knew Paul was scouting the V-2 behind our house, although he said little about it. Sometimes he hid in the bushes for hours watching the rocket lift off. Later he would make contact with a circling British plane. Often he returned home soaking wet from being out in the rain, groaning from a sore back and coughing horribly as the old bronchitis flared up again.

"I'm so scared," I told him one night as one of his strange visitors left the house after a whispering session in the dark corridor. That day the paper had carried another list of Dutchmen who were executed. "How long can we be lucky?"

"I'm trying to be cautious," he would reassure me.

Once when I insisted that he was taking too many chances in the mud, he said, frustrated, "Jesus, Babes, this is so important. It just has to be done, and I have the perfect setup to do it. Since I'm a patrolman I can legally be out at night."

I leaned my head against his shoulder, "Darling, I really believe in you, and I'm so proud of you, but please don't take unnecessary chances."

Paul put his finger over my lips to silence me, but I brushed it aside and hugged him, holding him as tight as I could. "Paultje, my dear, I love you so much. I don't want to lose you!"

We snuggled for a moment. Then Paul held me at arm's length and looked into my eyes. He frowned, and said, "It's dangerous everywhere, sweetheart. Anything can happen to you or me, at any time, but I worry most about what could happen to you!"

I contemplated his danger and thought about his strange visitors.

"How can you be sure, without knowing names, who belongs to your group?"

Frowning again, he explained, "I know the top man, a friend of mine for many years. He used to be in the Dutch counter intelligence. And now I know the man under me. We each carry half of the same coin." He produced half of a penny with a jagged edge. I recoiled, thinking that whoever carried the other half must never be caught, or talk under torture. Once before a whole unit had been betrayed, and most of the men ended up in front of a Nazi firing squad.

"Paul, why didn't you go to England with the others?"

Paul sighed deeply, his eyes sad. "My God, I was dying to go, but Holland is in a hell of a mess, and some of us have to help here.

The group chose me to stay. You have no idea how much I wanted to join the RAF and fight the bastards again."

"But now, d'you think all you're doing is really accomplishing anything?"

"I don't know, but a man has to take a stand. This one is mine. I believe in Holland. I believe in our democracy. None of us can live under these Nazis. I'll do my damnedest to free our country. We can't just sit and wait for the Allies to free us. We've got to help and let the Allies know we are with them. We've got to prepare for a possible invasion." Then he added solemnly, "And as far as this danger is concerned, if you play this game you have to give it your all. You're either black or white. There's no grey!"

I thought that over for a moment. "I'm glad you stayed here. We wouldn't have met otherwise."

"Oh yes, we would've found each other! Some day, some time. I would've grabbed you no matter who had his arms around you!"

"You're sure?" I teased.

"You're damn right I am."

Wassenaar was a "no man's land." When other homeless families tried to move into the empty houses still standing in this desolate area, our neighbors quickly reappeared to reclaim their own property. We helped them move in, grateful that we all could be back in our area with no V-2, no N.S.B., no German goose-stepping, and no marching songs.

Paul and Ysbrand were relieved to stop guarding their neighbors' houses. But this happiness did not last very long. One evening Ysbrand came home later than usual. Although it was already dark he could still see the familiar grey shadows of long trailers slowly navigating the corner.

"They're back!"

He entered the kitchen looking grave. We were aghast. Could we never have peace and quiet? The V-2's stayed only that night. The next morning they were moved to a new site, and then they were rotated daily.

We had a pretty good idea where they were: the Beukenhof, Raaphorst, Duindigt, Vreugd-en-Rust, all well-known estates around The Hague and Wassenaar. No matter how dark the night, we could still see the moving convoy. The three long trucks which carried the V-2's were unmistakable. They were followed by three tank cars, holding liquid oxygen, alcohol and other fuels; a generator truck, and a couple of staff cars brought up the rear. The crew was either in the tractor cab or walked beside the long procession, as they slowly wound their way through the crooked streets of Wassenaar.

Paul always became excited when he saw them coming, quivering like an animal spotting his prey. He would leave the house soon after their arrival.

OPERATION MARKET-GARDEN

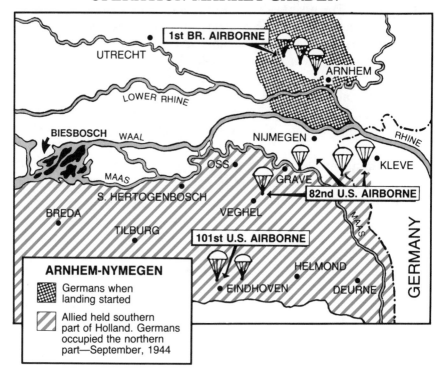

17

Those lucky Belgians! For them the war was over. We were still occupied. Freedom seemed so close, but still so far away!

We were all disappointed and frustrated. This caused the first real fight between Paul and me. I screamed, slammed doors and stomped upstairs. The Galemas and Paul just shrugged their shoulders and paid no attention. They had heard louder screams and louder noises every day in the agony of the war.

Upstairs in the freezing cold I calmed down quickly. We seldom argued for I conceded that Paul knew more about the world than I did; besides, we never had time to quarrel. There were bigger problems to solve every day. Sometimes we were frustrated with the Galemas, too, but we had made up our minds never to have words with these strangers who had given us refuge. There wasn't really much you could do if you were upset. You couldn't call a friend and complain about your husband, the neighbors or anything else. No one had time to listen. So we all made the best of it and became tolerant of each other. Together we complained about the Krauts, or the food shortage, and this was a good outlet. On the whole we got along remarkably well. Janie, the maid, was the most nervous. She would cry for no particular reason which really annoyed us, as our nerves were also on edge. Once in a while our dogs became excited and forgot they were housebroken. Then Hanneke and I glared at each other, depending on whose dog it was.

But our life was certainly not improving. Our Dutch language, always quite explicit and colorful, didn't get any better either. We never used the word "German" or its synonyms alone but unfailingly combined them with a few swear words. Irritability also sprang from our hunger or minor ailments. It was no use going to a doctor because we knew that lack of sleep and improper diet — especially the lack of fats and oils — was what gave our insides the sensation of being lined with sandpaper. The absence of many pharmaceuticals and some medicines was also very uncomfortable, as nothing could replace them. Serious illnesses flared up. Tuberculosis, always a menace in our damp climate, became rampant. For the first time in my memory, diphtheria and typhoid shots were advised for all.

Somehow we struggled along, trying to keep our sense of humor, until suddenly on Sept. 17, our life changed drastically again. After four and a half years of war, this Sunday morning we saw a tremendous flight of planes, towing gliders, between masses of grey surging clouds. Were they coming? Were the Allies really coming?

My friend Oda called and told us that a huge airborne army was now landing around Arnhem, about 75 miles from us. I had no time to ask how she knew. For an hour and a half the sky was filled with a ferocious roar that even the downy clouds could not muffle. The phone rang.

"The British are here!" friends from Arnhem yelled. "It's fantastic! Thousands of colored parachutes coming down all over. Yes, yes, we saw them ourselves. From our balcony! Yes, I'm sure they're our Allies! The Germans are shooting like mad! No, no! Sure, still more are coming down!"

Then we heard a loud crackle and the line went dead. Paul and I looked at each other numbly. Okay. So the Allies were in Arnhem! Good luck to them! We weren't going to believe it until we saw them ourselves. Though feeling exuberant, I wasn't ready for another Mad Tuesday.

But skeptic though I was, I couldn't doubt my eyes. Overhead flew a genuine invading force. We were told later that it was the largest daytime airborne assault ever mounted: two thousand planes and gliders from the south of England, destination Arnhem, a lovely town on the Lower Rhine. Their mission was to capture, undamaged, five major bridges to open a corridor for tanks coming from the south. The tanks would then drive through the city of Arnhem and turn east from the Rhine beyond the Siegfried Line, into the northern plains of Germany. From there they would speed past Hanover and hopefully celebrate the peace of Christmas in Berlin.

Stories about Field Marshal Montgomery, with his sporty beret, started to circulate in Holland. He was the one who proposed this daring attack to Eisenhower. He had reason to be confident. In

North Africa he had outfoxed the German Desert Fox, and at Normandy he had led a successful part of the invasion. Eisenhower's greatest asset was the ability to bring independent and stubborn leaders together. He recognized animosity between generals of different styles, but the plan was strategically sound. Patton was wary, and he objected with his characteristically strong language. Nevertheless, Eisenhower wanted to stop the dreaded V-weapons and bring the war to an early end. Thus the plan continued with the enigmatic name of "Market-Garden."

Overhead, the planes headed east. Ahead of the bombing at strategic points in Arnhem and the surrounding countryside, thousands of leaflets were dropped from the planes with Eisenhower's greeting to the Dutch:

"THE HOUR FOR WHICH YOU HAVE WAITED SO LONG HAS STRUCK."

The following instructions were written: "Stop Germans from ruining factories and plants. Act only according to the accepted war code and document enemy actions which do not adhere to the code. Refrain from unnecessary violence and sabotage. Heed instructions from the BBC and the American radio."

Late in the afternoon we had our first request from the Allies, relayed to us by our Dutch government in London. We were stunned to hear that our 30,000 railroad workers must go on strike so our trains could not transport German troops and V-weapons to the coast. This was the first serious request from our government to defy the Nazis. We knew that this would be the only effective help we could give the Allies, and so, without much ado, the strike was mounted. Actually, many railroad workers were glad to retaliate after being forced to transport prisoners to Germany for so many years.

At first, the toughest part of the strike was how and where to hide the 30,000 brave strikers in our flat country. Meanwhile, the British 1st Airborne Division landed without much trouble at the farthest end of the corridor in the heather and moors west of Arnhem.

Everything seemed to go according to plan, they told us later. The 82nd Airborne dropped between Nymegen and Grave to secure the Maas and Waal bridges. On the way to their landing near Eindhoven, the 101st American Airborne flew over the British 2nd Division ground forces, who waved at them from the top of their tanks. They seemed ready to drive up to reinforce them as scheduled.

An officer of the 101st told me personally that their drop was also unexpectedly smooth. The only German they saw was a soldier in the marshes, his head sticking out from an unbuttoned tank. When captured, this lonely figure turned out to be AWOL, not a fighter but a lover, on his way to visit his girl in den Bosch! The Americans were also surprised to find a well-camouflaged airfield — an innocent-looking farm with haystacks which hid German fighter planes.

The Dutch, not expecting a landing sixty-five miles behind enemy lines, rushed out to greet the red-bereted Tommies with tea, cookies and anything else our pitiful pantries still contained. British Headquarters was established at the Hartenstein Hotel in Oosterbeek. This well-known country manor hotel had been German headquarters and the surprised German Kommandant, General Model, fled just in time to avoid capture by the Allies.

The Dutch were finally able to help. Many eagerly became involved, describing German positions, directing the Allies to the bridges, and assisting them in any way possible.

Meanwhile, General Model rushed to the eastern corner of Holland. From there, he ordered his crack units to attack the British ground forces driving on the narrow country road towards the bridges. Before the Tommies came to the Maas, they were besieged by S.S. Panzers. This unexpected attack unfortunately delayed their advance by two days.

While the Allies desperately fought to hold the Arnhem bridge, the Dutch civilians shivered in their cellars with little food or water, not knowing what dire events raged over their heads. They soothed their own crying children and tended to the Tommies, carrying wounded into their homes. Bombed-out families tried to escape and suffered greatly. The towns around Arnhem were now burning while their residents fled along the road to Apeldoorn.

Women and children walked or crouched in carts, draped with white sheets to show they were refugees. Believing themselves safe, the sad caravan crawled along, accompanied by men on foot or on rickety bikes. Amid the chaos nobody noticed the planes returning. Before the refugees could scatter, a rain of gunfire fell from the sky. In one vicious second, men, women, children and horses were strewn over the road in an unforgettable carnage. In the confusion we were never able to verify that the planes were German.

Some friends of my parents from Nymegen were among those

who fled. With three other families they huddled in their cellar for nearly a week until the Germans ordered them out. They were told that if they refused to leave, they would be considered *franc-tireurs* and shot on the spot. My parents, watching the homeless trek by, happily recognized this family of four. They took them into their little cottage, where they lived together until the end of the war.

During the night of Sept. 25, eight days after the Arnhem drop, Montgomery ordered the troops to withdraw. They had suffered tremendous losses, later estimated to be greater than on D-day. General Urquhart's British 1st Airborne Division was almost completely destroyed. In the pouring rain, less than two thousand of his ten thousand men managed to escape across the rivers to the south of Holland.

Jeopardizing their own lives, the Dutch hid many injured soldiers and nursed them back to health. When they healed, the indomitable Resistance guided them through secret waterways and enemy lines to rejoin their units south of the rivers. We were deeply shaken by the deaths of these young soldiers whom some of our friends had greeted so enthusiastically just a week before. Many showed their compassion by writing to the soldiers' families, and later by tending to the graves as if they belonged to their own sons. Some deep friendships were formed between the Allies and the Dutch at that time.

We, so close to the scene and so hopeful for success, didn't understand why Market-Garden failed. As we sifted through eyewitness accounts of fighters, Resistance men and friends, and read the newspapers, we were even more astonished. The Dutch Resistance felt that Allied Intelligence had not heeded their warnings of German Panzers appearing unexpectedly in the Veluwe area north of Arnhem. Were there other reasons? Was there a betrayal by a double agent? Was it a German soldier's possession of the complete dossier of Market-Garden he found in a downed glider? Or was it something as simple as the weather, which prevented supplies and reinforcements from arriving?

To us, the daring plan seemed sure to succeed with its elements of surprise and synchronization of air and land troops. But the land support did not make it to Arnhem in the scheduled two days. The sky-borne soldiers were forced to defend, that last bridge, that long bridge over the Rhine, without enough artillery or tanks. Why did ground support start so late?

"They probably stopped for tea," the unhappy Yanks said later.

Unfortunately, the unexpectedly strong Panzer attack held up the advance of the British Second. The heroic RAF tried to save the situation. Many soldiers watched while the supply planes flew low to try to help out troops vainly awaiting support from tanks. The pilots did not know that the drop zones were in enemy hands and alive with deadly flak.

Among the heroes was a British pilot who steadied his flaming craft during drop after drop of supplies, without trying to bail out himself. For his heroism RAF Flight Lieutenant David A. Lord was posthumously awarded the Victoria Cross.

For the Dutch, the unsuccessful Market-Garden operation was a far greater disaster than we could have imagined at that moment. We suffered heavy civilian and military losses, and many towns were in ruins. But the biggest tragedy was still to come. Our country was now divided. The vindictive Germans were north of the rivers and the Allies were regrouping south of them. We knew that the Allies would now concentrate on clearing the Antwerp channel. Only by using Antwerp as a northern supply harbor could a final assault on Germany begin.

"Terrible timing for us," Paul said, as we discussed the dwindling supply of food one day. He and Bouman, his boss, had hoped to be able to transport some of the newly harvested potatoes in eastern Holland to the big cities in the west and stockpile them there for the winter. Unfortunately they were too late. With no trains running, our trucks confiscated and our rivers frozen over, we had no way of shipping anything.

When the Netherlands goverment-in-exile conveyed the Allied request for a railroad strike, they must have realized what the consequences would be for us. Within a week, the entire railroad system was at a standstill. It was a severe setback for the Germans. An infuriated Seyss-Inquart ordered the Dutch newspapers to print a warning to end the strike immediately. Otherwise, he said, we would be threatened with starvation. When most of the newspapers ignored him, a Nazi squad marched into "The Haagsche Courant" in The Hague and blew up the presses. This initiated a new round of terror. Not only did the Nazis ride around picking up people, but they destroyed factories, hauled machinery to Germany, and flooded thousands of acres of farmland. They ripped up the quays, cranes and warehouses, and sank ships to block the harbor.

Our situation became rapidly worse. The wolf of hunger, for the last year held just one step away from our door, now moved in. Everything the Germans could use was hauled away. Every striker caught was shot and there was no longer any pretense of justice. During this disastrous period, some of us wondered if the consequences of the strike were worth the sacrifices. In a broadcast from London our respected Prime Minister Pieter S. Gerbrandy vehemently urged us to hold out. It would not help to give up now, he admonished, as the Allies would bomb all moving trains anyway. Dr. Louwes, still chief of the Food Distribution, knew the situation best, and he agreed completely. Although our population in the western provinces was indeed starving, he reasoned that if our trains could carry food to us, the Germans would use them to take anything edible across the border into Germany. Shocked by this caution, we realized that the war would not be over before Christmas. Instead, we faced a merciless cold winter and inevitable starvation.

18

As predicted, our devastating Hunger Winter was now starting. For us and everyone else in western Holland, acquiring food became a daily problem, especially in the cities. We were constantly scrounging around for everything, going from store to store all over town. Paul finally managed to buy two dozen eggs from a friend. We carefully dropped them in a crock filled with *waterglass*, a syrupy liquid which seals the shells and keeps the eggs fresh for many months. Only on rare occasions did we eat one of them, and then it was with great ceremony.

By mid-October, the distribution of gas for home consumption stopped entirely. As most homes had only gas stoves, we could not cook anymore. We were able to buy a little miracle stove. It was built of two steel drums, one inside the other, with a grate above the hole in the side. Some stoves were homemade from garbage cans. They would burn anything. One time when I visited Oda, their stove was burning at full tilt and a strange smell permeated the house. I enviously asked about this glorious flame and she whispered that her father, a retired government official, was burning the old archives to heat their living room.

When the electricity ran out, we bought a carbide lamp. It gave light but also a putrid smell, one we never got used to. It was better to do without light and go to bed. The only handy thing was the Philips "knypkat," a flashlight called a "squeeze-cat." It gave light when the lever was squeezed, activating a dynamo, and made a purring sound.

As soon as it was dark, the streets came alive with shadowy figures sneaking around with their "knypkats." We would hear them purring past our house, as everyone hunted for food, wood, or coal. Respectable citizens now chopped trees or carted away fences from around parks and homes, even digging out the stumps. This desperation only came after the burning of their own doors and stair banisters. Pigs and cows were stolen and slaughtered right on the spot to cook over those fires. Whatever could be hacked off in a hurry was taken. Few people worried whether it was good or bad to steal. When a horse was killed during a bombardment people swarmed into the rubble with knives and saws, more ferocious than a pride of lions attacking a wildebeest. In a short time parts of the poor horse were being carted away on their bikes.

No cat was safe. They appeared on restaurant menus as "rabbit." After that they were called roof-rabbits. Soon there weren't any cats around. Dogs were kept inside to escape a similar fate.

Each day our situation became more precarious, but even so we did not give up hope. Paul and I talked about the possibility of starving to death in a philosophical way, wondering what we could do if it really came to that. Which one of us would last the longest? Thinking about it upset me so much that I didn't want to talk about it anymore. Not talking about the problem didn't make it go away. We saw more and more examples of it in the street. People were often too weak themselves to help a fallen person and just left him on the side of the road.

Paul had many disconcerting experiences. He often did not want to tell me about them. But one morning he saw some young children listlessly playing in the street. They looked pale and thin and obviously did not have much energy. A little boy of about ten years old just stood there and watched. His much too big clothes were hanging from his skinny shoulders. He held a paper bag with a few sticks of wood in it. Suddenly he turned, stumbled to the portico of a house and laid down, curling up on the cold brick. Paul ran over to cover the tiny, shivering body with his coat, while others ran for help. It was a long wait and he hunched down, cradling the frail little boy. He whispered not to be afraid, "I'm right here with you." The boy's tiny lips trembled, and a faint smile appeared. Then he didn't seem to hear anymore, and his body went limp, a forlorn, starved little figure. Paul stayed on his knees for a long time, shaking uncontrollably. Finally a Red Cross truck pulled up. The boy's body was covered with a blanket and carried off. No one even knew his name.

Paul slowly walked home. He went straight to our room and broke down. "Oh God, Babes," he sighed, "I still can see that tiny little bump under the blanket."

I cringed and thought of his sister Gerda's very thin newborn baby, who needed a special milk to survive. Carefully I told Paul about this new problem. He looked at me, half dazed. I didn't know what he was thinking until he suddenly got up and left, carrying a pair of shoes, determined to find the goat's milk for his baby nephew. He did. Hours later he succeeded in exchanging the shoes for a few cans of this life-saving sustenance. It was only enough for a couple of weeks, but Paul promised his sister to find more.

An unmerciful darkness now settled over our country. Strangers would shuffle past our home, selling or swapping anything from food to razor blades. Once a tired-looking man came by to sell tulip bulbs. I traded a woolen skirt for a few bulbs. Although he looked as if he would collapse any moment, he still rode his bike north to where the tulips thrived, in the flat lands behind the dunes.

Defying the Germans, roadblocks and Allied air raids, hordes of city people swarmed across the countryside, begging the farmers for food, or just taking anything edible they could find. The sad procession of "hunger trippers" crawled along the byways, pushing hand carts, baby carriages, or pulling sleds, shivering, their bodies hunched against the biting cold winter wind. Some still had bicycle bags filled with articles to barter with. But many had nothing and just hoped some compassionate farmer would give them something to eat.

Eventually Paul and I began our own hunger trek. As we trudged along we passed many older people, struggling to get on, or sitting in the dirt next to the road, utterly exhausted, a picture of untold misery.

I was tired, cold and hungry myself, but Paul dragged me along, refusing to let me sit down and rest. As I had never been a good walker, he knew that once I sat down, I probably wouldn't get up anymore.

We finally made it to the farmer who knew Paul. Although there were many other people waiting for a hand-out, he invited us in and gave us a glass of milk, which we drank immediately. Unfortunately he had nothing to sell anymore and we left with empty hands. I was near tears and on the verge of collapse. Allied planes flew overhead and dove down trying to hit the German anti-aircraft. Bullets were striking the ground around us. It was pure luck that we were not hit.

Everyone returning to The Hague tried to elude the roadblocks. The Food Distribution control officers and Dutch Nazis who manned them would confiscate everything we had gathered. People crawled through the fields, hiding behind bushes, trying to make it to the city somehow without being detected. Paul and I, having nothing to hide, went through the roadblocks. Surprisingly, we were not even searched, as the guards had their hands full with others who were violently resisting search and seizure.

That evening we decided to try the tulip bulbs I had bought at the door. A government pamphlet told how to fry or boil them, if you were lucky enough to have fuel. If not, you had to eat them raw, after first removing the bitter yellow core. We were also warned against the poisonous hyacinth bulb, which would cause violent stomach cramps.

Kip, our pet chicken had died. We had cooked her a few days earlier. As hungry as I was, I just couldn't swallow a piece of this faithful bird, which had become a friend. Ysbrand dismantled the coop, which gave us some wood to cook the bulbs.

Each of us had our own idea how to prepare this strange food. Not having butter or lard anymore, I melted a piece of white candle, sliced the tulips and fried them in the wax, afterwards sprinkling a little curry on them.

Paul grimaced, "They taste like a slap in the face," he moaned, using an old Dutch expression.

When I used the last part of the candle to grease the pan that night, I remembered a friend who had just told me that he had done a terrible thing.

"You killed a Kraut!" I anticipated, my eyes widening.

"Good Lord, no! Far worse!" he said emphatically. He then described to me how he had crawled out of bed one night to find something to eat. Downstairs there was nothing but a lone candle. He devoured it in the dark, careful not to awaken his wife, since they had promised each other to eat the candle together when the meager food ran out. His wife woke up anyway and called downstairs to ask what he was doing.

"Nothing," he lied.

His wife would never know, she was blind.

Listening to his story, I could see he was distraught with guilt. The next day when Paul was lucky enough to get some potatoes, I gave him two to take home — a king's ransom!

That night, after eating the tulip bulbs, Paul threw up and lost his dinner.

Pretty soon the situation in Holland was changing again. We saw fewer Nazis around. Most of them were sent to the front as Germany was now attacked from three sides. Those who remained seemed to be more lenient. They still had enough food for themselves, and some were embarrassed to see us starving. This was probably lucky for them because by that time nothing would stop the Dutch from fighting back. We were desperate, hunted like animals, constantly moving under the threat of shootings and bombardments. Always hungry, always tired, we were determined to escape the Nazi vengeance, deportation, death.

We became thinner by the day and had a constant gnawing in our stomachs. A Dutch winter means rain, wind, cold and more rain. With no heat the house was cold and damp. Clothes mildewed in the closets and we felt like mushrooms ourselves.

Despite all the miseries of a cold and hungry winter, babies were still being born. Even women who had not been able to conceive were suddenly surprised with pregnancy. Perhaps it was our diminished amount of food or the eight-hour curfew. Paul thought it was the good Lord giving new life for the lives we lost.

Every day the signs were worse. People had swollen faces, wounds that would not heal, and legs hideously bloated from hunger edema. Deaths happened so fast that the bodies had to be laid in churches as well as in mortuaries. Finally there were no gravediggers left, and no wood for coffins. The great Dutch statistic system collapsed because people would not report the death of a family member in order to keep the ration card. The indignities of death were compounded by terror. When a Jewish person who had been hidden for many years died, his body might be carried out by night and simply shoved into a dark, murky canal.

Paul became very calm and philosophical. I was proud of his strength. He always seemed to say the right things at the right time, was never doubtful or afraid, and that gave me confidence and courage. I could trust him and lean on him. He was nearly always able to analyze a difficult situation and decide on the right action.

On my birthday at the end of October, we decided to celebrate with the last of the eggs. Realizing that we both had become ferocious when we saw food on the table, Paul said calmly, "Babes, we can't become worse than animals. The difference between us and animals is that we are supposed to have wisdom and restraint. If we become beasts and attack this food, dirty and grubby as we look now, we degrade ourselves. Let's try to act like ourselves under all circumstances. Let's put on our best clothes, and eat with a table-cloth and candlelight. This'll be your last birthday in this situation. Next year we'll be free or we'll be dead."

Half an hour later we both appeared in the living room, Paul impeccably dressed in a worn blue suit and I in a red evening gown. We set the table with our one and only candle, a slice of bread toasted on the stove, and the one hard-boiled egg nestled in a pretty porcelain egg cup.

For a moment we just stood there, looking at the table and at each other. How handsome he was, I thought, even though terribly thin! His dark, thick hair with the white streak looked matted. His skin was yellowish-grey, but his eyes sparkled and he watched me lovingly. He surveyed the tiny feast and, with intense concentration, began to divide the bread. We chewed slowly to savor every morsel. After we finished, we were still hungry and looked despairingly at the crumbs on the round bread board with the letters carved into the border. "Give Us This Day Our Daily Bread," the board read. I stared at the words pensively. They had never meant more to me.

We sighed. Paul then turned the board over on his plate and counted the crumbs. He put one crumb to one side for me, the next one to the other side for him. The last two, he gave to me. This gesture of pure love made me weep, and our eyes met in a long exchange. We seemed to be thinking the same thing: life had changed so much that dividing these small crumbs made all the difference.

We slowly embraced. Paul blew out the candle and put his arm around my shoulder as we walked slowly to our bedroom. Thank God we had each other. He was my man, and in the bleakest of worlds, his love still made my life worthwhile.

We were not the only ones who were famished. Mice were coming to the second floor looking for food, so Paul set a trap. In the morning we saw that three hungry mice had attacked the bait simultaneously and were caught by the spring. The trap had not been able to close completely and the three were still half alive.

We stared at the poor creatures on the floor. They looked up at us with their beady eyes and started to struggle again.

"Look at these poor devils. They're just like us, rats in a trap, half dead and still struggling to be free," Paul said.

I turned around not willing to look any longer, hoping that

Paul would put a quick end to their suffering.

That night I couldn't sleep.

Just like us, just like rats in a trap!

I saw the mice struggling in my dream, mice with human faces, and I awoke with a scream.

19

In November 1944, Paul faced Louwes in a room haunted by the faces of hunger. The powerful head of the Food Distribution had spent many sleepless nights wrestling with the prospect of certain starvation for the Dutch in the North.

When Paul walked in, Louwes was absorbed in his thoughts and didn't seem to notice Paul at first. After a minute he swung around and fixed his eyes on him.

"Paul," he began with the barest tremor in his deep voice, "I need a man who knows about food distribution and who also has the guts to go through enemy lines."

"I know one," Paul answered, without hesitation. Louwes' serious face relaxed at the implied offer and he seemed almost youthful for a moment. Then he smiled, putting his big hand on Paul's shoulder.

"I hoped you'd say that."

Louwes, worried that the Dutch were now only able to get about 500 calories of food per day, knew that in three months there would be nothing left. He had been hoping for a miracle, but now as he stared out of the window he realized that the bleak fall landscape gave only a hint of the future. Because of the railroad strike, organized looting by the Germans, and deportation of Dutch workers, our food distribution was in chaos. The desolation of the coming winter would be compounded by misery and death from hunger. Louwes' records showed that, after the first week in January, there would be no butter, oil, margarine, or meat, and very little milk, even for babies and expectant mothers. The records listed a limited amount of grain, but there would be neither coal nor gasoline to mill it, nor means to transport it.

He had foreseen these problems and had already sent A. H. Boerma, his colleague, south to Brabant. There Boerma was to organize a relief plan tailored to the special needs of the north's

starving people. That turned out to be a shrewd move when com-
munications to the South ended after the battle at Arnhem.
Boerma was the only one out there who knew how bad the situation
in the North was. Louwes reasoned that even if Boerma knew how
critical their plight had become, he would have to have substantial
documentation to convince the Allies of their impending death by
famine. Someone had to get through enemy lines and Paul van Dillen was that man.

Paul joined Louwes in scanning the fall landscape and shivered, thinking of the cold winter ahead. "Once there, Mr. Louwes,
what do you want me to do?" Paul spoke with a calm certainty and
cool confidence that cheered Louwes.

"We need to fill them in fully about our situation. You and
Boerma must plead with the Allies. Tell them we have hunger
edema at this moment. You must start an organization to get food
to us, not — " he paused, his voice full of emotion, "not in months,
not in days, but in hours!"

The task was exciting but Paul hesitated, considering the best
way to voice his concern. Finally he said bluntly, "What about my
wife?"

"These are details," Louwes said with a wave of his hand. "No
problem. I'll take care of her. Let's start the big plan."

Paul came home and related the details of his meeting. I knew
that this could be the most important thing any of us would ever
do. The fate of so many Dutch depended on it. Paul was determined to do this job, although he didn't want to leave me in danger
in the North. When he disappeared, the Gestapo would become suspicious. They would probably come looking for me, pick me up,
throw me in jail and, if I didn't give satisfying answers, torture me.
This had happened many times to others.

Paul paced the room as he talked, then came over and sat
down.

"Babes," he said, banging his fist on the table, "I really want
to do this, but I have to know that you'll be taken care of. I don't
want those damn Krauts to lay a hand on you!"

I loved him for his concern and I gave him a quick kiss.

"Go ahead," I urged him. "I'll be okay."

He saw me smile and, for a second, weighed my answer. Then
he leaned toward me. "What do you mean, 'okay'? What do you
want to do?"

I looked straight into his eyes and my smile vanished. I was
never more serious.

"I'm going with you."

Paul related our conversation to Louwes the next morning, who approved our plan so speedily that it surprised him. Apparently Louwes had been thinking about his off-hand reassurance of my safety, and realized that he didn't want such a responsibility. Instead he said that, no matter how dangerous the trip, it would be better for me to go along.

Every morning for the next two weeks Paul talked with Louwes about the trip. He memorized all the information, since carrying any kind of papers was too dangerous. He was instructed to approach the Allies, to organize a food distribution system as Louwes foresaw that the Dutch would be far too weak to organize themselves.

Both worked grimly, knowing their failure would wipe out most of the population of northern Holland. The trip assumed even more importance when the Allies became aware of its purpose. They saw a golden opportunity to get fresh intelligence on the rivers and activities of military interest. And so, aside from one identification paper, we took along some military information typed on thin copy paper which we could swallow if we were caught.

As a farewell present Paul's friend in the Resistance gave him two cyanide pills. I shivered as I looked at the innocent-looking capsules in the palm of his hand.

"I'm going to keep both of them for a while," he informed me. "I don't want you to do anything drastic before you have to."

Later in the trip, when he saw that, in the face of the enemy, I became a calm and cool "line-crosser," he gave me my own pill. I took this sign as a compliment as he now respected my judgment.

Two days before we were to leave, the Nazis started another clean sweep of young men in Rotterdam.

"Razzia!"

The word struck terror in our hearts. We knew now that a young man heading toward the rivers on the empty streets of Rotterdam would be as conspicious as a black bear on an ice flow. We had to think of a better way to travel south.

Louwes found a solution. He bribed a German official, who was responsible for feeding the Dutch-based German army, with half of any potatoes purchased by Paul in return for getting us through the German checkpoints. Herr Woltheim had known Paul in the Food Distribution center and had recognized his value in the Dutch food crisis. We suspected that it was Woltheim who had probably helped get Paul out of jail the year before.

The German was interested. In private life, Woltheim was more concerned with hunting on his estate than with politics. Nevertheless, he knew how dangerous it was to get along too well with a Dutchman. He also knew that the Gestapo was watching him, for he was in love with a Dutch girl. But, as a true army man, he wanted those extra potatoes for his soldiers, and this made him agree to escort us. Thus Woltheim gave us what we couldn't do without — his personal protection, and a German soldier as a chauffeur.

"We're going with two Germans," Paul said that night.

I stared in disbelief. "Paul, ben je gek!"

"No, I'm not crazy," he said grinning. "No, not really. Can you think of a better way?"

I shook my head and said, "Perhaps it is a smart move. But you know what I'm thinking? What'll we do with the dog? I know Hanneke won't keep him; she has her own to feed. What shall I do?"

"My dear," Paul sounded relieved to hear that was my biggest concern. "I've thought of that. Louwes promised that whoever cared for the dog until we came home would get some extra potatoes every week.

Armed with this offer, I felt free to ask our army friends, Han and Annie, to take Terry. Han, a true buddy, immediately agreed when he heard the reason for our trip. He thought it would be only for a short time. We didn't know that it would be the longest six months of our lives. Nor did we have any idea that they would have to watch out for hungry people who might try to steal and eat the dog.

After taking care of Terry I got busy with what to take on the trip. I decided on a very small bag packed with underwear, a toothbrush, and an extra sweater. Paul would take his trench coat and I would wear my Persian lamb. Paul did not like the idea of the fur coat, but I wanted it to keep me warm, knowing I also could sell it, if necessary. I tried to think of everything and even went to the doctor asking for something to stop my monthly period. He gave me two pills I had never heard of.

"One to stop and one to start it again, just like a faucet," he said smiling, and wished me good luck.

The day of November 13 started out badly and left me shaken and numb. With my packing behind me, I sat down for a moment and looked about the room. I still had to resolve where to store our furniture without a permit. Sipping my bitter ersatz coffee and idly turning the pages of the newspaper, a name leapt out at me. In a black bordered announcement, in between many others, was his name: Frits Ruys, executed . . .

The blood drained from my face as I stared at the print. Closing my eyes I let the awful truth sink in. I sank into the chair devastated, cradling my face in my hands, sobbing uncontrollably.

Frits, one of my dearest friends, always friendly, always helpful! Frits . . . I saw him standing in front of me, persuading me to type some secret papers. What cruel fate had been dealt to him! I just sat there; my head seemed full of cotton and I could not even think anymore. The grief was overwhelming and I had never felt more helpless. What could I do? What could I say? How could I express my feelings to his family? I wanted to go to see his parents, who were living close to us in Wassenaar.

While I sat there Hanneke came into the kitchen and told me that Terry seemed to be sick. My sobbing had subsided and she didn't notice my tear-streaked face.

Wordlessly I picked up the dog and took him to the vet around the corner. The gentle old doctor was preparing to move because the V-2's were now being launched behind his house. He checked the dog, gave me some pills for him, and wished me well. I could only nod and smile a faint thanks.

After this visit I made up my mind and ran over to Frits' parents home. They both saw me coming and opened the door before I rang the bell. Silently we embraced. Together the three of us stood in the hall with our arms around each other, Frits' mother's head on my shoulder, a torrent of tears rolling down our faces. There was nothing to say. We all three felt the same deep searing pain in our hearts. The 13th was a dreadful day!

On the way home I felt lost and longed for Paul. From our balcony I finally saw him coming, his old trenchcoat flapping in the wind. Because of the job, his bike permit had been renewed. He spotted me and waved with both arms held high, pedaling with no hands, like a kid showing off. Paul was always full of enthusiasm for everything he did.

Seeing him cheered me no end. The dog ran down to greet him and I followed. Every day we were grateful to be together. Every day we were fortunate that we had not been killed one way or another. Paul took one look at me and immediately sensed something was wrong. I snuggled up to him, and we embraced as if we would never see each other again. When I could, I told him about Frits. He just stared at me for a second and winced, his lips pressed together. He then shivered as if to shake off the bad news. When he recovered, he said in a voice more determined than ever, "We're leaving Thursday, three days from now."

I was full of questions, but Paul would say nothing about it just then. The trip was dangerous and the more people who knew about it, the more chance there was for the Nazis to find out. Ever since he had been released from jail, he was sure that they had been keeping an eye on him. If they saw anything unusual, they would be sure to investigate. Either they would tail him or they would come in the middle of the night and snatch him away.

"You'll find out soon enough about our plan, dear," he said gently, after refusing to give more information. "We'll have to tell the Galemas something, though. We can't just disappear. They would contact our families to find us."

Before dinner we told our friends about our plans. They were silent and I could see disbelief in their eyes. They could not imagine us as "line-crossers," young adventurers who sneaked across the rivers to join the Allied armies. Paul did not try to satisfy their curiosity. He only said "we were asked to go." Ysbrand listened, and in the end his only question was whether they could go along. We hated having to tell them this was impossible.

That night in bed, snuggled under the warm blankets, Paul told me a little more. The Nazis planned a razzia in The Hague for the coming Saturday. Because Paul's assistant was a prime target for these sweeps, he wanted to go along on our trip. Bob would be a help in our project, but it meant we had to leave before Saturday. We talked most of the night, unable to sleep. There was so much to think about, and Thursday was only a few short days away.

I started worrying about everything and everybody. I felt like I was suffocating, and finally I started to cry very softly. Paul became irritated. He had his own problems and felt badly at having to put his wife through this new hazard. But after I had expressed my worry, we both felt relieved and finally fell asleep in each other's arms. That was the last time I cried about the trip. I made up my mind that I would not be a burden after that.

I spent the next day sorting out our belongings, deciding to put them in storage with a company owned by the same family which was taking the dog. Their personnel was reliable and they would not breathe a word about getting an unexpected batch of furniture. Such irregularities were supposed to be reported to the Germans. Paul, watching me prepare the list for the movers, suddenly looked glum.

"We certainly can't come back, can we?"

I just shook my head, not trusting my voice.

While I was busy, Annie came to pick up the dog. The minute Terry saw her, he knew. His tail went down and he wagged it feebly. I hugged him, ruffling his fur. "Be a good dog," I whispered close to his ear.

The dog looked at me, and I felt miserable at leaving him behind. Annie quickly snapped Terry on the leash and left, waving at me while closing the door behind her.

"Bye, Terry," I mumbled to myself, feeling more and more depressed.

At noon, like a lightning bolt from out of the blue, Paul's mother arrived by bicycle from Leyden. It was a long trip for an older person, especially one weakened by lack of food. She always had had an incredible intuition about what was going on. Sensing that we were up to something, she came to find out.

"Just what I suspected," she said softly when she saw me packing. When I admitted our plans to her, she embraced me, fighting back her tears. As always we felt very close. When she promised not to tell anyone, I invited her to come and see us off the next day.

Paul came home, sorry to have missed his mother. He then asked if I was ready. After he inspected my bag, he added some medicine, and wrinkled his nose at the fur coat again.

As we sat in the front room that evening, the Galemas put their last logs on the fire, and we opened our last bottle of wine. Although we wanted to be together, we weren't in the mood for a party, as we were seriously worried whether we would make it alive. We gave them the rest of our meager food supplies, then sat quietly, just thinking. We couldn't even bring ourselves to discuss our favorite subjects, food and religion. Soon we said good night and went upstairs.

Before going to bed I knelt, closed my eyes, and said a simple prayer. Then I quickly crawled into bed next to Paul. We would need a good night's sleep to be ready for our dangerous journey.

Morning came quickly, and we tried to suppress our nervousness while we dressed. Luckily we had some dry toast to eat as suddenly an extra bread coupon had been rationed to us. Although it was only made from flour and sawdust, it filled our stomachs a little. Over an awful-tasting surrogate cup of tea, Paul told the Galemas that we had decided on a code to indicate that we had reached Allied lines. Only Dr. Louwes knew the code, and when he heard it over the BBC he would tell them of our safety and send a note to our parents.

It wasn't easy to create a code. We had discarded many a catchy sentence before deciding on a simple phrase. It was the BBC's custom to repeat the codes three times right after the news. We were always thrilled to hear the deep voice of the announcer say in his measured way, "This — is — London — the — BBC." After the news he would add, "And now some special messages."

The Galemas listened attentively to our explanation. I saw a wistful look come into their eyes when I told them our code was, "Give Terry A Bone."

Paul's mother came again at noon just as we finished cleaning the rooms. She was happy to have this one last moment with her son. They chatted until Bob came. A young bachelor, Bob regarded the whole thing as an exciting adventure. Paul, on the other hand, viewed it as the serious business it was. Mother started to sniffle when Paul said good-bye.

The German came exactly on time in a Dutch car with a German soldier as chauffeur. When he was introduced to Bob, he objected, pointing out that such a young person would cause problems. Paul, knowing that Bob's life would be in jeopardy if he stayed in The Hague, refused to back down. Woltheim finally consented, and we were off.

Mamma, as we endearingly called her, and Hanneke hid behind the curtains at the window. Would we ever see each other again?

20

We drove through the lowlands south towards the rivers. The chauffeur and Woltheim sat in front; Bob, Paul and I in the back. Now and then we were stopped by guards behind wooden barricades. Woltheim would show his Reichskommissariat identification card through the side window. His card was impressive enough to let us through immediately. All went well until we hit Rotterdam, where a Nazi razzia had raged a few days earlier. The streets were deserted. We drove along in silence, haunted by memories of razzias we had seen.

Germans stood clutching their guns at all major crossings. The closer we came to the rivers, the more roadblocks there were.

At all these checkpoints Woltheim held up his card, and most guards waved us through without any question. At the entrance of the Maas tunnel, we were stopped by a young soldier who looked like a country boy from the fields of middle Germany. He glanced at Woltheim's identification and became very officious.

"Halt!" He saluted, then held out his hand for the card and examined it carefully. Pursing his lips over the stamps and swastikas, he appeared satisfied, when suddenly he turned and demanded, "Who are these people?"

We shuddered in the back seat. We did not have a permit to be in this area. Woltheim took over. He straightened up and hesitated only briefly.

"These are my guests."

The guard became suspicious. Even though Woltheim indicated that he was an important man, he wasn't impressed at all. Like a terrier, he held on.

"What are these people doing in your car?"

Woltheim crawled out of the car. His six-foot-three frame made the guard look smaller.

"Soldier," he said threateningly, "what's your name? You

seem too stupid to understand who I am. I'll report you to your commanding officer."

The guard got red in the face, stammered something we could not make out, and stepped back. Woltheim told the driver to proceed and we quickly drove through the tunnel. I breathed a sigh of relief and looked at Paul, still shaking.

Bob leaned toward us. "That dumb little shit nearly did us in," he whispered. "Can you believe it?"

Paul sighed and nervously stroked his fingers through his hair, saying, "Heck, that little nitwit wasn't so dumb after all."

I gazed over the open country of Dutch polders, meadows surrounded by dikes and interspersed with canals. I knew Allied airplanes would be our next problem. We were open targets. They knew that all Dutch transportation had stopped. If they spotted a train, truck, or car on the highway, it had to be German.

I imagined it was a delightful moment for a pilot when he saw a car on an empty road. I could hear them in the cockpit, saying, "There's a Kraut flirting with death! Where does he think he's going? Let's give him a goose!"

They would then dive over the car, spray it with bullets and soar upward, leaving behind a smoking wreck and a dead passenger.

It was dreadful to be stalked by the Allies as if we were Nazis, but we had no choice. Woltheim had also thought about the problem and found the solution in a hitchhiking German soldier. We took him along and stationed him on the bumper. Every so often our sentry would point to the sky. We'd jerk to a halt and hit the ditch flat on our stomachs, waiting. The plane would swoop over us, but aside from a few stray bullets, we escaped harm. Luck was with us!

After Rotterdam we went east towards Gorinchem. Fear kept me from talking. With the German soldier on the bumper, I realized we were even more of a target than before. Paul's face was ashen-grey and his mouth twisted nervously. Bob looked no better. Woltheim was silent, too. At the beginning of the trip, he had discussed Paul's job and the buying of potatoes, but it was apparent his heart was not in it. I looked at his broad back and wondered what he was thinking. Did he suspect that Paul and I were trying to escape?

As we neared the city of Gorinchem he asked, "Where do you want to be let off?"

"I'd like to see Terwilligen, our agent of this area," Paul said.

"He knows all the farmers in the neighborhood and we can probably stay at his place. If you want to drop us there, we'll see you tomorrow."

"That's fine," Woltheim replied, without asking us what time the next day.

As we were parting, Paul emphasized, "Tomorrow, late in the afternoon."

Woltheim just nodded.

"Good trip!" he said.

Paul and I walked toward the house, arm in arm. Bob followed.

"About Woltheim —" I began. Paul put his hand over my mouth and mumbled, "I wonder if he really knows."

Klaas Terwilligen received us warmly, although he hadn't known we were coming. Nobody was surprised when people appeared unexpectedly, especially in the country, where city people went for food. Terwilligen knew Paul from the Food Distribution and he welcomed us without question. We had a wonderful dinner with his wife and four young kids. The children were excited to see us and we all had to write a short poem in their albums.

After dinner Paul told Klaas the real reason for our trip. While he listened he said little but looked concerned. After our story he left the house for a few hours.

"I don't think you can leave here sooner than tomorrow night," he said when he returned. "The river is too high today!"

We stayed overnight. Paul and I went to bed early, worn out.

The morning dawned grey, but we were treated to breakfast with the family. It was a Dutch breakfast of white bread with butter, cold meats, cheese and an egg. We had not eaten like this for years. We had not known that people in the country were so fortunate.

Terwilligen left after breakfast to arrange to get the underground's help in getting us across the river. He wanted to help us, but he also wanted to get rid of us as soon as possible.

It was a long, dark day for us. The weather was dreary, and so were we. The little girls tried to entertain us, which only made it worse. I had little interest in their school stories. Paul made the best of it, letting the girls explain how to play the small organ in the living room. Soon he hammered a tune on it, proudly adding this instrument to his talent on the guitar. This diversion made the day go faster and calmed his nerves, but it drove me crazy. We waited and waited, not knowing what was being planned. I tried to visualize the rest of the trip. How would we get over the rivers?

Could we trust these people? Klaas finally returned at dinner time, and announced, "You're leaving at eight-thirty tonight." He paused and added, "By car over the dike to Hardinxveld, then by boat across the river."

Which part of the river? I thought. But I didn't ask, thinking, the less talk, the better. I only knew that the Allies were on the other side of the Maas and that the Germans were heavily defending the banks of the Lower Rhine and the tributaries in between. Actually we weren't even sure *where* they were.

Terwilligen was a man of few words, a good habit to have in the underground. I felt uneasy, not knowing exactly what was going to happen, but years earlier I had learned to make my mind a blank when I was scared. There was no turning back now. We had to go fast, and we had to trust those who would lead us. This was the most difficult part of all, especially for Paul. He was a leader himself and felt uncomfortable depending on others. Paul was the kind of planner who did not take unnecessary chances. Now he was taking the biggest chance of all, depending on people he had not met. Would these guides have the knowledge to get us through?

We knew that the Merwede river was much wider at this point than where it became the Waal. The danger was doubled here, because the westward current swept along, merging with many tributaries. At high tide, the meeting of the incoming North Sea waters and the outgoing river created whirlpools, troublesome for a big boat, and disastrous for a small one.

We could only hope that the river men knew what they were doing.

It was pitch black and stormy outside. At the stroke of 8:30 a small car appeared in front of the house with Klaas at the wheel. We said good-bye to the family and ran through the pelting rain to the waiting car. Although the weather was unpleasant, it was a good cover for our escape. Slowly we drove over the basalt-bouldered dike, built strong enough to keep the river from inundating the lowlands. Terwilligen had a permit to drive a car, but we were still scared of Allied planes. Our headlights were blacked out, except for a little slit where a small beam shone through. It was hard to see the road, and Klaas drove slowly, steering carefully, to stay on top of the dike. This gave Paul a chance to spot anti-aircraft batteries and other military installations. He was also looking for the fake factory with a noticeable tall chimney the Germans had built somewhere along the river.

Suddenly Klaas stopped the car.

"We have to pick up three K.P. men," he said. We were surprised. He had not mentioned anything about the tough K.P., the "Knokploeg," meaning "fist-fighters." In this area it was secretly known that this underground group had ambushed many an unwary German patrol and kept them prisoner on a dilapidated houseboat hidden in the marshes. Knowing they would come along with us made me uneasy.

We waited a minute close to the silhouette of a wooden barn. Hearing the warble of a water bird, Klaas answered with the same soft call. At once, a dark figure in a black trenchcoat loomed beside us, a floppy hat hiding his face. He jumped to the car, quickly swung open the door and a long cold thing landed on our laps — a Sten gun!

"Good evening," the voice under the hat said cheerfully. "Hold this gun for a minute, will you?"

More dark figures appeared, tossing a couple of handguns inside. Two of the men flung themselves on top of us in the back, another in front. Off we went! I was dumbfounded.

"Did you bring any guns along?"

"No," said Paul.

"Well, that's too bad," one commented mournfully. "Then we won't start shooting right away."

For God's sake, what have they planned? I wondered, hoping they weren't going to fight the Krauts! This seemed exactly what they were anticipating!

It certainly was not Paul's plan. He purposely had not taken a gun along. He knew that we would be shot if we were caught with weapons and it would be useless to claim to be innocent potato buyers.

Silently we drove along. Ten minutes later we stopped again, this time at a small house built below the road. There was often a narrow strip of land in between dike and river, where shipyards and repair shops served the river boats. In this case it was hard to see the big wharf behind the house where barges were moored to the piers.

Here many underground people had found a haven. The men who were living on the barges were a rough bunch of young workers. Unlike the elite Nazi troops of The Hague, the German river patrol were farmers themselves, drafted into the army. Afraid of being beaten up and thrown into the river, they didn't dare come too close to the barges. Aside from a few cursory inspections now and then, they left the river people alone, and the barges became a great hiding place.

We stumbled down small wooden steps leading to the lower level of the house, which was a barn lit only by candles. After getting used to the darkness, we saw a group of men sprawled on the floor, cleaning and assembling machine guns and loading their revolvers. I gripped Paul's hand a little tighter. At first the men just glanced up at us. Then they noticed a woman in the group, and they stared at me. A few made a vague move to get up and introduce themselves. I tried to remember them, but it was hard to identify the faces in the dimly lit barn. The K.P. men seemed to know them, shaking hands and laughing heartily.

"Hey, you sonsabitches, are you still around?"

The meeting was joyous, with many ribald remarks.

From the barn we walked a few steps past the outhouse to the well-lighted home. Like all the other houses in Holland, it had blackout curtains across the windows. Inside we met the owner, Bas van Mill, a good-looking man with dark brown hair and a strong but friendly face. We liked him immediately. But he was not to be our guide; we were waiting for another person, skipper Jan.

In the corner of the room we noticed the wife of the owner. She didn't say a word and silently kept on spinning on an old-fashioned spinning wheel with wool from a few self-raised angora rabbits. She totally ignored what Bas and his friends were doing. That was a man's world; her world was feeding and clothing the family and helping anyone who needed it. Her two small children and a baby were tucked in their beds in a back room somewhere. More people seemed to be hiding on the premises, but I never found out much about them.

I, too, sat quietly while the others talked noisily about daring trips to return downed Allied pilots to England. I felt they had done this many times and probably could be trusted; nevertheless, I still hoped they knew what they were doing.

After an hour or so, skipper Jan arrived, followed by two men. Although they tried to look like Dutch burghers, they looked very British. No one asked any questions. Jan began to outline our escape route on a dirty, crinkled map.

"The river is damned dangerous," he started. "First we have to row about 400 meters upstream. That seems like a short distance, but you have to row goddamn hard to make it. Jesus Christ, Pieter, will you listen!" This outburst was directed at Piet, who was talking, having heard it all so many times before.

"Rowing up stream," Jan went on, "we'll have to get across, around these blasted islands, into here. Those damn Krauts are holed up there. You can see them patrolling on the dike. I don't know how many of the bastards are there. It changes every time. But they're sure looking for us, firing at the first sound they hear. Their searchlights scan the waterline, and if they see the boat, rat-tatatatat! It's curtains for us. They'll just blast us, no questions asked. For Chrissakes, guys, will you shut up!"

He glared at Piet, who grinned back, unconcerned.

"When we get here in the Merwede, we'll be okay. It's duck soup, from there. We don't have to row at all, the river will do the rest. But the current is strong there, and we have to be careful that it doesn't float us out to sea."

Jan cleared his throat, spat into the fireplace, and went on explaining the rest of the trip.

"Across there is Brabant. There's where the Canadians and the Poles are. If we make it, we're goddamn lucky. That's free country, and they have some damn good cigarettes."

This information was given to us with many grunts, groans and swearwords. Paul and I just listened, not saying a word. After a few moments of silence, van Mill said quietly, "Hey, Jan, if I were you, I wouldn't curse the Almighty God so much. You'll sure need him on this trip!"

As Jan talked, Paul made notes on his official papers. He had noticed German anti-aircraft on the dike and had made a mental note. Now he wrote it down, asking the wharf owner how many men he thought the Germans had in their area. When everything was written down, he asked for a piece of rope and tied the papers to a brick, to be thrown overboard in case of capture.

We were going with only two boats, and I realized that there would be no room for our bag. I left it after I put on two sets of wool underwear, which made me look like a barrel. Our pockets held a few pills, a toothbrush and some cosmetics. That was all we could carry.

Around midnight we said good-bye to the wharf owners. I embraced van Mill's wife, who still had not said one word. Silently we looked at each other, a warm, understanding look from one woman to another, and I saw tears glistening in her eyes. It was a good thing that I didn't realize she felt our trip was far too hazardous, and she worried that we wouldn't make it alive.

It was pitch dark and raining outside. Two by two we walked over the gangplank to one of the barges. Paul and I held hands as we followed the skipper, who held a small flashlight to lead the way. Water sloshed under us; the rain and wind hit us in the face. I thought I would never make it. We went over another long plank to another barge, moored alongside the first one. This time I walked by myself as the plank was only wide enough for one person. Paul pushed me ahead of the others, thinking he could save me if I fell in the water. The others couldn't have cared less. It was each man for himself and nobody would look back. You either made it and stayed with the group, or you didn't.

I carefully inched over the plank thinking it was all over, when I found myself being led to the third plank. Each plank seemed to get longer, the water under me rougher, and the wind stronger. A gust of wind nearly blew me off into the river on that third crossing, but I balanced myself against its force at the last moment. Jan waited a minute for me. With his tiny flashlight he pointed to a rowboat next to the barge, many feet lower. I didn't believe in what I could only dimly see. I heard the slapping of the waves against the boat and saw a dark outline of where I was supposed to jump. I was paralyzed when I heard Jan whisper, "Just jump, right now! Hurry up!"

He pointed his flashlight into the boat for a second, then everything went dark again. He never turned the light on again. German flares were being shot off in the distance and caution was imperative.

In the darkness I groped over the side, hanging onto the barge for as long as I could. Then I jumped, tumbling into the rocking dinghy. I made it. Paul landed almost on top of me. The three others followed in quick succession and we pushed off, neither hearing nor seeing how the other five men and Bob fared in their boat. We did not look back.

"Who is going to row?" Jan asked.

Paul, who thought the others had this all planned, didn't answer. The other three set themselves noisily to the oars.

"Okay! One-two, one-two, pull," they whispered. The boat creaked, and we moved ahead slowly. Everything seemed to make a great deal of noise. It was fortunate that the wind blew from the direction of the Germans, so they could not hear us from the dike. Jan placed the Sten gun on the bow. The handguns were on our seats, to be thrown overboard in case of imminent capture. That was my job. I also guarded the brick with the secret papers and

The hand-drawn map the Underground gave us. November 1944

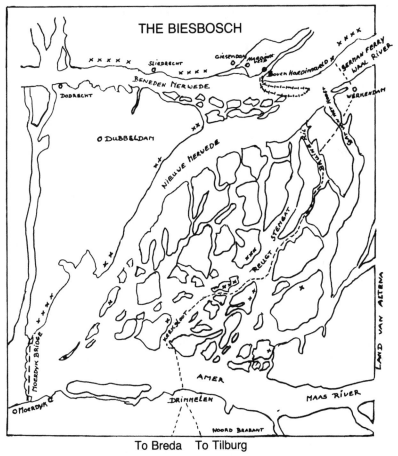

THE BIESBOSCH

To Breda   To Tilburg

xxxx   German military installations and posts
⊢⊢⊢⊢   our first trip (aborted)
----   our second trip

three boxes of ammunition.

It was tough rowing against the current and hard to tell if we were making any headway. The flat countryside all looked the same, lowlands with masses of high reeds bowing down from the wind. Soon we came out of the sheltered tributary into the open water of the Lower Merwede. It was the first river we had to cross to the islands. The wind and the rain blew in our faces. Every time the oars went into the water, the spray covered us. We could see only the white caps on the waves. The weather was worse than expected, but it also shielded us from detection.

In the distance we saw lights on the river, which disturbed us. We had no way of knowing which one was a German patrol. I became fascinated by a flashing beacon stuck on a dark piece of land in our path. The skipper was also worried. He leaned down, mumbling that he didn't trust this new beacon and that I should tell the rowers to stick to the left bank until he could identify the light. He did not know it was a ferryboat landing the Germans had reactivated.

I tried to tell the others, but in the thrash of wind, rain and waves, they could not hear me. They rowed on, not realizing that instead of going forward against the stream, we were going backward, the current proving stronger than we were. Inescapably we drifted toward the flashing light and the German post.

A big swell rocked us and the skipper chose that moment to whisper that we were lost! I turned around and looked across the heaving waves. I couldn't see the shore. The Germans had cut the reeds on both sides of the river. The landscape was wide open, unrecognizable, and even more frightening without any place to hide.

Our luck held. The boat stopped with a jolt, stuck on a sandbar. Without this break we would have drifted to the German ferry landing. We were completely out of control. The rowers stood up to push the boat off, but we only slid deeper into the sand. Frightened, someone screamed that a German patrol boat was coming, but it turned out to be only the sounds of the waves battering the side of the boat.

Reluctantly Jan and Paul dropped into the icy water to push the boat off the sandbar. We then floated around helplessly at the mercy of the current, the wind turning us first frontward, then backward. Having no idea of our location, all we wanted was to return to a safe shore. Instead, we wallowed along downstream in the blackest of nights. Suddenly a dike loomed up. I hoped and prayed it was the dike we had come from. The men rowed toward it like mad. As soon as we came close, Paul jumped into the shallow water, followed by two others. They would explore, and if they found it safe, flash a signal to us.

While we waited there with machine guns and revolvers, someone asked me to find his paper bag with candy. Candy? I asked. Yeah, he said, he had hidden some forty bullets in between the candy. I groaned inwardly, imagining what the Germans would do if they found our boat contained ammunition. I frantically groped around until I found it, and gave the bag to its owner. Leaving the sten gun behind, I grabbed the handguns and waited for the signal. Finally I saw a little flickering light. I clambered out of the boat, slipped, and fell flat on my face. The muddy water splashed against my head, and I lay there for a minute, gathering my wits. The water was freezing cold, but I was so numb from fright that I did not notice it much. Listening to the sounds around me, I recognized the unmistakable voices of German soldiers right over my head. I froze. I didn't move a muscle, just listened. The last man crept out of our boat with the sten gun. He, too, slipped and fell next to me in the murky water. When he looked at me I pointed to the top of the dike and he motioned that he was also aware of the soldiers. For a moment we just lay there. When we didn't hear anything more, I got up and he followed me through the mud toward the large bazalt boulders covered with rolls of barbed wire.

"Don't touch!" I heard him whisper.

I stopped in my tracks. Running into charged wire scared me half to death and I wished Paul were with me. I didn't know that Paul had already discovered some wooden steps leading up the dike and was looking for me. When we finally found each other in the darkness, he pulled me up by the arm and led me towards the steps, telling me that the soldiers were gone and the wire was harmless.

Reaching the road on top of the dike, the three of us snaked along on our stomachs and elbows until we reached a small cottage where our companions waited. One of the men whistled a few soft notes, waited and repeated it twice more. The door opened slightly and a familiar face peered at us. With a big smile the owner of the wharf welcomed us back. We had landed at the other side of our starting point.

I had no idea where we were and couldn't imagine what would have happened if we had not reached this secure haven once more. The other boat had capsized earlier and the men had to swim ashore, retracing their steps to the wharf-house.

Relieved but utterly exhausted, I fell into the arms of van Mill's wife. She was genuinely happy to see us, even though we dragged lots of mud into her house. She scurried around finding dry clothes for everyone.

That night our friendly host showed us to a room in the attic. It had a double bed and a chair. The men offered me the bed with a half comical, half courteous gesture. Paul and I jumped in. Two other men followed. We slept packed like sardines in a can, keeping each other warm, but it was better than lying on the bare floor. After the two men fell asleep next to us, Paul looked at me and winked. I knew what he was thinking and I grinned back at him, while he put his arm protectively around me. Overtired, we soon fell asleep too. The rest of the group snored in chorus on the floor.

We woke early in the morning and I crawled over the others to get out of bed. While I washed myself in the downstairs bathroom, I smelled something delicious, something I had dreamed about many times. No! It couldn't be! I must still be dreaming. But when I entered the kitchen I saw it was true. Right there, in the middle of the table, was a stack of golden pancakes, neatly spread over the back of a plate. Next to them was a bowl heaped with fresh butter and a blue-and-white pitcher of syrup.

I blinked at the scene in amazement. The story of our futile trip had gotten around. The burly men hiding on the barges had found out and with the help of the women, they surprised us with this special treat. Smiling, they stood around to watch my reaction. I beamed, tears of gratitude streaming down my cheeks. They laughed and I hugged the one closest to me. They were not used to a city girl and stared at me curiously.

After breakfast, I helped with the dishes and I felt at home. Mrs. van Mill's warm personality made me feel comfortable right away. She offered for me to stay with them, while Paul went on his mission alone, but I declined her friendly offer.

A little later we had a chance to talk to Bas van Mill alone. Paul said that he had decided to cross the rivers in his own way. Bas listened to Paul's plan to go to the Germans and tell them, as he had told Woltheim, the fake story about getting potatoes. He would then ask them for a permit to cross the first river, the Waal, the large tributary of the Rhine. Then we would be in the Biesbosch, the delta between the Waal and Maas. In this region of low, swampy lands it would be easier to hide.

Bas thought about the area with its maze of connecting channels and small ditches, bordered by eight foot-high reeds, and the nearly impenetrable willow-scrub, a tangled mass of low growing brush. At high tide some of the land would be under water. It was indeed a difficult place for the Germans to patrol. Not only was he willing to help us, but he wanted to go along, presumably to reestablish his own contacts in the Biesbosch. He had lost this link in the underground chain and was now going to find it again.

While we were talking, Klaas Terwilligen appeared. He looked surprised to see us. He expected that we were either dead or in Allied lines. Klaas suggested another way to cross the Merwede by boat, but Paul did not listen. He had made up his mind.

Our conversation was interrupted again, this time by two German soldiers. They came to confiscate tarpaulins from the barges, demanding one per barge.

"How many boats are there?" one of them barked, striving for confidence. Bas got up quickly, saying he would give them two right away. He wanted them gone before they snooped around and found the next room where the other men were cleaning their guns. The soldiers considered this immediate offer.

They chose to leave, sensing that if they tried to find more, they might be ambushed by tough "partisans," who were surely hiding on these barges.

We winked at each other and smiled when they retreated. They looked so young, sixteen or so, inexperienced and frightened. We guessed that they were some of the fresh new troops recently arrived in Holland.

After a long talk, Bas and Paul decided to go from Hardinxveld over the Merwede by ferryboat. This required a German permit. Once in the Biesbosch we would figure out our next step.

We reasoned that with Paul's official papers we should be able to get that permit. Sunday would be a good day, because most of the German brass would not be working.

Wasting no time, Paul and Bas walked to the German commander's office in the next village, and presented their plan to get potatoes for the German Army from the plentiful supply in the Biesbosch. At first the Germans were very suspicious, but Paul urged them to check his story with their headquarters in The Hague. That was a daring move, but he gambled that no one important would be in on Sunday. It worked. Nobody in The Hague knew anything about it, but it sounded all right, they said. By now, the Germans began to think that we were doing them a favor. Not only did they give us a permit, but they also offered a special P.T. boat to run us across. We were embarrassed to accept but too scared to refuse!

"When would you like to go?" they asked.

"One o'clock," Paul said without hesitation, explaining that we needed an hour to get ready. He told them he would be joined by his wife and an assistant. The Germans smiled knowingly. They knew all about taking girlfriends along. With a wink to Paul they nodded, "Ach so! Sure, take your wife along!"

At this point a Dutch government official in the next office was summoned to discuss the quality and the transportation of the potatoes. All of them bent over charts and acted very officious. The moment the Dutchman was alone with Paul, he gave him the name of a reliable man in the Biesbosch. He also typed an explanation of Paul's alleged purpose for the mayor of Werkendam, the main city of the Biesbosch area. After all was arranged, our two men strode home, chuckling that their ruse had worked.

21

Just before one o'clock, we embraced van Mill's wife and walked with her husband over the dike to the ferry landing. This time we didn't have to crawl. Now we had papers. I took my bag along, which looked very businesslike. While we walked we had a good chance to look around. In contrast to the spit and polish of the Nazis in the cities, the German soldiers here looked disheveled. They stood around in grubby uniforms, talking to each other. Bas said they seldom marched in military formation. It was a far cry from the Nazi Elite Corps which we had seen in The Hague.

As we approached the landing, we were startled to see our transportation. The old ferry had been replaced by a sparkling white, powerful German patrol boat, with swastika flags fore and aft. Two soldiers stood at the entrance to the gangplank. They saluted smartly and took my arm to help me aboard. Two military policemen greeted us inside and motioned us to sit. The boat took off. While we nervously sat on the edge of our chairs looking at each other, we crossed the large, fast-flowing river. Fortunately the sky was overcast, because when it was clear, Allied air attacks on any water transport were quite accurate. While I worried about this, the Germans started a conversation. Suddenly one of them asked Bas what time we wanted to return; they would wait for us!

Bas looked uneasy, but he recovered and said quickly, "About six o'clock."

We were silent, realizing that Bas would be the one to return alone to face the waiting Germans with the fact that we were missing. Fortunately, we heard later that he had returned safely, having made up a convincing excuse for our absence.

It was very unusual to arrive in Werkendam in a German boat on a quiet Sunday afternoon. Bas van Mill, wearing wooden shoes, his faded brown cap deep over his eyes, jumped ashore first. A well-known skipper from "across," he hoped nobody would recognize him. Paul and Bob, two young city slickers who were now slightly muddy, leaped after him. Finally I stepped ashore in my expensive fur coat. We certainly were an odd-looking group. People were leaving church as we arrived, and everybody stared at us. The parishioners, in their Sunday best, wore dark clothes with sensible black shoes. We looked strangely out of place. Children ran up to us and gaped openly. Were we German, American, or what?

Bas, embarrassed to be seen with us, said a quick goodbye and disappeared, planning to meet us later at the other side of town. The three of us wandered through the streets, heading toward the village center. We walked slowly, looking around us. Instinctively, Paul knew someone would show up. After a while we noticed a young farmer leaning on the fence of his front yard, nonchalantly smoking a pipe. Our eyes met. He stared at us intently and Paul walked up to him, whispering van Mill's name. The man acted surprised. He said he didn't know van Mill, but that if we needed a place to stay, he might know about that.

We followed him to the tiniest house I had ever seen, built on a little crooked street with cobblestones. It had a small front yard surrounded by a white picket fence, which was covered with rose vines. One entered through green double-Dutch doors directly into the hall, which also served as the kitchen. Behind that was a living room and a bedroom.

It looked like a delightful playhouse. We met the farmer's wife and children in the kitchen. After some back and forth exchange, Paul told the man that we had to cross the river, and fast. The Germans would be waiting for us by the ferry at six o'clock.

Our host looked somber. Puffing heavily on his pipe, he said that he knew nothing about people "going across." He was just a farmer minding his own business, he said. Paul kept on talking, probing, attempting to find out who he was. Finally, Wim, as he called himself, said he had a friend who might put us up and that Bob could sleep in his house. We were disappointed at this vague reaction, for it looked as if we had met an unmovable obstacle and had little chance of getting further.

Wim offered to take Paul and Bob to the Visser family. As he left, Paul scratched his nose, a sign to me that I had to be careful. After half an hour Bob returned with Wim to share his bed for that night. Wim's wife was to sleep with the children in the living room, and I was to join Paul.

As I walked to the end of town, I saw no Germans. Where were they? The village ended at the Visser lot. Beyond that were the lowlands of the Biesbosch. Reeds and grasslands stretched as far as the eye could see. Some of the area was cultivated, but the largest part was still wild. It was getting dark. The black outline of the brush and the gnarled willow trees, etched against the grey sky, slowly darkened. The shimmering water in ditches and creeks seemed to lighten. It looked like a fairyland, mysterious and eerie.

On the left stood the large brick house of the Visser family, my destination. It all felt very strange, but the family greeted me warmly in their spacious kitchen, the only heated room. They sat around a large stove with a water kettle steaming on it. The senior Vissers, who must have been in their sixties, had grown sons and daughters. One of them was Kees, a tall, blond, broad-shouldered man. We guessed he was the head of the entire Biesbosch Resistance. In addition to the family, two other men were present. They looked like they were from above the Moerdyk, the bridge which spans the river dividing the north region from the south.

Paul had established his identity, so Kees took out a map and explained the escape route from island to island. We would sneak through the Biesbosch and finally cross the Maas River to the province of Brabant, a distance of about 25 miles.

I started to feel tired and a little faint, and asked if I could lie down somewhere. Paul got up to help me and Mrs. Visser led us downstairs with a lighted candle. Our room was in the "sous-terrain," a cellar which was somewhat below ground. It was built with tiny rectangular windows just above street level. The windows were blacked out, and we used candlelight so no one would know the room was occupied. There was only a small double bed, built into the thick double walls for warmth, a typical farm innovation. To reach the cupboard-like bed, I climbed up three short steps, opened the wooden sliding doors and crawled in.

Paul still wanted to talk to Kees alone for a while. He gave me a quick kiss and left me alone in the dark. I felt lonely and forlorn. To make matters worse, my head started hurting and I was getting cramps. Crawling out of bed with the tiny candle, I tried to find the pills my doctor in The Hague had given me. I quickly swallowed one without water and returned to bed. The pill made me feel worse, but I fell asleep in the funny little bedstead, exhausted from all the day's emotions. Paul startled me by nearly stepping on my head, trying to climb through the narrow doors in pitch darkness. We both started to giggle.

"Darn it! How come you have your head at the wrong end?"

This was typical of Paul. How incredible men are, I thought to myself.

"Everybody sleeps with his head on the left side of the bed," I quipped.

"Who is everybody?" Paul's standard answer was always a conversation stopper, and we both burst out laughing.

I knew that he was in a happy mood and I began to share his feeling. Paul stepped more carefully as he wiggled his body through the small opening. Banging his head against the roof of the cupboard, he swore in the dark. I laughed even harder, holding my hand in front of my mouth to muffle my giggles.

"Dammit," he muttered, finally plopping down and closing the door. "Good grief, now I know why these people have so many children. These beds are made for love. They are the damdest, coziest beds I have ever seen!"

He put his arms around me and drew me close. His warmth made me feel a little better. I snuggled comfortably against his strong body. For a moment we were quiet and I felt secure and content. But we could never really relax as we were always aware that something unexpected could happen. We always had to be on the alert, always ready to fight or flee. Paul was still tense and I softly massaged his neck and shoulders. Eventually he felt like talking and he told me what had been discussed in the kitchen.

Kees had been far from enthusiastic about helping us, Paul said, but he finally warmed to the idea when he heard the reason for the trip.

"Of course," he had said, "there are many people who want to get out in order to join the Allies, or just to escape."

The boat people of the Biesbosch had helped many across, but lately it had become a lot tougher. Now, Kees explained, they were only willing to risk their lives for men escaped from prison camp or wounded Allied soldiers left behind and hidden at Arnhem. Kees agreed that Paul's job was important, but taking a woman along was out of the question. They had had nothing but problems with city women, and were not going to risk their lives for this unnecessary ballast.

When Paul persisted, Kees finally admitted his real concern: two weeks earlier a woman had betrayed the area's entire Resistance group. They had all known and trusted her, but she fell in love with a Nazi officer and Kees had smelled trouble too late.

I could feel Paul tremble as he retold Kees' story. Although they were careful and changed hiding places, Kees had not counted on the Nazis' thorough search. With a list of names they tracked through town and country. They surrounded each house with at least ten soldiers and routed out the inhabitants in the middle of the night, taking young men at gunpoint without asking questions. If there was any resistance, they burned the house down. The town was still in shock and the Resistance itself was decimated. There were not enough people left to be trusted, Kees said. Some had been shot and others had left the area, knowing they would be next.

Paul said he had listened silently and then told Kees the reasons I was different. He pointed out that I knew the game, had played a major part all along, and that having worked for the food distribution for three years, I understood its procedures. When we reached the Allies and started to list our needs, I could help save children, because I knew the proportions for baby food as well as their diet during the hunger years. Kees politely acknowledged my value, but he was not convinced until he heard the story of the blankets. Then, Paul said, his serious face crinkled into a big smile and he agreed I should come along. In the next moment, my valiant husband was asleep, while I was now fully awake, alone with my fears and worries.

It had happened just before we left Wassenaar. The Germans ordered us to give up our blankets and coats. We would be allowed to keep only one blanket or one coat for ourselves. On a certain day everyone was to bring these items to schools and halls around town. In exchange we would get a card to hang in the window of our house, indicating what we had donated. While we wondered what to do, our London government told us to refuse, and the Resistance began to forge receipts. Within a few days Paul came home with ten forged cards, adorned with swastikas, Nazi seals, everything except the signature of the S.S. Commander of our collection center. That we had to get for ourselves.

Paul and I volunteered for the job. All we needed to do was get just one copy of that all-important signature. We had no warm clothes left, having given anything extra to the underground, so we took two blankets to the Nazi depot and returned with our trophy. We were elated to see that the real card and the forged one looked identical, except for the missing name. On that signature rested the well-being of ten families.

I was a pretty good artist and Paul asked me to copy the signature. I practiced for a long time, becoming increasingly nervous about my task. When I was finally satisfied, I started on the real thing. Paul and the Galemas stood around me. Perspiration trickled on my forehead. I concentrated as hard as I could, but my hand wouldn't move.

"You can do it, Babes. Just pretend it's your own name and write it," Paul said encouragingly.

I couldn't do it. Finally I asked everybody to leave. Then I composed myself and took a deep breath. I dipped the pen in the inkwell and let the ink flow quickly over the paper in a perfect copy of the signature. The next ones were easier. I quickly did the nine copies for our neighbors. We sent the original card to the Resistance, who used it for others.

Of course, very few blankets were handed in and the irate Germans started a thorough search, barging into houses, shooting through stairs and closet doors. Our poor friend Guus got caught this way. He was hiding in the closet when the Nazis shot through the door, hitting his leg. Even so he kept quiet, but he was betrayed by his blood trickling under the door.

When I saw the German army truck come down our street, I went out boldly to meet it. I told the soldiers that we had been the first to give up our blankets. Proudly I showed them our card, talking them out of checking our home. They went by waving at me. Paul and the Galemas watched incredulously when the truck slowly passed.

I remembered the whole episode as I lay in bed in the Visser's home. I became excited about it all over again, staying awake for a long time while Paul slept.

The next morning we had a farewell breakfast with everyone in the house. Kees and Wim made plans to go in two boats. Another young man from Werkendam joined us, who would man the second boat. One of them had checked the whole trip earlier. It looked the same as before, he said: no German posts had been changed nor had any been added. Today seemed to be the best day to go. The weather was not perfect, but it was good enough. It was raining but was supposed to clear later in the night. What good planning compared to our first trip! The risk for our hosts was so great, we were thankful they were willing to take us.

The two strangers accompanying us introduced themselves. We understood they were not using their real names, but no questions were asked. It came out that they had escaped from a German prison camp, taking three months to reach the Rhine. They tried to cross the same day we did, but their boat was swamped, too, and they swam to shore. We heard from them our first account of the cruelty in the camps. The story of the women in Ravensbrück forced from their barracks to line up naked in the snow for roll call haunted me for years. There were far worse stories, but the two men did not want to tell them to me then.

Thus we passed the day waiting, the tension mounting. This time when Kees and Wim returned from their reconnaissance, they brought us high rubber boots for treading in the mud and shallow waters. We got a last warning to be completely silent; across the water any noise carried far. Then it was time to go. As I stood up, someone handed me a box of crackers and a bottle of Dutch gin. Finally came a whispered, "Let's go!" and with a sigh of relief we moved off into the darkest night I could remember.

We walked single-file through the garden as the wind blew and the rain fell. We crossed the road, slushing through the mud. After ten minutes in the meadows, we arrived at a narrow canal. Kees motioned us to wait. We stood silently, looking at the water, the mist hiding all recognizable shapes. The tension was nearly unbearable.

We peered through the fog, trying to make out the shape of a rowboat. Finally, we heard a soft bird call, then silence, then another call, then silence again ... Kees answered the call with a short little chirp. Nobody can imitate the waterbirds as perfectly as the people of the Biesbosch; they grow up with these sounds.

A shape appeared. It was a man pushing a boat into the reeds. He offered his hand as we climbed in. We had to be rowed across in two groups. After landing safely, the man and boat disappeared into the mist again, just another link in the long chain of courageous Resistance people. We slopped our way across the bigger island and on to the next canal. Thank heaven for the rubber boots. With every step we were mired in the sucking mud, sometimes as deep as our knees. Speed was vital, for we had only half an hour before meeting the next boat.

The weather grew worse. I followed Paul like a robot as we trudged along. When we made it to the next canal we flopped down on the dike of the Bruine Kil. Paul produced an umbrella, and the three of us huddled under it while our skipper went off. In the distance we saw a burst of tracer bullets and the flicker of gun flashes, reminding us that they were fighting an "above ground" war at the other side of the rivers.

As I sat there on the dike my thoughts ran wild. One moment I felt like I was outside looking in on an old spy movie. The next moment I was scared back to reality as errant gunfire whizzed by overhead. Finally I decided to make my mind a blank, avoid thinking of what could happen to us and just follow the others.

We sat for what seemed like a long time but was actually only half an hour. We were glad when we finally heard soft noises above the sloshing of the waves against the dike. Grey shadows appeared and the two fugitives from the concentration camp got up immediately. We peered into the darkness as the shadows came closer. Would they be friend or foe? At last we heard the familiar warble of a waterbird.

Kees and Wim arrived in two rowboats. They took our rubber boots for others to use again. Wim motioned me to sit in the stern, where he had kindly put some straw under a small canvas roof. Kees carefully pushed a lead-weighted package next to me. It was to be thrown overboard in case of danger as it was filled with military information from all over Holland. Besides their classified papers and pictures, we carried our own bags and papers, and we prayed we wouldn't be caught with these incriminating documents. Finally the box of crackers and the Dutch gin were stowed under the seats.

We were now ready to go. It was too dark to see what the other boat was doing. "Every man for himself, and God for all of us," I thought, telling myself not to worry about other people. The two men took the oars, carefully covered with cloth to lessen the noise. The oarlocks themselves were wound with rope to make them smoother. Paul and Bob swallowed their anti-cough pills. Both had a smoker's hack which had to be suppressed completely.

First we rowed upstream. The rain suddenly stopped and the moon tried to peek through the clouds. I had memorized the route and tried to orient myself, but the sameness of the area made it difficult. Everywhere was water and masses of reed, with a low mist hanging over all. The boatmen had to navigate very carefully, staying close to the shore and hiding in the shadow of the reeds. At the same time we had to be careful not to startle the sleeping wildlife, as their noisy quacking would wake up the German guards. Then we would be the most frightened birds in the water!

The men rowed with short, powerful strokes in a rhythmic pattern, so the boat did not sway. Ever so gently, they put the oars into the water to avoid splashing. From my straw bed I could peek around the small canvas roof at the purple sky. Once in a while a heron would fly over, slowly flapping its wings, its long neck outstretched. The only noise was from the frogs, which were holding a late night concert. They were big, fat, bright green Dutch frogs.

There were no German posts at the beginning of our trip and we got used to the boat and the darkness. Very carefully we travelled, expertly guided by Kees, until we suddenly stopped. Kees pointed to a black outline of a guard house ahead on the dike. A German post!

We rested for a while, preparing ourselves for the ordeal to come. Then I dove under the tarpaulin and the rowers crouched as low as possible. Softly we floated along, close to the bank. The lights were on in the little house and a soldier stepped outside, followed by another one. They talked together but didn't turn our way. We knew that if we made any noise the searchlights and machine guns would find us, giving us no chance to shout or wave a protest. In the bright light cone we would be a shiny target to be destroyed, shot to pieces. Then the soldiers would probably laugh and go back inside to their beers.

It was easier for us to see them than for them to see us, and we watched, mesmerized. The moon lit up the area; the house and the soldiers looked like a faraway picture.

As we stared in terror at the dike, a big, black cloud passed over the moon. It became dark just long enough for us to float by without being discovered. God was with us, and we all thanked Him for our good fortune. We thanked the moon, too, and the sky, breathing a little easier when we were finally out of sight.

We reached the Stemgat and took the southern passage through to the high reeds of the Reugt, resting and taking advantage of this shelter. The night was bitterly cold and we quickly passed the bottle of gin. I took a big slug, which made me feel warm and velvety inside. My legs were numb from not being allowed to move, and I wiggled my toes to keep the blood streaming. Fortunately the fur coat kept my body pretty warm.

We stayed in the reeds about half an hour. The moon was out again, but it became obvious that God had us in his sights that night. Whenever we had to pass by German guards, the clouds obliged by covering the moon as we slid by in the darkness.

Floating past the military posts, I felt like a duck in a pond watched by eager hunters. In this area the Germans called their dikeguards "partisanenjäger," hunters of the Partisans. After passing two more German posts, we arrived in the Kerksloot, the last leg before the river Maas, which was called Amer at this point. It seemed endless and I feared we would never get there, that somehow we would get lost. There was no chance for that, though, as our guides knew every ditch, every inlet, and every possible hiding place. But the sky was slowly brightening, which made us more visible.

Near the end of the night's trip we came upon a suspicious-looking farmhouse. My heart started to pound. We were so close to freedom, but this last building on the point looked like a fake. Were German troops hiding there? We never knew.

Suddenly we heard the sound of a motorboat. German police!! Alarmed flocks of water birds fluttered up, squawking loudly. Kees instantly turned our boat and we shot into the overhanging reeds, the high stalks closing behind us. There we waited, completely silent, barely breathing. The men listened, bent overboard to better hear from what direction the Germans were coming. Was it a patrol, or was it just a few soldiers hunting duck?

They were now very close. Did they notice the bent-down reeds? Could they possibly see a shadow of our boat?

We held our breath. We could hear them talk and laugh only a few feet away from us. After a few seconds, which seemed to us an eternity, they passed. They hadn't detected us. We listened to the sounds fade until we could not hear them anymore.

We all let out our breaths and slumped down on the bottom of our boat to wait. Kees then decided to change the route and push the boat forward through the mud and reeds to reach another creek, thinking it would be safer. It was hard work pushing and pulling through the dense stalks and plumes around us. Finally we reached open water again, and looked around. Wim picked three slimy leeches off his leg. These horrid creatures were lurking in the mud by the thousands.

Worried the Germans might return, we were watchful as we silently floated along, staying as close to the bank as possible. The waves became higher as we neared our last river crossing. A fierce wind from the North Sea was blowing over the open water. The little dinghy bounced along. Once in a while a big wave pitched us up, only to smash us down again, my stomach going along with it. But the men rowed calmly on, and after an hour they found a hidden spot in the reeds on the bank of the Amer. Here in the lee, we waited a few hours for daylight and the incoming tide, far away from the last German post.

Our guides were sure that the Germans would not venture out

this far to catch us, and they felt it was now safe to talk.

"Basically they're afraid of water," Kees told us, "They're like the Russian guards on that count."

"Russians, guarding our dikes?" Paul asked incredulously. "For crying out loud, I thought the Russkies were our friends?"

"Yeah, I guess so, but these are POW's. Either guard duty in Holland, or starving to death in prison camp somewhere."

"Jesus, what a choice! I wonder how reliable these chaps are! If I were a German, I certainly wouldn't trust them!"

Paul and Kees traded places with me. They stretched out on the straw and began to tell each other Resistance stories. I now sat on the bottom of the other side of the boat, leaning against the seat. Quietly by myself I found my mind drifting. I looked at the sky, watching a cloud, small, white and woolly, a loner, cruising along in the blue. A rustling in the reeds at my left attracted my attention for a second. It was only a heron searching for breakfast. When I glanced back at the sky, the cloud wasn't alone anymore. It had been joined by two RAF planes, the round circles on their wings looking as feisty as the cloud looked peaceful. I wondered out loud if that was our old friend Erik, who had escaped earlier in the war flying over us.

Paul perked up and stared intently skywards. He had the same reaction and said, "Jeez, it's probably Erik, lucky bum! Flying up there, while we're stuck in the mud!"

I glanced at Paul. A look of longing had come into his eyes and I remembered how much he wished he could have escaped long ago and joined the RAF, too. Now we all watched the sky. I could picture Erik confidently in the cockpit, large round goggles hiding most of his face. It seemed a million years ago that we had talked with him on the beach in Scheveningen.

As the planes neared the Moerdyk bridge, a sudden barrage of German flak exploded in the sky around them, chasing them into the safety of the clouds. While I pensively studied the red, white, and green sparks bursting into the sky, I wasn't so sure that being up there was so much better. A sudden chill crept over me and I pulled my coat closer around me, which somehow made me feel more secure. I recalled those happy and innocent years so long ago. After a while I heard Paul call to me to change places again. His seriousness brought me back to our own danger. We weren't out of the woods yet.

As we shifted from one hard plank to another, I noticed that the men were much more relaxed. We were about to start our last river crossing. The wind had died down; it was daybreak and the Amer was as smooth as a lake. Through the morning mist we could see the other side, where the 21st Army Group was stationed. It combined American, Australian, Canadian, Polish, New Zealand, along with some Dutch forces, a true melting pot of Allies.

We floated on the strong current of the incoming tide at a remarkably fast pace up the river to the harbor of Drimmelen. The pressure was off, and we laughed, sang and started shouting when we noticed some soldiers standing on the dike. It was a sight I will always remember.

"We made it," Wim said with a happy sigh, "let's make a lot of noise and sing the Wilhelmus so they know we're Dutch!"

We boomed out our national anthem, singing it slowly, the way you have to sing this stately song. Our bodies swayed along with the rhythm. Paul sat up straight and acted as if he was conducting an orchestra. Never had anyone sung it with more feeling and more enthusiasm.

Trying to find a landing place in the small harbor, we saw no opening through the barbed wire, just shadows of people on the dike. Nobody seemed to pay the slightest attention to us.

Finally two uniformed men came closer, bent over to look at us and shouted, "Halt!"

After the trauma of German control we had forgotten that the command is the same in Dutch. For a moment we thought we were in German hands again!

"We are Dutch linecrossers!" we hollered, in Dutch of course. Then an unmistakable Dutch voice shouted, "Verdomme man, dat zijn Hollanders. Okay! Come on here!"

They showed us the way to climb up through the barbed wire. Arriving on the quay, we realized we had made it. We were free, at last really free! No Nazis, no secret police! No razzias!

We put our arms around each other and danced around, hitting each other on the back. Paul held me so tightly I nearly choked. Then we shook hands with the Dutch guards and introduced ourselves, using our real names. Although we were on Dutch free soil, we felt strange, as if we had landed in a foreign country.

We couldn't figure out who these Dutchmen were. They dressed in the same kind of uniforms as Allies, but they had an orange band around their arms. Paul found out that they were the O.D. (Orde Dienst), a unit which had been very effective in the Resistance. Once liberated they had acquired uniforms and were run by different men.

Their reaction to us was strangely cool. They did not seem to care about our stories of starvation in the North, nor about the dangers of our trip. When we went to their offices, we saw secret messages openly displayed on their desk for everyone to see. Guns were thrown any old place. We were shocked that they seemed so unorganized. These couldn't be Resistance men! If so, how quickly they forgot! Had we jeopardized our lives to see our secrets treated like this? That piece of paper nonchalantly thrown on a desk could mean a whole string of death sentences up north!

We had a sinking feeling of despair and complete frustration, a feeling of being let down. Kees and Wim found some old friends, Resistance men from the north. They started an animated conversation, had a good laugh, and completely ignored the others.

When a group of Polish officers arrived, we felt better. They had liberated this part of Holland. The commander produced a staff map and we explained in English what we had seen on our trip. He offered us our first English cigarettes, Pall Mall, which tasted very different from the strange concoctions we had rolled ourselves.

Paul, who had the most information, was asked to go to Polish headquarters. The rest of us stayed behind and had lunch. For the first time in my life, I saw packaged bread, corned beef and Spam. It tasted delicious to me. I wolfed everything down but unfortunately paid for my gluttony later. My poor undernourished stomach couldn't take the rich food.

The officers didn't know what to do with us. They released Wim and Kees, having met them before. The two brave men returned through the lines to their homes again. Paul, Bob and I were driven to Breda, where the Canadians were to interview us at their headquarters.

Driving down the roads of liberated Holland was a new experience. We saw the ravages of actual fighting in the fields, the woods, the cities, everywhere. We passed by hundreds of burned-out tanks, demolished cars, and bombed-out houses. We saw gaping bomb craters on the roads and in the meadows, but it was not the desolate picture that I had seen elsewhere. This was a panorama of Allied armies readying themselves for a final push over the Rhine river into Germany and northern Holland. It was also a scene of busy Dutch citizens, trying to rebuild the farms, round up their cattle, and start a new life.

We could not believe our eyes when we saw the amount of Allied war materiel. The ingenious Bailey bridges looked like a bigger version of the ones we used to make with our erector sets. The steel prefabricated bridges were pushed over the smaller streams and canals, or put on pontoons and floated in the larger rivers.

There were even Burma Shave advertisements on the roads. We laughed when we read the whimsical verse as we sped by. This is how I had pictured the Americans, always active, always inventive, and full of humor. How often had I dreamed of this moment. How often had I imagined myself meeting Americans for the first time. I wondered why they intrigued me. Was it their dash and panache, the way I had seen them in the movies? Or was it because they were unknown? I had met Britishers through the years, and I always liked *them.* They were Europeans and I knew them, but I had never seen a real live American! Nor had I ever seen any of those handsome Canadians, for that matter.

Driving through it all was terribly exciting. Huge tanks, like great big mildewed monsters, reaching to the second floor of the houses, whirred and clanked down the narrow roads. Little khaki-colored jeeps scurried in between the hundreds of large trucks and amphibious cars. Every car had the white star emblem of the invasion painted on its sides and top, so it could be seen from the air. Together they formed a dizzy stream of green and white. Men, guns, tanks, cars, army vehicles — this was the liberation army!

I felt like screaming for joy. I wanted to embrace everyone out of sheer happiness and ecstacy. To think that all these Allies had come to Europe to liberate us!

It was a fantastic display of power that eclipsed the German army's drab, shabby uniform, stolen bikes with wooden wheels, and cars fueled by coal.

Right then I fell in love with the jeep. For me this spunky little car with the big white star was the symbol of Holland's liberation. When I later managed to get one for myself, I treated it with honest affection.

In the beginning it was difficult for us to identify the different nationalities and their uniforms. The Allied soldiers and officers in the cities looked clean and healthy. Not having seen healthy people in a long time, I kept staring at them. They seemed to me to be the real Super Race rather than the Nazis which Hitler had tried to create. The tall men in their Eisenhower jackets — God, they looked great!

After about half an hour we arrived at the Canadian intelligence office. Two officers asked us in and offered cigarettes and coffee. They interrogated us in English, writing everything down. They went into the smallest details and questioned every sentence. My exuberance changed completely when I found out that they did not believe us. At first I thought they were kidding. They asked us stupid questions about how we reacted to the Nazis. I felt silly, thinking they should know by now how we felt. Once in a while they looked at each other with knowing glances. I couldn't tell whether they didn't know what was happening in the north, or were just pretending. They had never heard of Dr. Louwes or anybody in the Food Distribution Service!

We were bewildered. How could we prove to them we were okay? Or even prove who we were? With so many fake papers floating around, they didn't believe anything or anybody. After the debâcle in Arnhem they were extremely cautious. The Secret Service was working overtime, questioning persons, ferreting out traitors. Anybody coming through the lines was suspect.

Paul became obstinate. He refused to mention any names of Resistance people who were still in the German-occupied territories. After so many years of covert activities, we were hesitant even to tell our own names. After seeing how the Dutch were treating our secret correspondence, we became more careful. We couldn't make them understand how dangerous it was to name names. It was clear that the Allies had no idea how bad the situation was in northern Holland. The courier service was only between the Dutch. The Canadians had obviously not been informed.

After conferring with each other, the intelligence officers decided to keep us in the Civilian Interrogation Camp in Tilburg until someone at Dutch headquarters in Brussels could identify us. They were very polite and apologetic, saying, "There's a war goin' on, you know."

"Yes, yes, we *do* know, only too well!"

They further apologized for the building where we would stay. A buzz-bomb had landed there a week ago, and the building was half burned out.

Paul and I were exhausted. Right now we were not worried about ourselves but felt our mission to inform the Allies was more important than our personal comfort. We knew that one day they would understand, but for the moment, we were guilty until proven innocent. We were prisoners.

22

The Civilian Interrogation Camp was set up to get information from escaped civilians and also to house men and women who were thought to be spies or collaborators. Starting in France, the camp moved with the troops. Consequently, there were prisoners of all nationalities behind the high iron fence on the Bredasche Road.

The two officers took our few belongings, including my small diary containing my most intimate thoughts. I started to cry. Paul glared at me. He had warned me not to bring it along, but I felt it was safest with me. While still sobbing, I was frisked and measured. They looked in my mouth, charting the fillings in my teeth. It was humiliating. A guard was called and we were marched to the barracks which were to be our temporary home.

The big building had been used by the Dutch army, then by the Germans, and now it was in Allied hands. We saw that it had been severely ravaged by a V-1 bomb meant for Antwerp, that had missed by miles. The women's quarters were on the right, and the men's on the left. The halls in between were under water, due to the rain coming through a big hole in the roof. Balancing ourselves over wobbly planks to get to our respective sides, Paul and I looked at each other as we parted. Paul's face was terribly drawn and thin, with hollow cheeks. How he suffered as I was led away.

Too tired and upset to make a fuss, I meekly followed directions to a first aid station where I was given two very thin blankets and a rubber sheet. The guard then led me along the water-filled corridor, past the inundated washroom, and up a few steps into a big, dry room, which was the women's hall. As we entered the room fifteen women prisoners silently stared at my fur coat and at me, distrust in their faces. I could feel their hostility. They had all been picked up at night, lifted from their beds with only their night clothes. Was I an informer put in their midst?

The guard pushed me into the room. With a "Good luck, young

lady," he closed the door behind me.

Nobody said a word as I stood there in a state of shock. Finally an older Dutch woman came up to me and asked, "What's your name?" I stared at them for another second before answering softly, "Babes."

The others giggled, but the older woman ignored them, pointed to a steel bed and said, "This is your bunk. You can make your bed any way you want to."

The others laughed again. There were no mattresses or sheets on the steel cots lined up on both sides of the room.

"The straw mattresses were burned in the last bombardment," she explained. "This is all you have, and no pillow either. It's freezing cold at night. As you can see, we have no glass in the windows. It blew out."

"How do you sleep, on this iron thing?" I asked meekly.

The heavy-set woman eyed me coldly for a minute. Then her eyes softened, and she said, "That's your problem, kid. It ain't the Palace Hotel. You can either put your blankets on the steel to make it feel softer and be cold on top, or you can put your bones on the steel frame and be warm on the top. These two holes between the iron plates hit you just wrong. You either put a shoulder in the first hole and your hip on this steel bar, or the other way around. Both ways are bad, but you get used to it. You're lucky, you have a fur coat, so I wouldn't complain if I were you!"

She pointed to a huge oil drum with a low stepping stool in front.

"This is the john. You just jump up and hang on."

I stared in disbelief, wondering how I would ever "just jump up and hang on" without falling in. My tour conductor did not notice my anxiety.

"This is only for the night," she continued, matter-of-factly. "During the day, you can ask the guard to take you to the can outside."

She then showed me to my corner, "This is the shelf where you put your stuff. We clean the room every day. Tomorrow it's your turn."

"What'll I clean it with?" I asked, seeing neither cleanser nor rags.

"With a rag and water, and a broom for the floor," she said. "The cooks bring two pails of water every morning, one for drinking and one for cleaning. You can get your own pail to wash yourself in from the washroom."

We moved to the other side of the room where some of the women sat on two wooden benches around an old-fashioned stove. They looked at me coldly and asked why I was there. I tried to explain, but they did not understand the situation at all. They all had collaborated with the Germans, and couldn't understand why I would jeopardize my life to fight the Nazi occupation. Some of them had earned their living by fraternizing, living off the Dutch, French or German men. The German officers were the most generous, they said. Only three of the women were Dutch, the rest were French or Belgian. I spoke French, and the Belgians understood some Dutch, since they were Flemish; but it was still hard to converse. They kept staring at my fur coat, and I wondered how soon they would try to steal it.

Uneasily I sat down on the bench and looked at the red bricks lying on top of the stove. Finally I asked what the bricks were for.

"To keep your feet warm," one of them answered. "We put them in bed like a hot water bottle. It works fine — you either burn your feet, or you burn a hole in the blanket. It's worth it, though. You'll find out tonight!"

I looked around and saw a hole in the wall. They had pried the bricks out of the wall. The older woman followed my gaze.

"You can get your own brick, if you want to. But it takes a long time to get one out with a spoon."

I was too tired to worry about it any further and decided to go to bed. Quietly I got up, said good night, and drooped towards my iron cot. Passing the oil drum, I decided to wait it out until dark.

I put the rubber sheet on the steel, and my fur coat on top of that, with the two thin blankets over me. The straight bars were unbelievably hard. After a few minutes I tried the floor. That was softer, but colder. I tried all different systems, but could not sleep that night. Finally I put my coat on and realized how nice it would feel to have a warm brick near my feet. That would be my first task in the morning.

The night was very, very long.

Two Belgian girls slept together in the cot next to me, to keep warm. They whispered and giggled for a long time. Next to them was the older Dutch woman. She not only snored, she grunted, groaned, whistled and ground her teeth, once in a while emitting a startling loud snort. Somebody finally threw a shoe at her head. She woke up, sat straight up in her bed and yelled one obscenity after the other. I closed my ears to it all, too tired to worry about what was going on around me.

The temperature was below freezing outside, and inside it was not much warmer. I dozed off a couple of times, but my stomach started to kick up and then suddenly began to turn. I ran to the oil drum just in time to lose my first good dinner. Some of the girls swore at me a couple of times. My heaves were not too attractive. After three more runs for the drum, my stomach quieted down, and I had a few hours of fitful sleep.

Wake-up started at six o'clock with a lot of racket. I arose hurting all over. The head cook, a jolly roly-poly Belgian prisoner, came in with the pails of water and a friendly word. He eyed me curiously, and made some casual remarks to the other girls, who were in all stages of undress. At 6:30 the staff sergeant came in for roll call. After that we were allowed to go to the washroom, a typical old-world barracks lavatory with a long row of faucets hanging over a steel sink. The floor was under water, so we walked on mildewed raised planks.

While I was in the lavatory getting water, the men entered. Most wore only their pajama pants, but I hardly looked up from my chore. In less than twelve hours, I was already losing my sense of propriety, which is the most dehumanizing experience in prison life. Suddenly I felt a touch on my shoulder and then an arm close around me. My gaze traveled up long, bare legs to a familiar old trench coat, to see the worried face of Paul.

"Are you all right?" he whispered. I couldn't answer. Instead I threw my arms around him, and hid my face against his chest.

For some reason, the guards thought this his-and-her spy team was hilarious. What did we care! We held on to each other as if we were the only two people in the world. After that I felt a lot better. We talked while Paul washed up, and then he asked the guards permission for me to see his room.

The men's quarters certainly looked better than ours. It held about twenty men, mostly Dutch linecrossers, who were a far more congenial group. They had escaped from the north intending to join the Princess Irene Brigade. The unit was originally created for the Dutch who arrived in England to fight for Queen and country. It had participated in the D-Day landings at Normandy.

Paul was shocked when he heard my story. When I told him how bad my cot was, he winced and wanted to give me his bed.

"Oh, no," I gently refused his offer, "The other women would kill me if I have anything better. They're already upset about my nice warm fur!"

He was now even more determined to get me out and started

to complain to the guards, demanding to speak to the officers. However, nothing could be done until we had been questioned again.

Some of the women in my room came from Paris or Brussels and had consorted with the Nazis. They had been picked up by the Allies, who hoped to get information about the whereabouts of their lovers, either high ranking Nazis, or collaborators. Often the women had been caught at night, which explained their outfits.

Then there was Monique, alert and adapting to her new environment. She had helped a high-ranking pro-Nazi escape from Paris and was later caught by the Allies to be questioned for information. The Canadians grilled her constantly. She spoke only French, repeating that she didn't understand the interpreter. She was playing for time, intending to divulge nothing until she was sure her friend had reached safety.

Monique managed to get more favors than anyone else in our quarters. She had led a good life during the German occupation. As a result of having had enough to eat, she still looked healthy. Her auburn hair was shiny, her skin luminous and her blue eyes lively. She was sensuous and attracted the eye of every man. When she managed to get a pass to go home for a change of clothes, we all stared at her beautiful wardrobe. Every morning she put on lipstick and brushed her hair one hundred strokes. We knew instinctively that she would always get her way. Even the tough-looking women in our camp kept a respectful distance from her. They were all extremely jealous of her. I only envied her lipstick. When I was free, I vowed, that would be the first thing I would buy.

Another of the French girls was equally attractive. Every morning the cook brought her a pail of warm water so she could wash herself in our room. We were all envious, but I soon found out that she returned the favor at night.

"A man is a man," she told me simply, "and I like all men."

I asked Paul if he knew anything about a blonde girl in the room, the youngest one there. Paul was told by the cooks that she was the girlfriend of a Belgian contractor. He was an economic collaborator who had made millions supplying the German Wehrmacht and building part of the Atlantic Wall. Together they had led a very good life. They could buy anything they needed during trips to Brussels and Paris, and it was all paid for by the Germans.

She saw nothing wrong with her opportunistic way of life and described it to me in glowing terms. I couldn't believe her total lack of conscience.

Two other quiet women were British who had been caught

working for the Nazis. After a short while they were sent back to England and tried as spies.

Paul and I discussed the three older women. During the day they shuffled around in curlers made of strips of cotton cloth. Just before dinner they would take the curlers out of their hair and primp themselves up with whatever cosmetics were on hand. We called them "Les Papillottes," the French word for curlers. I wondered what had brought them here.

Our three cooks were prisoners in for collaboration. One was a manufacturer for the German Wehrmacht. He was not really pro-Nazi; he had just gambled on the wrong horse and lost. He had believed the Germans would win the war, and he would be rich. Now, all his funds were confiscated and his family was under house arrest, waiting to be tried by Belgian courts.

When I returned to my side of the barracks after visiting Paul, I received an icy reception from the group. They made me feel very uncomfortable. Finally the Dutch woman, who had shown me around when I arrived, pointed to the oil drum and said sternly, "You got this thing dirty last night, so you can damn well clean it!"

Fifteen pairs of hostile eyes were watching me and they convinced me to do the dirty job immediately. I dragged the drum out the door, where one of the guards helped me carry it downstairs. We dumped the contents into the outside toilet and cleaned it out with a hose. Now I knew better than to use the drum again, even if it meant waking up the guards in the middle of the night to be escorted outside.

On the afternoon of the second day Paul and I were interrogated separately. I was led to a small room in a building across from the courtyard. Two Canadian officers sat behind a desk and motioned me to sit down. One of them was an interpreter. They were very pleasant and offered me a cigarette.

They showed me my diary and asked me if this was my writing. Though I could speak and understand English pretty well, I was so nervous that I just looked at them questioningly. The interpreter repeated the question in Dutch. I nodded. When they told me they had read my diary I was terribly embarrassed. Suddenly, I felt as though I was standing naked in front of them. Paul was right, I should have left it home!

Fortunately they did not react to the contents, but said only that they were surprised there weren't any names in my private little book other than my husband's.

I shrugged my shoulders. "I wouldn't have taken it along if

there were other names in it. This diary is private, it's just about us," I said icily.

They exchanged glances and smiled. After thumbing the pages, they changed the subject and showed me a piece of paper with a long list of names.

"Your husband told us that these were some of his friends. Do you know them? If so, please tell us about them."

I did not recognize one single name. I wondered why Paul had never told me about these friends. Who were they? Was I supposed to know them? Were they in the Resistance? Were they the ones who came to our house at night?

I racked my brain, but none of the names rang a bell. I shook my head. They asked me again, but feeling positive, I indicated I had never heard of any of them. The interrogation stopped abruptly and they led me back to my room. Paul told me later that they had used an old trick. Those names were all known spies. If I had thought that I'd even heard of one of them, that would have been the beginning of serious trouble for both of us.

When it was Paul's turn to be interrogated, he took the chance to complain about the fact that they had put me together with a group of pro-Nazi women. The Canadians apologized profusely again, saying they had no other room. They said they had tried to contact Dutch Army Headquarters in Brussels, without success. The Germans had started an offensive and the Allies had more important things to do.

We tried to understand, but we felt rotten about it. We were just stuck there and wasting precious time.

Back in the women's room I noticed two new faces — a Dutch mother and daughter from Heusden, a town near where the Germans still held the bridge on the banks of the Maas. With the help of the underground they had just escaped from one of the Nazis' most inexplicable acts of cruelty. Numbly, they told me that during the dawn of November 5, the town was rocked by two blasts followed by an incredibly loud third blast. The Germans were blowing up all the lookout posts. First to go were the steeples of the two churches. Then they closed in on the town hall, where 150 people were hiding from Allied shelling.

As a final act of vengeance in the face of the approaching Allies, the Germans blew up the whole building, covering 134 bodies with tons of debris. The woman and her daughter miraculously survived and escaped through the cellar window. When they realized the other women in our room were pro-Nazi, they stopped talking about their experiences, and I never found out how they got out.

Mother and daughter were quiet during the day, but at night they started singing, at first very softly. As we applauded, they took heart and their singing became louder. As I listened to their beautiful harmony I felt a ray of pure happiness that such joy could penetrate this dreadful place. Soon the door opened, and the cooks and guards came in to listen, too. That night I almost fell asleep happy. Instead, I found that the nostalgic songs made me remember the family I had left behind up north, and I wept bitter tears.

Every morning Paul and I were interrogated for hours at a stretch. As the Canadians became friendlier, I thought they had finally come to believe that we were loyal Dutchmen, and they were just waiting for proof. We talked about other things, and ended up drinking a cup of tea or a glass of gin and smoking a cigarette. They told us that because we had been so reticent to talk in the beginning they were distrustful.

"You're not sitting in front of the Gestapo, you know. We are your Allies," they told us over and over again.

We begged them to understand that for over four years caution had been our watchword and we had learned through bitter experience not to talk, not to say anything. One word could mean death to a lot of other people. Perhaps later, after the North was liberated and they could see the situation there, they would understand.

I had to tell them my whole life's story: where I was born, what schools I had attended, all about my parents, my vacations, and so on.

"Oh, you were on vacation in Germany, just before the war!"

"No," I said, "It was not a vacation. We were in Baden-Baden. My father needed gold treatments for his arthritis." They wrote it all down, jumping at every hint that might prove we weren't the couple we claimed to be. Finally they became interested in my stories about the V-2 behind our house.

I told them about the difference in the V-weapons, that the V-1 was a buzz-bomb and the V-2 was a rocket. As I remembered Paul saying that the Allies were interested in the missiles' remote control, I told them what I knew about it. Paul knew a lot more, I said, because he had transmitted the dimensions of this rocket and its launching sites to an Allied plane which was circling the area. At night, Paul would ride his bicycle to charge the battery for this transmission. He would come home late at night, soaking wet, after having crawled in the rain toward the V-2 pad behind our house.

He also took pictures with a camera in a cigarette box, repeating this routine in the rain for many weeks.

The Canadians were impressed by this and their attitude changed. I think they started to work seriously on our release. During one of the sessions another officer barged into the room, saying excitedly that they were having a big fight in the men's dorm. When he noticed me he stopped in his tracks.

I ran to Paul's dorm where everybody was indeed very agitated. It seemed that the Allies had caught a Dutch Nazi who had not only helped the Germans round up Jews, but had also betrayed many other people. Paul and the others complained about this new prisoner, as "they didn't want the sonofabitch in their room." When no action was taken, they took matters into their own hands and threw the man out of the second-story window.

"Good riddance," Paul said matter-of-factly. I winced.

Walking back to my quarters I thought about my own situation. It was just the reverse! The Dutch mother and her daughter and I were the odd ones in the lion's den.

The days went by slowly. Five days had passed since we had landed in our "free country." Not free for us, yet. Every day was the same, but at least the food was plentiful and good.

I started to look a little healthier. Although still hungry most of the time, I was careful not to overeat and stuck to a diet of toast, cheese, and tea. I toasted the bread on the coal stove for Paul and myself. Once we even managed to get some flour and raisins from the cook, and I made pancakes on the small stove in the men's quarters.

The atmosphere in the women's side became worse as time went on. There were constant fights about trivial things. One fight became quite serious when a pair of scissors was stolen from a newly arrived prisoner. The girl, who was no shrinking violet, started such loud screaming that the guards came rushing in, probably thinking someone was being murdered. We never knew who took the scissors, but they showed up again the next morning.

I finally managed to pry a brick from the wall for my own "heating pad." It kept me warm at night, although on my first try I burned my foot and on the second, burned a hole in the blanket, just like the others had said. Eventually I found out how long to heat the brick on the stove to get it to the right temperature.

I also took a "bath." It was a three-pail affair. Paul brought two pails of warm water to me. I hung my blankets over one of the drying lines to give myself a semblance of privacy. Then I stepped

into my own empty pail, cleaning myself with the pail of soapy water, and rinsing myself with the clear one.

The camp became more bearable as the weather improved. As
it warmed we were allowed to exercise in the yard twice a day,
stepping single file in a circle. Dutch burghers stared at us through
the tall iron fence in disgust. They threw stones and spat at us. I
felt terrible, wanting to shout: "Stop that. I'm more loyal than
you!" But I didn't want to start a commotion now that we were so
close to getting out. In my heart I was glad that the Dutch were
unforgiving of our traitors. I knew I would be the same; I would
never forget.

At last Paul and I were called in together before an interrogation board. The board members still wondered why Paul had taken
me along and why he had so few identification documents. We
were asked to describe Louwes, who had sent Paul to go south as a
member of the Food Distribution.

Paul explained the dangers of leaving me behind and indicated that he felt one signed letter would be sufficient. The board
finally agreed, and said we could leave the next morning. We
thanked them, but we really didn't know for what.

During our last evening there a new prisoner arrived. She was
a thin, nervous woman with a scared look in her eyes. She told us
the story of her life and ended by saying nobody had ever liked or
accepted her.

"And so that's why you joined the Dutch Nazi Party." added
the cook who always seemed to be hanging around our room.

"Perhaps," the new girl said thoughtfully, "With the glorious
Party I was somebody. I was part of a group and we did everything
together."

Her story did not surprise us. She seemed the type: happy to
follow the Nazi discipline, never asking questions, not even knowing what they stood for. To her it was kind of a grown-up girl scout
troop. After she told her story, everyone ignored her. There was a
great distinction between being Dutch Nazi or being an opportun-
ist. The two groups did not want anything to do with each other.
Even in this camp, this sad woman was not accepted.

The next morning the staff sergeant told us to pack. He returned my diary, my wedding ring, and the little money we had.
That, with our toothbrushes, medicines, and the extra set of underwear, were all our earthly belongings! On our way out, the officers
bade us a warm goodbye.

Paul asked them why they had kept us so long. They finally

told us that when we arrived, they had received a secret message that a Dutch couple known as notorious spies had disappeared from their home. Presumably they were escaping to the south, so the Canadians had to be certain of us. Finally a telegram arrived from Major General J. J. Kruls, Head of the Dutch Military Forces under Allied command, requesting our immediate release.

We left, accompanied by two Canadian soldiers who were to drive us to the Dutch police for our identification cards and a certificate of "political trustworthiness."

It was miserable weather. Sheets of rain clattered on the brick pavement. Paul was coughing badly. He didn't feel well at all. We looked for a drugstore to get some medicine for him, but they were all closed. We were free, but we felt completely lost. Carrying our new police papers, we finally managed to find our way to our contact, Mr. Boerma. It was past six, after office closing time, but fortunately everyone was still there. We were delighted to get a warm welcome and to be able to tell all, and be understood this time.

One of Paul's friends took us home for the night. Although we were exhausted, we never felt better than when we saw a real bed with clean sheets and thick Dutch blankets. What luxury!

We had been told that Queen Wilhelmina had arrived in Holland and that she would speak to the nation that evening. Knowing we could now listen openly to the radio, made us finally feel really free. Her voice halting with emotion, Her Majesty delivered a personal greeting to "my people," as she always called us. Our national anthem followed. Paul and I stood up and sang along, holding hands.

"We made it, Babes; we really made it!" Paul put his arm around me. I nodded and leaned my head against his shoulder, closing my eyes. When the broadcast was finished I changed stations to the "sound of the big bands." We sat quietly and listened to the wonderful music. Close to tears, I felt a tremendous joy in my heart, when I suddenly heard the orchestra play one of my favorite songs, "Kiss me once, and kiss me twice, and kiss me once again. It's been a long, long time . . ."

Paul looked at me, his eyes moist. When I smiled at him, he lifted my face and kissed me on the nose. Tenderly his arms wrapped around me. While locked in this embrace, laughing and crying at the same time, we fell backwards on the soft bed and loved in a free-spirited whirlwind of happiness.

23

The following morning Paul began a round of frantic activity. He started by driving to Eindhoven, requesting the radio people there to broadcast our secret code. The arrangement had been to send the message to the BBC so that our parents and Dr. Louwes would know we were alive and well. His reception was disappointing. The radio staff was unwilling to broadcast our code, saying they had to check us out first. After weeks of not knowing whether we had been cleared, we were so busy that we finally forgot about it.

While Paul went to the office, I walked to the Red Cross to get some clothes. Sorting through a pile on the floor, I found two discarded cotton dresses and a worn rayon nightgown, which I cut down to a slip. Paul was lucky enough to meet a factory owner willing to sell him shirts and slacks. When I arrived at the office, Boerma promised me that I could buy a new wardrobe in Brussels later that month.

We sat down and Boerma gave us a rundown of what had developed in Holland while we were in the interrogation camp. Large areas of Zeeland and the province of South Holland had been flooded by the Germans. People ran for their lives. He told us how the Germans had sent over a special demolition squad to systematically destroy the Amsterdam and Rotterdam docks, cranes and warehouses. Obviously the oil refineries would be the next to go, but currently they were still intact. We listened stoically to the account of the devastation until we heard the description of the destroyed harbors. Then, observing the shock on Paul's face, I realized that he, too, was thinking that we had jeopardized our lives for nothing. The docks and warehouses we had noted on the thin paper we carried across the enemy lines had been blown out of existence during the week we were imprisoned.

After telling us what had happened in the North, Boerma turned his attention to the South. First he warned us that German soldiers were still sneaking across the river to blow up strategic points. He then explained that the whole world was now aware of the plight of the starving Dutch.

In England, Queen Wilhelmina received promises from the London War Office, the Ministry of Food and the Supreme Headquarters Allied Expeditionary Forces (SHAEF), that after the liberation, supplies and transportation would come from Montgomery's 21st Army Group and the United States would provide most of the food.

We were happy to hear that American food had been gathered and was waiting on docks and airports in England. At our first meeting with the Allies, we had learned that the relief offered by the Red Cross organizations of Sweden and Switzerland was now inadequate and no plans for distribution had been made.

Boerma then told us about other authorities involved. They included the Dutch Military Authority (Militair Gezag), the Allied Civil Affairs, a unit of SHAEF organized to help civilians during and after the fighting, the Food Distribution in the South which Boerma himself headed, and the one under Louwes in the North.

"So, Paul," Boerma sighed, "I think you should start an outline for our distribution plan. Don't worry about anyone else. If you offer these organizations a good plan, they'll be happy to accept it. Then later of course, they'll get the honor!"

He smiled and tried to look comforting.

Dismayed, Paul was ready to leave the confusion and go fight alongside the Allies. But instead, sitting on a rickety chair in Boerma's office and working on a corner of a table, he devised the CNV-B2 Master plan. CNV were the initials of Commissariaat Nood Voorziening, the relief organization, and B2 was the Allied code for our particular area.

Finding competent leaders willing to give up their time to help our plan was a first priority. I made a list of large companies in the South and we drove to one of the biggest factory complexes in the world, Philips Gloeilampen N.V., the Philips Electrical Works, in Eindhoven.

The directors were seated in the safety of their board room in a partly bombed-out plant when we came in. Paul knew he had to get their attention immediately. He started his speech by saying:

"Have you ever seen a starving woman drop dead in the street right in front of you?"

He paused. "Have you ever had a hungry child die in your arms?"

Paul slowly eyed every member of his audience. "That's starvation! And that's what is happening in the North — in your own country — right now!"

He had captured their full attention and continued, "For once in your life you will have a chance to help your fellow men. Not for profit, not for glory, not for fun. It may even turn out to be a big headache. But, later, when you see hope come into the eyes of the hungry, you'll never forget it. You will know then that this was the most important effort you could *EVER* have made."

There was a stunned silence in the room. Then they all questioned him at once. At first they thought only of their own plants which had to be rebuilt, but in the end they only asked him when they could start.

"Right away!!" Paul answered. "The ultimate goal is to feed an estimated four and a half million people up north. One of the biggest problems is that we do *not* know when the war will end and we can start; we do *not* know the circumstances; and we do *not* know what we will find there. The only thing we do know is that these people will need an easily digestible ration of 1800 calories per person per day, as soon as possible. Not a simple assignment gentlemen."

They looked pensively at each other, now quite aware of the problems.

Encouraged by this success, Paul and Boerma went to the small town of Oss. There the Hartog factory, part of Unilever, the giant Anglo-Dutch consumer products company, was headed by M.M.van Hengel. A handsome man, who stood straight as a candle, van Hengel agreed to help almost immediately, also offering the assistance of his office staff.

With these manufacturing giants behind us, we had a good start and we were even more elated when van Hengel assumed command. For six months these men, on loan from their companies, masterminded the project. We called them the "Brain-trust," and Paul was proud to be one of them. With their un-bureaucratic planning, they made quick decisions and believed nothing was impossible.

Van Hengel turned out to be our "Eisenhower," having to lead and pacify the ten strong-willed members of the Brain-trust, who had been used to taking command themselves. He also had his disappointments when he tried to get action. He was outranked by the

Dutch Military Authority, which was formed in England and had not suffered from a Nazi occupation. But they, in turn, had to take orders from the Allied 21st Army Group. However, van Hengel kept the main goal in sight and refused to be befuddled by a few who wanted personal gain. He succeeded. When it was all over he had the satisfaction of hearing that the B2 plan had worked well, and the starving people of the North were enthusiastic about the fast provision of food without governmental delays.

"And with glowing enthusiasm we started," van Hengel would say in his farewell speech eleven months later. "Often we had violent arguments, but our cameraderie never left us."

Indeed, we were quite congenial, having a common goal much larger than ourselves. We had no time to squabble. We needed all our energy to help get food to the North as soon as possible. Paul and I had to tell our story at least a hundred times. Every time we spoke, another person offered help.

Outgrowing the abandoned textile school where we started, our next office was the convent, Ave Maria. With a name like that we had to watch our language, which was not easy. The place was cold, drafty and miserable. We could never find each other's offices in the maze of halls, stairs, and secluded rooms. We ran out of tables and chairs, and sometimes had to sit on the floor between piles of files. But we continued working, even on weekends and holidays, often in unheated rooms. Our biggest worry was that our efforts would be too late.

After a lengthy talk with Queen Wilhelmina, Winston Churchill was made fully aware of the desperate situation, and he sent a letter to President Roosevelt. Describing the starvation in western Holland, Churchill cautioned, "I fear that we may soon be in the presence of a tragedy."

And then there was Henkie, one of the many big-eyed, hollow-cheeked little boys who hung around to do odd jobs for a piece of chocolate. He was special with his blond curls and deep blue eyes. When someone said, "We like little boys," he responded seriously, "But I am a *big* boy!"

The men, perhaps thinking of their own sons, spoiled him. After a few weeks it was heartwarming to see his little cheeks fill out, and get some color, and his eyes begin to sparkle. Little Henk became our unforgettable mascot.

I started out as Paul's secretary but was later put in charge of housing. Armed with American army blankets, I convinced reluctant home-owners to rent rooms to our staff. But by far my most interesting job was working with the Information Department.

Through the Canadian Army we obtained an officers' mess. This bothered the civilians to some extent, as the Allies gave us some luxuries, but only we knew how hard we worked. We had no time to worry about our image.

As time went by the organization grew. Textiles, medicine and fuel came under our jurisdiction. Drivers, couriers and nurses were added to the staff. Paul found many Dutch specialists in the South: leaders in water transport, distributors of coal and textiles, and nutritionists for mass feeding. They became section heads. Ration cards were printed and flyers to explain their use, as well as signs and posters to tell the public where and when the food would be available.

In the kitchen of Ave Maria, a dietician developed recipes for people in varying degrees of starvation. Thirteen large cities were chosen as distribution centers in the B2 area and we hoped to use some of the men of the original distribution offices there. To transport workers and food, the Allies gave us trucks, motorcycles and gasoline. But we had to scout out our own private cars and chauffeurs. We even hired divers to remove the ships the Germans had blown up and sunk to block the harbor of Rotterdam.

All in all, the CNV-B2 plan became a large and vibrant organization. Because time was short, we made some mistakes and hired a few bad apples along the way, but most of the four hundred were honest and capable people. Without them, the relief organization for the three western provinces never could have been successful.

Our planning had just started when the Battle of the Bulge occurred. It nearly ended all hopes for timely help to the North, and worried many people in the South who had outwitted the Germans.

On December 14, the Germans launched their counterattack, intending to split the British and American forces and recapture Antwerp. Four Panzer Divisions rushed deep into Belgium, creating a "bulge" in the Allied line. Field Marshall von Rundstedt, whom Hitler had reappointed as supreme commander for the assault, was at first reluctant to use troops meant to defend German soil. Somehow a very annoyed Hitler quickly convinced him.

Helped by severe winter weather, which prevented air support to the surprised Allied ground force, the Germans crashed through American lines into the snow-covered Ardennes Forest. Repeating the trick used during the invasion of Holland, some German units wore American uniforms to spread confusion among the Allies. And it worked. It was tough enough to distinguish between the various similar outfits of our friends, let alone our enemy.

Paul and I were alarmed that all we had risked for, all we had worked for, might now be delayed just long enough to be in vain. We also worried that both of us could be caught again. We read in our Brabants Nieuwsblad of revengeful Germans shooting civilians and burning villages to the ground to punish anybody who had aided the Allies.

The Germans managed to penetrate nearly 60 miles before the weather cleared enough to permit the Allied Air Force into the fight. When the assault was finally stopped, the Germans had surrounded Bastogne. Battering the city, they demanded General Mc Aucliffe to surrender.

"Nuts!" was the American general's now-famous answer. We all laughed at that, convinced that he must have added a few more explicit words! Although their situation was precarious, the Allies held out until General Patton's fierce fighters came storming to the rescue, hitting the southern flank of the bulge. The Germans reeled back and Hitler's last gasp, the Battle of the Bulge, was over.

It was the middle of March, more than three months after we arrived in Brabant and submitted our code to the radio station. Slouched in an overstuffed chair, I idly turned on the radio just in time for the news.

"This is London, the BBC. Americans have seized the Remagen Bridge across the Rhine. Cologne has fallen ... U.S. bombers hit Tokyo."

The sonorous voice droned on with battle news from all over the world. I listened with only half an ear. Then suddenly ... "And now some special messages. *Give Terry a Bone!*

There it was, our secret code! I yelled for Paul, who came running in time to hear the repeat. *Give Terry a Bone!* We both burst out laughing and threw our arms around each other, hugging and kissing. What an emotion it was to hear our own code, planned what seemed an eternity ago. After our embrace we stood motionless.

For a moment I felt uneasy, but I shrugged it off. "Well, they finally came through. Paul, d'you think Louwes or anybody up north heard it?"

"I hope so, but maybe not. Not too many radios have batteries anymore. I can't worry about it now. I've got to go to Brussels to meet with the Allies." Paul soon left the house and I fell back into the chair, daydreaming.

Suddenly he returned. "You can come along. It's safe to go now, but hurry up!" he said, impatiently drumming his fingers on the door.

I rushed around, threw on my only dress and was ready. In half an hour we were off to Belgium in Boerma's car, driven by his loyal driver. Paul was to meet van Hengel, who had left earlier, Dutch Major Kruls, and the Allied commander of our area at Dutch Army Headquarters in Brussels. We didn't have time enough to get an official permit for the Belgium border, so the trick was to push our way into an Allied convoy and act as if we belonged. It was a scary maneuver, but it worked. We squeezed into a long Red Ball supply line of trucks and drove at a steady 30 miles an hour toward Antwerp. As we followed along, we noticed the real devastation which the V-weapons had caused. We cringed when we saw the demolished Rex theater, where seven hundred people, half of them Allied soldiers, had died.

From a bluff we overlooked Antwerp harbor, its docks and ships waiting to be unloaded. We watched little figures skittering about, like an accelerated Disney cartoon, lifting, stretching, heaving, unloading and loading, and moving out. Mountains of equipment from the generous United States were neatly stacked on the piers. Huge coils of wire and rope, piles of netting, and rows of oil drums lined one side; jeeps, trucks, cars, forklifts, rubber boats, bridge parts and pontoons on the other side filled an enormous area.

Jerry's V-weapons had been quite accurate lately. In the previous months Antwerp had been hit with over 500 buzz-bombs, and later with at least as many V-2 rockets.

But nobody stopped working. They went on as if disaster from the sky was not possible. It was an unbelievable sight. We now understood what a tremendous logistical feat the whole invasion was.

"To think the Allies would do all this for us," Paul said with reverence. "Look at these Yanks, all the way from the States. They probably don't know any more about us than we know about them. Look at them, Babes, these men have all the guts in the world. Guts and dedication! God, how can we ever repay them!"

Paul was impressed with what he saw that he couldn't help philosophizing. "Can you imagine all this was necessary to beat this Heinie-bastard? If only we had stamped this miserable carpet-chewer, this Hitler, into the ground. If we had opposed him right away, we wouldn't have needed all this. We wouldn't have spilled all the blood. It's still unbelievable how many people danced to his tune, and still do!"

We were fortunate to be behind the scenes during the liberation. Many people saw the Allies march into town, but they never saw the staggering amounts of material, the ingenious equipment, or the enormity of the whole operation.

I had looked forward to the filled stores in Brussels, finding healthy people and a normal life, but after seeing this, none of it seemed important anymore. We both wanted to get to work as soon as we could, excited to do our share in the liberation. We had committed ourselves to helping those people in northern Holland who could not help themselves. This was our challenge.

Brussels was a wonderland. The stores were filled with merchandise and it took me a while to make up my mind what to buy first. Unfortunately I never finished my shopping because, while I was there, a V-1 dropped on a department store nearby. In panic I ran back to the car. I was lucky to find the parking lot and our chauffeur in the mob scene. We sped to the outskirts of the city where Paul and van Hengel were meeting. Two more buzz-bombs exploded in the center of town that day, making me think that all the beautiful stores were not worth the visit. The Germans obviously had made Antwerp and Brussels their new targets.

While Paul and van Hengel discussed their meeting with the Allies and expressed their delight with the promised help for the B2 plan, we enjoyed a perfectly delicious dinner. I nearly felt guilty savoring the fabulous dishes and the excellent wine.

Back at the heatless hotel, I showed Paul the two identical pairs of white flannel pajamas I had bought for us, the only ones in the store I could find in a hurry. He laughed at this ridiculous purchase. Sitting in bed in the pajamas that evening, we looked like a couple of bookends.

It was freezing outside and in the middle of the night our room was so cold that we asked the hotel staff for more blankets. There were none, so we pulled the large Persian rug from under the furniture and piled it on top of the bed, where it stood like an Arabian tent. Suddenly the bookends were gone; a sheik in a white burnoose beckoned me inside the tent, and I wriggled in.

24

When we returned from Brussels we started each day determined that the food be ready to go north at the shortest notice. Each night we were depressed because there were no Allied victories to speed us along. Only later did we realize that the emphasis of the war had been shifted to the southern part of the Rhine, the Ruhr and the Saar areas. In our part of the river the only action was infiltration by a few Germans. Such bravado seemed to be just isolated cases. Why were these Krauts fighting so hard, knowing in their hearts that the game was over?

I found one answer while having lunch in the officers mess. Scanning the newspaper, I spotted a headline, "The Forgotten Front." The story told of a tenacious group of German soldiers at the naval base of St. Nazaire, who, although surrounded by Allies and French Maquis, refused to capitulate. Their loyalty to Hitler was reinforced by the threat that the family of any soldier, who gave up, would be seized by the Gestapo and shot. It was just not an idle warning. Most soldiers had heard that when the German commander of Paris, Dietrich von Choltitz, disobeyed Hitler's order to destroy the famous buildings and monuments before surrendering to the Allies, his wife and children were picked up from their home and executed. This dreadful story went around and we believed it to be true.

Hitler was expressing his mad viciousness in other ways. He ordered a "scorched earth policy," obliterating everything while retreating, so the incoming Allies would find a "wasteland." In Holland this meant more flooding. The dikes of the huge Wieringermeer polder were dynamited. The water gushed across the meadows, drowning hundreds of cattle and destroying thousands of acres of fertile land, Holland's bread basket. Within a few days the water rose to the second floor of the farmhouses, ruining everything inside. The owners fled for their lives. It also flushed out

many unfortunate underdivers. We heard so much bad news from
the north these days that we became frantic, feeling utterly
helpless.

In our first weeks in Brabant Paul and I had no time to look
around. Later, when the organization was rolling, we went out and
spent some weekends with old friends. While we were out of the
office we noticed more of what the Allies were doing.

On Sunday we were inspired to see the soldiers kneeling in the
rubble of a church to receive communion. Many were Poles who
were part of the 21st Army Group. We all felt sad for them when
they explained that they still were not free, for the Russians now
occupied their country. The people of Brabant took them in their
hearts, happy to see their girls dating someone of their own religion. Watching the Poles with their blonde dates, our chauffeur
said dryly, "In the next war Poland can just send uniforms down."

One sunny winter weekend we spent with friends on their
beautiful estate in Rysbergen, a small town near the Belgian border, where we met many Canadian, British and American guests. A
few Aussies arrived later, truly a wonderfully wild bunch. They got
the party going in no time! It was interesting to watch the different
nationalities. They were like a breath of spring air after the dour
Nazis. I admired the way the British officers handled the relation-
ship with their batmen. They went to the same parties and had a
jolly-good-old time; the next day neither one talked about it and
they both knew their place again.

Not all was fun and relaxation on our visit. As Rysbergen is
only a few miles from Antwerp and right on the path of the V-1's,
we heard many come over. Two fell short of their destination and
exploded in the thick woods around the house. That's when we huddled in the cellar again, holding our breath, listening to the chucking sound of this eerie monster, and the rattling of our anti-aircraft
batteries. After a while we refused to let the doodle-bugs, as the
British called them, bother us. To stay sane, we needed a few hours
to forget, so we shut out the sounds outside by turning the phonograph louder, laughing and kissing, while dancing cheek-to-cheek.
The Allies amused themselves thoroughly. Paul was no slouch either. He found some attractive and healthy-looking WACs.

The British showed us the Lambeth Walk; the Americans
taught us how to jitterbug, and we hopped along until our feet
could not move any longer, and it was finally time for all to go
home.

"Don't cross the white ribbon along the road," our host warned us casually when we left, "There're mines on the other side!"

After a few hours of fun in the evening, we faced some grim problems the next day again. Every morning the news from the north grew worse. More executions, more flooding, more razzias. Schools were closed. Children foraged from garbage cans, scraping the sides of the empty soup kitchen drums hoping to find a tiny morsel. Hungry men, plundering a food store, were shot on the spot; their bodies, a grisly warning, left in the store's window all day and night. The food distribution ration was down to 300 calories per person per day, mainly sugar beets with a few potatoes. There was no electricity, no gas, no form of light or heat. We tried to ignore these horror stories by working feverishly.

The only good news from the outside world was that the Allies, surprised at finding a bridge intact at Remagen, had suddenly crossed the Rhine and established a beachhead into Germany. Despite a press blackout, we knew that the spring offensive had started. At night we heard tanks rolling by, pelted by incessant rain. Because of the storms, they were heading north without air support. That worried us and we said an extra prayer for them.

When the press ended its security silence, we heard that Zutphen and Deventer were in Allied hands. Hurrah! My sister and her family were now free. In two more days of tough fighting, the Canadians liberated Voorthuizen where my parents lived. By March 26, the thousands of concrete pillboxes, bunkers and other obstacles of the formidable Siegfried Line had been overrun. The British, French and Americans rushed through the German countryside to meet the Russians who were storming through Poland towards Berlin.

Some concentration camps were liberated. Allied soldiers were shocked beyond words when they saw the carnage. Now they knew what they were fighting for! Who could ever have imagined the extent of man's inhumanity to man!

Although tragedy and death seemed to be our constant companions, it was still a great shock when Franklin D. Roosevelt died. Sad that he had not lived to see the results of his tremendous effort to free the world for democracy, we stood with all the rest of free Holland for a few minutes of silence to honor the American president.

As the action crept closer to the end, van Hengel felt we could no longer operate without a uniform, and so I was measured for one and inducted into the army. Persons of recognizable rank, such as van Hengel, flew to London for installation. He was awarded the rank of full colonel. Paul, deemed too young to be second-in-command, was made van Hengel's adjutant with the rank of captain. All department heads and other administrators were made instant majors and captains. Five of us women were given dark blue Eisenhower jackets and blue skirts with patches of CNV and the Dutch lion on our sleeves and beret. We had no official rank, but we considered ourselves to be lieutenants. Because it was flattering and easy to take care of, I was delighted with the outfit. We learned to salute and often giggled when the Allied officers invariably reacted in mock surprise. No wonder we all fell in love with the Allies!

To celebrate our new ranks, some generous co-workers dragged a case of wine into the restaurant we used as our mess. That evening we all drank too much, but it only served to regenerate the spirit of brotherhood, which had been lost during the frenzy of organizing.

At that exuberant moment, Paul's brother, Rob, looking thin and wan, suddenly appeared. After three previous attempts, he had finally escaped over the rivers. We were thrilled to see him. Rob fell on the food. Utterly exhausted, he nearly passed out after only one glass of wine. He did manage to give me the latest news from home before he fell asleep on a sofa in the hall.

In the last weeks many desperate people tried to escape. Hunger forced them to take terrible chances. In the end even our brave river pilots loaded their boats with their own families and, once they got across, stayed there.

Our family in The Hague suffered greatly and Rob was not sure they would survive. His sister and her husband were so weak, he said, they could barely lift a small bag of coal to fill the little stove for their family Christmas. Huddling together, they celebrated this holy feast with a pathetic dinner of soup made of sugar beets and one measly kohlrabi.

Rob's description of their starvation was very depressing. No wonder we had estimated that to satisfy the hunger pangs of about four million people, we would need six and a half million pounds of potatoes each day. That would give each person only one and three-quarter pounds. We asked ourselves again, would we be able to do it? Would we be ready in time?

In the meantime the Allies pushed on. They bypassed the strongly defended western part of Holland and went deeper into Germany, expecting the Germans to surrender. We were delighted

The RAF dropped little bags of tea over Holland with the inspiring words: "Keep the Spirit".

Paul was promoted to captain in March, 1945.

LEGITIMATIE-BEWIJS

Houder dezes

M.A. van Dillen-Schoorel

Persoonsbewijs No G 41/322679

is werkzaam bij het Militair Gezag (Commissariaat Noodvoorziening) en is bestemd standplaats te nemen

te Utrecht (Staf)

Te Velde 1 Mei 1945

o.l De Res.Kpt.   De Commissaris Noodvoorziening
                        De Reserve-Major
                        De Res.Lt.Kol.
(Ir.M.v.Wesel)   M.M.v.Hengel

IDENTITY-CARD

Bearer

M.A. van Dillen-Schoorel

Civil id. card number C 41/322679

holds an appointment with the Netherlands Military Authority (Relief Organization for the B 2 area) and is

liable to go to Utrecht (Staf)

In the field 1 Mei 1945

p/o The Res.Kpt.   The Commissaris Noodvoorziening
                        The Reserve-Major
                        The Res.Lt.Kol.
(Ir.M.v.Wesel)   M.M.v.Hengel

duimafdruk

I am in the Army now, inducted by the B-2 Relief Plan, April, 1945.

VERSPREID DOOR DE GEALLIEERDE LUCHTMACHT   LAATSTE NUMMER, 10 MEI 1945

DUITSCHLAND CAPITULEERT

In den nacht van Zondag 6 op Maandag 7 Mei 1945 onderteekenden generaal Jodl en admiraal Von Friedeburg op het Geallieerde Hoofdkwartier te Rheims de overeenkomst waarbij alle Duitsche strijdkrachten zich onvoorwaardelijk overgeven. Midden tegenover de Duitsche gedelegeerden zit de chef van Eisenhowers staf, generaal Bedell Smith. Vierde van rechts is de Russische vertegenwoordiger, generaal Souslaparov.

Het Derde Rijk onderteekent de onvoorwaardelijke overgave — eerst te Rheims, dan te Berlijn

In een eenvoudig klaslokaal van een Fransche ambachtsschool in de buurt van Rheims heeft Duitschland zich onvoorwaardelijk overgegeven. Tegen een achtergrond van het verlichte stafkaarten zaten vijftien mannen rond een oude gro_ten tafel, die de sporen droeg van honderden schouders, die er hun messen in hadden zitten kerven. Voor de fotografen en filmoperators was een speciale verlichting geïnstalleerd, die de gezichten der deelnemende scherp afteekende. Aan den muur een kalender met den datum: 7 Mei 1945.

Keitel, chef van het Oberkommando der Wehrmacht, geteekend dezen Wereldoorlog, onderteekent te Berlijn Duitschlands onvoorwaardelijke overgave

Aan de rechterzijde der tafel zaten de drie Duitschers, Admiraal van Friedeburg, Jodl en hun adjudant. Tegenover hen zaten Gen. Bedell-Smith, Chef van den Staf van Generaal Eisenhower, de Fransche Generaal Sevez, de Russische Kolonaal Souslaparov en nog eenige andere hooge officieren en tolken. Zoodra verscheen te doen de teekening was het gedaan.

Half drie 's morgens komt de Geallieerde delegatie binnen. Generaal Smith, de ambtenaren aan het fort. Eisenhower, het teeken. De strenge verlichting maakt het geheele fort nog helder. Om precies 2 uur 39 minuten de Duitsche gedelegeerden binnen en blijven staan achter hun stoelen staan tot Generaal Sevez hen met een teeken uitnoodigt plaats te nemen. Zes minuten geheele de onderteekening. Generaal Smith vraagt hun of zij de beteekenis van het document begrepen hebben. Zij knikken en gaan weder zitten. Het wordt twintig voor woord zonder te zeggen uit te wisselen en zonder iemand aan te kijken. Dan te spreken aanvoerdende onderteekening. Om 2 uur 41 heeft Duitschland gecapituleerd.

IN DE RUÏNES VAN BERLIJN

Op 6 Mei arriveerde in Berlijn Sovjet Geallieerde vertegenwoordigers, vertegen aan de hoofdstad van de overwonnen Duitsche Rijk Duitschlands capitulatie te teekenen. Het eenige moment werd een gebouw en zonden der een aantal te gecombineerde met waren van 11 November 1918 wel herinnerde aan den ellende Duitsche geteekend. En hoewel Engeland en Amerika vertegenwoordigd waren in bestond-te om 13 uur de troepen de secretaris generaal kon de rede er nog enkele andere kamers naar onmiddellijk Keitel kreeg het van de Duitschlands onvoorwaardelijke Keitel overgave alleen in wereldgeschiedenis teeken...

De overwinnaar Generaal Dwight D. Eisenhower heeft zich in weinig jaren tijds opgewerkt tot opperbevelhebber van een leger hetwelk geschiedenis gemaakt heeft. Het is een brillante carrière geweest van een werkelijk groot man.

The last edition, May 10th, 1945 of the Flying Dutchman newspaper, dropped from planes by the Allied Air Force. The headline says: "Germany Capitulates."

Food by air. An Allied flier explains "Operation Manna" to his surprised colleagues. "And then I dove to 100 meters and dropped two thousand loaves of bread right on target."

Canadians arriving in Amsterdam, May 18, 1945.

The first Canadians arriving in Holland, April, 1945, Voorthuizen.

The German Surrender
At Field Marshall Montgomery's 21st Army group HQ on Luneburg Heath. Montgomery is seen reading the surrender terms to the German delegation.   IMPERIAL WAR MUSEUM, LONDON

Germans surrender to Canadian General Foulkes in Hotel De Wereld, Holland.

Seyss-Inquart (with glasses), the Nazi Reichskommissar for the Netherlands is arrested by Dutch police right after the war.

Paul in the liberated jeep, 1945.

Terry, after the liberation, May, 1945, on our army car with the invasion star.

The Wieringermeer polder. The Germans blew up the dikes and thousands of acres of lowlands were inundated, 1945.

"Operation Manna," food from heaven.

Food arrives in Rotterdam courtesy of the U.S.A.

Three generations, Bas van Mill and family with photo of his father, Bas, Hardinxveld, Holland, 1986.

Plate presented by Queen Wilhelmina after the war, honoring Paul and myself for going through enemy lines and organizing the B-2 food relief plan. Our names are inscribed on the back.

Delft Tile Plate depicting the ship's wharf (home and buildings) of the van Mill family as it was in 1944.

that the main battles were not fought on our soil. Radio Orange carried Prince Bernard's warning not to cheer prematurely this time.

The truth became stranger than fiction. While the Allies and Russians met in Germany, Seyss-Inquart had Dr. Louwes escorted through the fighting lines to arrange with van Hengel for an integration of the CNV-B2 plan. We heard conflicting stories about German generals attempting deals with the Allies to save their own skin, or at least not be delivered to the Russians. But General Montgomery made no promises. Instead, he told Seyss-Inquart that if he prevented assistance in bringing food *now*, he would be held responsible for the starvation of the Dutch and later be tried accordingly. Seyss-Inquart did not seem overly concerned and continued to be his arrogant self. After many talks he finally agreed to allow Allied planes to drop food in the North.

On April 29, nearly 4500 British Lancasters and about 800 American Flying Fortresses flew a designated corridor via Tilburg, den Bosch and Utrecht, to drop tons of dried food, along with packages of flour and tea, into the white painted circles of ten different areas. German Grüne Polizei guarded the spots. It was aptly called Operation Manna.

One of the drop circles was on Ypenburg where in 1940 the first Germans parachuted out of their Junkers. Another was on the race track near the Galema home. I could picture their joy watching something good fall from the sky for a change. On their way north the planes of mercy, with their black and white checkered wings, passed so close by our windows that we could see the pilots waving to us. We waved back at them, filled with emotion. We knew that for millions this would truly be "food from Heaven."

The pilots, with tears in their eyes, told us afterwards that the emaciated Dutch people ran along with the planes, cheering as much as their weakness would allow. Hearing them talk, I was sure the flyers would never forget this special mission of dropping food instead of bombs. On April 30, 1945, the second day of the five that the Allies parachuted food to the Dutch, Adolf Hitler shot himself in his Berlin bunker, bringing his evil life to an end.

It was the beginning of May and we were feeling pretty smug. Our supplies were stacked in warehouses around Brabant, waiting for Liberation Day. We thought we were completely ready, when van Hengel suddenly burst into Paul's office saying they were having transportation problems.

"We're short ten trucks," he announced bluntly. "I've talked to Brussels but the Allies are busy with the Russians and don't have time for our problems. Do you know how to get any?"

Paul, dismayed, drew a deep breath and swore. Not stopping to ask how the oversight had happened, he said, "I'll get those bloody trucks, but don't ask me how. Just give me ten F.N.'s and ten reliable drivers."

The encounter of the two sounded very familiar to me. I remembered another conversation eight months earlier when it was Louwes saying, "Paul, I need a man — "

Even before Paul had collected his ten handguns and left, van Hengel sought me out, asking my opinion on his chances of success. I thought for a moment. It wouldn't be the first time soldiers had traded war materiel, blankets, jackets, even motorcycles. The war was about over. No one would miss a few trucks, and the F.N. army gun was a desirable souvenir. Without hesitation I said, "I'm sure he can."

Van Hengel looked at me and smiled.

That night ten men, cocky and in great spirits, drove off. Two days later ten trucks pulled up outside Ave Maria. We cheered the whole happy lot of them, and they waved back with the victory sign. Van Hengel heard the commotion and rushed outside, beaming. He pushed his way through the crowd to get to Paul and thank him.

Years later, van Hengel visited us in the States. It was a memorable day. We reminisced about the experiences which had been such an important part of our lives. After dinner, as he walked toward the door to leave, he turned around with a twinkle in his eye. As if he had just remembered something, he said softly, "Just one more thing, Paul, how did you do it?"

Paul grinned. He had been expecting the question.

"Sorry, sir," he replied politely, as if van Hengel were still his superior officer. "If you mean the trucks, I made a promise then never to tell."

Van Hengel left, still puzzled, but smiling.

The trucks came just in time to go to Amersfoort and Utrecht, being the first distribution centers to be liberated. We loaded them with food and medicines, and sent them off with cheers and garlands of flowers. Surprisingly we saw them return the next day. They could go no farther than Arnhem as the Germans around Amersfoort had started to fight again, and the roads were packed with troops.

The drivers came back, even happier than when they left. Because overnight, in pure frustration, they had guzzled several bottles of Dutch gin.

25

Finally, after nearly five long, unbelievable years, the day arrived! Early Saturday, May 5, 1945, we heard that the Germans had surrendered Holland, Denmark and western Germany to General Montgomery in his tent on the Lüneburger Heath in northwest Germany. In the last issue of "The Flying Dutchman" we read the historic story of that cold and rainy afternoon:

In Montgomery's tent stood a simple wooden table covered with a blue cloth, and an inkwell in between two microphones. Earlier that afternoon, Montgomery had shown the Germans a map that proved the German position was hopeless. Now they were back with their answer.

Montgomery was busy when the Germans arrived. Without looking up from his papers, he made them wait 20 minutes, then went to greet them. Passing a group of journalists, he said, *"Gentlemen, this is the moment."*

Von Friedenburg, Kiensl and the others were there, waiting. Von Friedenburg looked upset and Kienzl was the model German officer, complete with monocle. Montgomery entered the tent, sat down and motioned the Germans to take their places. He slowly put on his glasses and said:

"I will now read you the conditions of surrender."

The Germans just sat there, no sign of emotion on their faces. Gravely, with the smallest note of triumph, Monty read the document. This was the moment he had been fighting for since El Alamein, Tunisia, Italy, through France, Belgium, Holland and Germany . . . One by one as the five Germans signed, not a word was spoken. Monty took the unpainted wooden pen and said, "And now, I'll sign for the Allied Commander, General Dwight Eisenhower."

This entire ceremony lasted five minutes and one million Germans had unconditionally surrendered."

The following day, at the small and unassuming Hotel de Wereld in Wageningen, our country's big moment came. A tired and nervous German General Blaskowitz surrendered his 25th Army to an unperturbed and poised General Charles Foulkes, Commander of the Canadian 1st Army. The latter had asked Prince Bernard to be present as Commander of the Dutch Forces of the Interior. We smiled hearing that our debonair Prince arrived in Seyss-Inquart's large black Mercedes, recognizable by the plate mounted in front with the letters RKI (Reichskommissar I). The Resistance had found the automobile somewhere in the North and had presented it to our Prince, gleefully expressing their feeling that it was the perfect car for this occasion.

When we heard the news, we whooped and hollered and ran through the mess, then sang the American, British, and Dutch anthems, holding glasses of wine. Thank God, the nightmare was finally over. We ran outside and joined the throngs of boisterous people dancing hand in hand in ever larger growing circles. We kissed and hugged, and carried on throughout the rest of the day.

Back in the office we heard that for our own safety, we could not enter the North yet. The Allies were not able to reach Amsterdam for another two days. In the meantime the Germans were shooting and killing the Dutch. It was a dreadful situation, now that it was supposed to be over. Only van Hengel was allowed to enter the distressed area. Our instructions were to stay in the office, so we could gather at a moment's notice.

We waited five long days while celebrations were going on everywhere. No civilian wanted to be out there celebrating more than I did, and no soldier was longing to get home more than I was. I looked dolefully out of the window at the wildly enthusiastic crowds of Dutch and Allies, who were carousing day and night, burning the air raid shelters and dancing around the flames until the last faint embers snuffed out.

The delay was unfortunate, but we couldn't do anything about it. Once in the North, we didn't lose a minute and worked with all our heart and soul. We knew the plan was successful when, after divers cleared the canal to Rotterdam, we watched the unloading of more than seventy Liberty ships and Dutch Merchant Marine vessels. The worst hunger was over after three weeks, and people started to regain their zest for life. Only much later did we hear the frightful statistics: more than 20,000 Dutch had died from starvation during the Hunger Winter.

Meanwhile, the Resistance leaders of Brabant were impatient. They wanted fast justice for Dutch Nazi members and collaborators, infuriated that these "wrong" people continued to walk around free after killing and betraying their countrymen for years. One newspaper defined the problem, writing, "What is to be done with about 10,000 political arrests in the South, which grew to 120,000 in our entire country, when the North was freed?"

Indeed, how to mete out justice for our fellow citizens was a challenge. It took a long time before these problems were solved, some never were. But those who were judged in court to be traitors went to jail or were executed. Those who were judged only by their neighbors wore the stigma of having been "wrong" for years to come.

26

On May 11, another one of those glorious spring days, we finally drove off with food and medicine.

"Hurry, hurry!" we goaded each other. Every hour someone, somewhere, was starving to death. There was no time for fights, petty jealousies, or wondering who was getting credit for what.

"Just get it done," said van Hengel, who never stopped shepherding the emergency food effort. Our first group of sixteen trucks roared off, garlanded with flowers, their canvasses flapping in the wind. Four dispatch riders, two ahead of the convoy and two at the end, kept us together. Allied billboards urged us to "Keep 'em Rolling" on the Red Ball Express Highway, as we sped over pontoon bridges that crossed our rivers. Finally the oversized trucks had to slow down to inch over the narrow dikes with flooded grazing lands on either side. Five years earlier, the Dutch had flooded these lands, hoping to keep the Germans out. Now the Germans had done the same.

I had requested to visit my parents in the country for a few hours, and so was able to ride with Paul in the first truck on the way to Voorthuizen, where they lived. Silently we observed the devastation in Arnhem, Nymegen, and Oosterbeek. We were again saddened by the damage done when the dikes were blown up to inundate the land.

I looked across large stretches of water that seemed endless. The bloated bodies of cows and pigs floated in a grotesque water ballet. The stench was overwhelming. Bare trees stood rippling in the man-made flood. Occasionally a brave little blossom sprouted just above the water line. I cringed when I spotted the body of an Allied soldier in the reeds. I was afraid to think how he got there.

Our trucks started to overtake a convoy of slowly rumbling tanks snaking through the flat country on our right. We slowed down. We crawled along behind the tanks, crossing many hastily made Bailey bridges of prefabricated steel sections, and finally reached the fertile area of the Betuwe. Before the war my parents had taken us children there to see the fruit trees blooming in a cloud of white and pink blossoms. Far away, against the horizon, the sails of a windmill were daintily etched against the sky. It was so quiet everywhere, and so dead. There were no herons standing on one leg in the ditches, no frogs plopping in the water to quickly hide under the lily pads. No aristocratic storks clapped their bills, perched on their nests high on a chimney. They were not the only ones who could not find their nests! Only the clouds moved, scudding white and grey surging masses, an artist's delight.

At the rim of the Veluwe, near Ede, Paul slowed the truck to a crawl and I jumped into a clump of grass, cushioning my return to free Dutch soil. Brushing the dust from my uniform, I watched the rest of the convoy go on. Allied trucks, rolled by, one after another, painted green with the white invasion star, which was the symbol of liberation for millions.

At every window my friends were smiling and waving and I gamely waved back at them. They were now going to The Hague without me. For five months we had planned, worked, and played together and now I was suddenly alone.

Pensively looking around for a possible ride, I saw a Red Cross truck coming my way. The driver was in a hurry, but agreed to take me nearer to my destination. After a short ride he stopped and pointed to a village in the distance. After I jumped out I just stood there for a moment in the pale light of the early sun, wondering how I would find my parents. A church steeple barely visible in the morning mist, appeared as if from a dream, still far away. Was that Voorthuizen?

As I started walking, a milkman with a small horse-cart came clopping along. He looked suspiciously at my uniform, then stopped and graciously offered me a ride. Did he know my father, Dr. Schoorel?

"Yep," he grumbled, starting the horse with a flick of his whip We bounced along in silence, milk cans rattling in the back. The gaunt horse trotted at an amazingly fast pace.

I felt a lump in my throat when I viewed the Veluwe landscape. It was a beautiful nature reservation, sandy with scattered Scotch broom, heather and birch trees, whose white trunks shimmered against the grey horizon. Here and there was a thatched roof farmhouse, quiet and restful.

Sudddenly the landscape changed. The peaceful view was

marred by many abandoned vehicles and a ragged bomb crater next to a blackened hulk stretched out in the sand like a giant dead caterpillar. I shuddered.

"Ho!" The milkman pulled on his reins. I leapt from the cart and ran toward the cottage, dodging the dry-looking heather plants which were all that remained of a once glorious flower garden. In the fall their blossoms would give the whole area a pink-purplish glow, but once the blossoms were gone, the tiny weekend house with its weathered brown boards looked quite dismal.

At the front door I took a deep breath. My heart was pounding. Without so much as a knock, I turned the knob and stepped in. A man was standing with his back towards me, wearing a familiar Harris Tweed jacket and grey flannel slacks, dirty and tattered. When he turned to me he looked as if he had seen a ghost, his eyes wide and unbelieving.

"My God, Babes, you're here, you're alive! Thank God. We worried so much. Your Mom could not sleep, always tossing and turning . . ."

The next moment we fell into each other's arms and I sobbed on my dad's shoulder.

"Thank heaven, you came back," he sighed, tears welling up in his soft grey eyes. I reached up and kissed him on each cheek, and then stood back to look at him.

"Dad, I knew you would make it through somehow," My arms tightened around him. "I was sure you would. How's Mom?"

"She is tired and a lot thinner," he said, sounding almost clinical, "but otherwise fine." We kept on hugging each other.

"Julie and Henk? And the baby?" I asked hurriedly.

"I know they're all right, but we haven't seen them yet," he replied, nervously pushing me toward the door. "Let's find your mother."

We rushed to the back of the cottage, which had been their home ever since they left their house in The Hague some two years earlier.

"Mom, where are you?" he called, but there was no answer. I ran through the kitchen toward the garden, where I spied her at last. She was watering their vegetable garden with a large can. She did not notice me at first and I stood back, letting the picture sink in. My mother looked so feminine, petite, and refined, thinner after a year of worry and hard work, as she bent to her task of survival.

When she spotted me, she let out a scream. We ran towards

each other, and I will never forget her warm embrace! She searched my face until, satisfied with my looks, she felt my uniform, the navy woolen skirt, short Eisenhower jacket, and jaunty beret with its brass lion pin. She touched the military patches on my sleeves, thoughtfully fingering the gold embroidered Dutch lion. I could see she was proud of me.

"Where's Paul?" Mother suddenly remembered my husband.

Beginning with the tale of my journey, we started talking and we could not stop, all the while looking, touching each other, finally just laughing because we were so happy to be alive and together again.

After holding their emotions in check for so long, my parents could not contain themselves. They hurriedly talked about the past year. About nearby Putten, where, in brutal reprisal for the assassination of a hated Nazi officer, the town's 600 men were carried off to a concentration camp and more than half the houses burned down. About the German train which, when strafed by Allied planes, exploded splinters of steel and parts of bodies in uniform into their garden. About the hatred and the pity of it all — the bedraggled refugees fleeing from Arnhem they took into their home; the wounded soldiers and the striking railroad workers they hid in a foxhole dug in the bushes; and finally about the retreating Germans, who drove their tanks right through their garden. While they told me about it, I could still see the fright in their eyes.

"We were so lucky that we were liberated first, a month ago. It took another month for the West to be freed, an awful long time when you have nothing to eat anymore," my mother said pensively. Then she smiled and said, "Those Canadians, they're so handsome, so kind, and so cheerful. They even let the children climb on the tanks! Of course we all thanked and kissed them!"

I smiled, I could just see my exuberant mother hugging and kissing delighted strangers.

After we had shared all, we were quiet, each with our own thoughts. Mother broke the silence, motioning us inside.

"You won't believe it, but I still have some tea left," she said cheerfully. What would the Dutch do without tea in the afternoon? Tea time is for sitting down, and having friends over. It's a moment of relaxation before the "lady" of the house has to start dinner. No matter how hard you worked, how much you scrubbed the floors on hands and knees, at tea time you felt like a lady. Pouring tea is a ceremony. As a child coming home from school, it was a warm, cozy, and comfortable feeling. The Dutch call it "gezellig".

Mother produced the familiar tray of cups and the teapot with the old Chinese silk teacozy. She placed the sugar and milk in front of us. We were ready to talk again.

But I was quiet. For months I had longed to chat with my parents, but now that I was with them I was happy just to be there and say nothing important. I was tired, and after seeing them healthy and well, I was ready for The Hague and to rejoin Paul.

Soon we saw an army truck drive up and Govert, our driver for the day, came to get me. A pleasant young man with his army beret nonchalantly on the back of his head, he greeted us. "Dag mevrouw, dag mynheer. Your husband sent me. We have to leave right away."

My parents looked disappointed, but I had to leave and waved at them from across the heather until the truck turned into the village. Once past the town, Govert ignored the roads and drove straight through the fields over rocks and holes. He insisted it was the shortest way to The Hague. Finally, where the area was ravaged with tank tracks and bomb craters, he slowed down and dodged charred vehicles, torn-up tanks and turned-over jeeps. I gripped my seat, staring at the horrible devastation. Then I turned away and asked, "How was The Hague?"

Govert shifted uneasily and said, "A bit of a letdown."

"What's the matter, something happened?"

"No, it just wasn't what we had expected. Considering what our cargo was, we didn't get a rousing welcome."

We were both silent.

"Govert, do you realize that it's exactly five years ago today that those Krauts burst into our country."

Govert shook his head. "No ma'am," he sighed, "and a lot of misery it was."

We had reached the macadam highway and Govert stopped. At the crossing near Utrecht the Canadian Military Police admitted us to a convoy, which we followed to The Hague.

I leaned back against the cool leather seat, my feet on my battered suitcase, and closed my eyes. My thoughts skipped over the last five years.

The war was over. Hitler was dead. Hundreds of thousands of people were dead. Some of my friends were dead. Most of my family was alive. Paul and I were alive. We were the lucky ones.

27

Whoosh!! A bunch of flowers flew through the open window and landed on my lap. I opened my eyes and saw a wildly enthusiastic crowd jumping up and down, dancing around, shouting and waving.

Govert shook my arm, "Ma'am, we're coming into town. We're in The Hague . . ."

I straightened up. We were there. My home town. I was back home! Thoughts raced through my mind. The Hague! — it was officially called 'sGravenhage, literally meaning the Count's hedge. There wouldn't be any hedges left now; they had all been burned for firewood. But the flags were not burned and they were flying everywhere. I looked at the men, women, children and even dogs running along with the trucks. Everybody who still had enough strength to stand up was out, cheering their gratitude to the liberators. Through my tears I watched some little boys try to climb on the hood of our truck as we slowed. They scrambled to pick up the shower of gum Govert tossed out of the window. What a welcome! I hadn't expected it, after what Govert had told me. Maybe they thought we were Canadians, too!

Slowly driving into the inner city I noticed a scattering of bombed-out houses. We passed an open area, the Bezuidenhout.

"Good Lord! What's this?" I stared horrified at the block of ruins. The houses, the church, the station — everything — was a mass of black rubble and twisted steel with only an occasional building still upright, its windows staring blindly out at the world. I felt my stomach tightening.

"That's the mistake the British made when they were searching for the V-2's, remember?" Govert said.

"Yes, I remember."

I was utterly depressed as we drove on. Eventually my spirits lifted seeing the happiness of the people, although they were thin, dirty, and hungry-looking. The children with their spindly legs and far too big clothes, were especially enchanting.

We could not run the truck into the narrow Spuistraat because it was already filled with cars, so we parked outside and walked through the street to our hotel. Within two seconds Govert had a girl on each arm, forgot about my suitcase, and happily sauntered off to other conquests.

Entering the Bock-Harrison Hotel, I stumbled on masses of army people and duffle bags. Looking around for Paul I finally spotted him in the background. Amidst the forest of khaki legs I also saw a familiar bundle of fur. Terry!

Paul, straining at the other end of the leash, let the dog go. Terry streaked through the many legs and leaped into my outstretched arms. After this joyful greeting we carefully stepped over the mess of luggage to go upstairs and see our bedroom. Our room had three double beds and two single ones, all close together.

"This one is ours," Paul said, pointing to the double bed near the window. On the ledge was a large vase with bright red flowers.

"The flowers are for you," he said. "Everyone still has them in their windows, war or no war. Sorry, I don't have any of those cigarettes and silk stockings the Allies are giving away."

"Thanks! How'd you get those flowers? And what about the other beds?"

"Two couples sleep in those over there and next to them two officers. I don't know them, but I sure hope to get a better room tomorrow."

"Sounds like one big family!" I laughed. Paul shrugged his shoulders. He was not happy about the accommodations.

The next morning he was even more chagrined to discover that one of the wives had left her husband's bed to join another officer in his single bed. I felt an iron hold on my arm as Paul steered me towards the door. Once outside he turned and said, ever so sweetly, "Babes, darling, if you ever do that to me, I'll kill you."

I groaned and asked cheerfully, "What did you do while I was gone?"

"First I got the dog, then I went to Rotterdam," he replied matter-of-factly. "We sent divers down to clear the harbor entrance. You know, there's typhus near Dordrecht. By the way," he said, peering at me, "did you get your shots?"

"When that horse-doctor stuck me with that enormous needle, I fainted, so I can't say for sure!" I said sheepishly.

"You and shots don't get along." Paul shook his head.

"Yes," I said, "I'm scared to death of them. But I wasn't the only one. Some tough-looking soldiers in line also fainted. Besides, we got all three doses in one time and the needle was blunt."

"You know what? I liberated a jeep," Paul said changing the subject. "Let's drive to our house."

We drove through The Hague, seeing all the damage, dirt, and garbage in the streets. I could have cried when we passed the Woods of Scheveningen, where we had played as children. It was completely gone. All that remained was acres of low stumps, the rest having been used for firewood. On the avenue, van Alkemade-laan, our home and the other identical houses all had their roofs blown off and no glass in the windows. Canadian M.P.'s had appropriated the house next to ours and were repairing it with bricks and anything else they needed from other homes. Behind us in the open field were stacks of goods ready to be carted to Germany, designated to grace the parlor of some victorious Nazi. Washbowls, bathtubs, pipes, lamps, curtain rods, drapery, and even kitchen tools, had been thrown on separate piles. All of them had been taken from our neighbors.

"I can use that thing over there, "I said to the surprised Paul, rushing out to pick up a serrated bread knife. Paul also got out of the jeep and poked around, taking along a souvenir or two.

"Looks like we have to do what the Canadians are doing," I said. "Fix up our house with the stuff from every other one. The last house is just going to be out of luck. The sooner we start the better, otherwise we'll be the last one!"

Paul agreed, happily. "Yes, later we can get some German POW's to fix the yard."

"Okay, that'll be interesting." I could picture myself overseeing a gang of German soldiers while they spaded and planted.

We jumped back into the jeep and drove a little farther. On a street corner, we saw several women with shaved heads being pushed around by a jeering crowd.

"I wonder if they're sorry they fraternized with the Krauts," Paul mused.

We passed Joseph Israel's Square, which was a mass of pink and red roses before the war. There we saw a vindictive mob milling around. Just before we had arrived, the mob had dragged a traitor from one of the houses and pushed him under a moving tank. I really didn't want to see it, and urged Paul to drive on. Despite his curiosity, Paul slowly turned the car.

As we began to move, we suddenly saw Robby down the street.

We honked and stopped. Our Jewish childhood friend came running over and we all shared the joy of being alive. We huddled together on the side of the road and exchanged news. As we were parting, Robby said,

"Well, I'm sure of one thing. I never want to see my children, like I saw my parents, go to slaughter. I shall teach them to fight to the death!"

"I hope there never has to be another war." I said, sighing and patting him on the arm. As we drove away in the jeep I turned around and watched his grieving figure until he was out of sight.

We headed toward the beach, past the Orange Hotel, the Nazi jail. Even with its horror fresh in our minds, its thick red walls seemed less formidable. Across the street, the dunes had resumed their serenity, accepting the violence of many a patriot being marched in and shot to death.

Paul stared with slitted eyes across the sandy area covered with tough grasses and low bushes. He muttered half to himself: "There're all kinds of ways to die."

When I looked at him questioningly, he told me of the awful experience he had had just a few hours earlier, when he helped a Red Cross nurse get a family to the hospital. Inside a dark house they found the whole family in bed — father, mother, and three youngsters. It was too late to save the father. The others, feeble from too little food, hadn't been able to move him, and kept the dead body in bed with them.

"Those doors hide a lot of misery, Babes. We see only the ones who can still walk. There's a health unit trying to find the others."

We were silent by the time we reached Scheveningen. Paul parked the car so we could see the sun go down. All along the wide yellow beach the waves rolled in slowly, leaving their foaming edges on the sand. The sound of the sea was soothing. For the first time in five years I felt a sense of tranquility. We were the only people there. Softly we talked about our families. Paul had seen his mother and had heard from his sister. They all had survived but he was shocked to see his mother so emaciated. She told him she prayed for us all the time and now her prayers were answered. Of our friends, those who managed to stay hidden, were still alive, but there was no news of those who had been sent to concentration camps. Paul told me that my friend Pico's husband had been picked up. The last she had heard from him was a crumpled note he had written and thrown from the train, on his way to a concentration camp across the border. We fell silent again, grateful to be together.

The weather was balmy. A soft breeze played through my hair and brushed my cheeks. The descending sun spread its orange and blue glow across the sky, getting ready to welcome the magic of a peaceful evening almost forgotten in Holland.

I snuggled closer, feeling Paul's heart beat. When I felt really cozy and warm, I decided that this was the right moment.

Paul seemed to sense my inner thoughts and looked intently at me, waiting.

"Paul, in spite of all the misery, there's something good for us.

His eyes widened.

I hesitated. I was about to tell him what I had known for more than two months. Now I felt a knot of doubt. How would he feel?

Times were still very unsettled — . I finally heard myself saying, "We're going to have a baby."

In what seemed like one move, Paul drew back, embraced me, and kissed me tenderly.

"I knew it! I knew it when you complained you didn't want to live like a gypsy anymore. I saw it in your eyes. That eternal nesting instinct was showing!"

He jumped up on the seat of the jeep, threw his arms in the air and let out a Tarzan yell, which reverberated against the empty fortifications around us.

"Yeahhh! My baby!"

I sighed happily.

"Our child," he murmured, sitting down again, "A new life for Holland, and a new life for us."

He shook his head not believing that such happiness could suddenly come into our lives. Then, caught up in the spirit of it, he wondered, "What shall we name our son? It should be short, and Dutch, and easy to pronounce in any language, wherever we might go."

I looked at him, loving him with all my heart. The tough experiences we had shared for the past two years had created a bond that could never be broken. Together we had survived in a world no one later on would understand. Who could be closer than we were at this moment; who could be happier?

"What if it's a girl?" I asked him.

We both laughed. Paul started the car.

"More boys than girls are born after a war," he said triumphantly. He turned the car, leaving the last sun rays to peek through the desolate row of bunkers on the beach behind us. We slowly drove back, noticing the road signs, which had been changed from German to English.

It made us feel good.

Suddenly Paul pointed, and I saw a small Dutch flag fluttering on a mass of rubble which had once been a building. It was a little bent, but still valiant. We stopped, and watched until the red white and blue was overcome by the night.

Then we turned and drove the jeep toward The Hague.

AFTERWORD

On my visits to Holland, I tried to find my friends. Some I had kept contact with, others had disappeared out of my life. Since the war everyone's circumstances had changed drastically and many had moved away.

Frits Ruys' family started a new life in Rhodesia (Zimbabwe). Frits, executed by the Nazis, was honored posthumously by having a street named after him in the city of Rotterdam.

Picolien Timmers Verhoeven had her baby, Caroline, during the worst time of the war. Her husband, Eef Duetz, was picked up by the Gestapo and died in a German concentration camp. He saw the Allies arrive, but did not make it home. Pico is remarried and lives in Holland.

Oda Lutjens married Kees Oorthuys, meeting him in the Underground telephone service, which they both manned for years.

Gerda Wijmans-van Dillen, Paul's sister and her husband, a surgeon, worked in an underground hospital during the war. It was located in the cellars of the Byenkorf, a department store in The Hague. She is a well-known artist. Her husband died after the war.

My sister Julie and her husband, Henk Thomassen survived the war in Gorssel, near Deventer. Henk had constant problems with the Nazis to keep his factory workers in Holland, and eventually he had to go into hiding himself.

My brothers, Kees and Akka Schoorel, and their families were in the Dutch East Indies (now Indonesia). They had an extremely rough time in Japanese internment camps. Men and women were in different camps and were constantly moved to other locations. In the large Ambarawa camp on Java, Kees' young son, Jemmy, died of dyptheria in his mother's arms, and was buried there. At about the same time the Japanese shipped Kees to a camp in Saigon. He did not know that his only son had died until after the war. Fortunately his three daughters survived the ordeal.

Erik Hazelhoff Roelfzema escaped from Holland to England and joined the Royal Air Force. Towards the end of the war he became adjutant of Queen Wilhelmina in London. In his book, Soldier of Orange, he describes his escape from Holland, the RAF, his time as a secret agent dropped in Holland, and his return after the war. The book has been translated in many languages and was made into a movie. He received the Militaire Willemsorde, the highest honor of the Netherlands, bestowed for bravery in action. He now resides in Hawaii, and still writes successful books.

The Galemas moved to Rome and after some correspondence, I lost track of them. Unfortunately I also lost track of the *Dingers* and I never heard from *Han and Anne Ahrends*, who took my dog, Terry; or *Bob*, Paul's assistant.

Jan Keunen, a physician, practices in The Hague. He remarried. I met both of them recently, and I still found Jan had a great sense of humor.

Mrs. Zuur passed away. Her daughter *Sabine* returned from a few horror years in the worst concentration camps in Germany.

Carry Vonck, with whom I went to Germany and saw Hitler before the war, married George Geysel and moved to Indonesia. A year later the islands were taken over by the Japanese. She, carrying her infant son, was one of the women who, for four long years, traveled by foot through the jungles of Sumatra, as the Japanese chased them from camp to camp. Neville Shute wrote the book "The Legacy," later named "A Town Called Alice" about her experiences, although placing the story in Malaysia. He mentions her name in the back of the book. A movie and TV-mini series made from the book were shown in the U.S. Carry passed away last year and I hope her husband will publish her memoires.

Dr. S.L. Louwes died a few years ago, a famous man. He received credit for organizing the Food Distribution during the war and for his successful negotiations with the Germans to keep more food in Holland. Without him we would have had starvation a lot sooner. Because of his leadership we had basic food items until the final months of the war.

Dr. A. H. Boerma also played an important part in the Food Distribution drama. After the war, I heard he went to Europe to administer the Marshall Plan, but I have since lost track of him.

Herr Woltheim (not his real name) was a gentle man. How much he was involved in Paul's release from jail, we'll never know. And if he ever went back to find us at the Terwilligen home, I never heard either. After the war, when we had moved to the U.S., the war trials started in Holland. The Dutch government requested us to give them information about Woltheim. Paul wrote them our story. He also said that Woltheim was as fair as possible in his dealings with the food appropriations from the German army and still leave enough for the Dutch.

My husband Paul van Dillen, with whom I shared so many experiences, passed away in California in 1964. He was 46. Scratched on the wall of a jail cell at Scheveningen are three little words: *My dear Babes.*

FACTS AND FIGURES

*From the Netherlands State Institute of War
Documentation, Amsterdam.*

Anton A. Mussert, head of the Nationaal Socialistische Beweging (N.S.B.) was executed by firing squad at Scheveningen in May, 1946.

Dr. Arthur Seyss-Inquart, Reichskommissar of the Netherlands, classed a major war criminal by the International Military Tribunal at Nuremberg, was found guilty and hanged.

Friedrich C. Christiansen, commander of the German Armed Forces in the Netherlands, who ordered the destruction of the village of Putten and the shooting of the hostages, was sentenced to 12 years in prison. Forty Dutch traitors were executed and 5 Germans, among others Hans Albin Rauter, Chief of the Nazi Police System in Holland.

Of the 140,000 Jews in Holland, 102,000 were killed by the Nazis. 12,000 Dutch died in concentration camps or work camps in Germany from starvation, hard work, and beatings.

Dutch killed in action, army and navy	5,200
Killed in action, merchant marine	1,600
Died in German POW camps	350
Dutch men and women executed	2000
Died in Dutch concentration camps	750
Died from bombardments and fighting	23,000
Died in Holland from starvation *during hunger winter*	20,000

Died in Holland from illnesses due to lack of
hygiene, lack of medicines, communicable diseases   50,000
Dutch killed in action in German services   5,000

About 150,000 pro Nazi Dutchmen were arrested after the war. Most of them were interned. Six thousand were deprived of their Dutch citizenship for entering a foreign military service. Their property was seized by the state.

Total material damage in guilders as a direct result of the German occupation has been estimated on 5.39 billion, among other damage to harbor installations, 300 million, and damage to roads and bridges, 100 million (at that time, 1 guilder was about equal to 1 dollar in buying power.)

One hundred thousand homes and churches were demolished; 50,000 badly damaged. Confiscated materials by the Nazis: gold, currencies and other valuable articles (paintings) estimated to 2.85 billion.